Fix It!
Grammar

Robin Hood

TEACHER'S MANUAL BOOK 2

Pamela White

THIRD EDITION

Also by Pamela White

Fix It! Grammar: The Nose Tree Teacher's Manual Book 1
Fix It! Grammar: The Nose Tree Student Book 1
Fix It! Grammar: Robin Hood Student Book 2
Fix It! Grammar: Frog Prince, or Just Deserts Teacher's Manual Book 3
Fix It! Grammar: Frog Prince, or Just Deserts Student Book 3
Fix It! Grammar: Little Mermaid Teacher's Manual Book 4
Fix It! Grammar: Little Mermaid Student Book 4
Fix It! Grammar: Chanticleer Teacher's Manual Book 5
Fix It! Grammar: Chanticleer Student Book 5
Fix It! Grammar: Sir Gawain and the Green Knight Teacher's Manual Book 6
Fix It! Grammar: Sir Gawain and the Green Knight Student Book 6

The purchase of this book entitles its owner to a free download of the *Robin Hood* student Blackline Masters.

Go to: IEW.com/FIX-2-E

(See the blue page for complete download instructions.)

Institute for Excellence in Writing
8799 N. 387 Road
Locust Grove, OK 74352

800.856.5815

info@IEW.com

IEW.com

Printed in the United States of America

Accessing Your Downloads

The purchase of this book entitles its owner to a free download of the following:

- *Fix-It! Student Book 2* e-book (132 pages*)
- *Mastery Learning* e-audio
- *But, but, but …What about Grammar?* e-audio

To download these e-resources, please follow the directions below:

1. Go to our website: IEW.com.

2. Log in to your online customer account. If you do not have an account, you will need to create one.

3. After you are logged in, go to this web page: IEW.com/FIX-2-E.

4. Click the red arrow, and then click the checkboxes next to the names of the files you wish to place in your account.

5. Click the "Add to my files" button.

6. To access your files now and in the future, click on "Your Account" and click on the "Files" tab (one of the gray tabs).

7. Click on each file name to download the files onto your computer.

Please note: You are free to download and print the student e-book as needed for use within *your immediate family or classroom*. However, this information is proprietary, and we are trusting you to be on your honor not to share it with anyone. Please see the copyright page for further details. Thank you.

  * If you would prefer to purchase *Fix It! Student Book 2* as a preprinted, spiral-bound book, it is available at this web page: IEW.com/FIX-2-SB

If you have any difficulty receiving these downloads after going through the steps above, please call 800.856.5815.

Institute for Excellence in Writing
8799 N. 387 Road
Locust Grove, OK 74352

Introduction

Welcome to *Fix It!*

Welcome to the second book of *Fix It! Grammar: Robin Hood*. As your students enjoy reading a sentence or two of this classic tale each day, they will learn to apply grammar rules to the writing. Over the course of the year, they will review the basic parts of speech and learn how to identify clauses and phrases, which will prepare them to learn the many punctuation rules needed in composition.

This book builds on the work that was started in the first *Fix It!* story: *The Nose Tree*. If you find that this book moves too quickly, it may be better to go back and complete *The Nose Tree*.

This is not a traditional grammar program, so it will not feel as if you are really learning grammar. Instead, you and your students will be internalizing the tools necessary for editing their own compositions, which is the main goal of grammar.

The Method: Modeling Proper Grammar within Stories

The traditional method of teaching grammar is to present a grammar rule and then have students apply it in a series of contrived exercises. When that grammar rule is learned, another is taught and practiced in the same manner.

Although students often do well on these traditional worksheets, the learning does not usually transfer to their own writing and editing. Why? The grammar involved in real-life sentences is usually much more complicated than what is in the grammar exercise book, so students are often unable to edit their own work.

Fix It! Grammar overcomes these difficulties by teaching grammar at the point of need. Instead of a page full of grammar exercises, students will tackle real-life sentences with limited instruction. Thus, students will learn to think about their writing and incrementally learn how to apply the grammar rules to written work. Moreover, it is this daily practice in editing that will help instill the habit of editing anything they write.

For this to work, you as the teacher need to approach this book as a series of modeling exercises. Discuss each rule as it is presented, and then model for your students how to label the sentences and make the corrections. As your students gain confidence, they will often complete the labels and corrections accurately, but that is not always the case. Consider that mistakes are an opportunity to learn. If your students mismark a word or miss a correction, laugh! Show them what they missed, revisit the grammar rule involved, and encourage them that they can catch it next time.

After all, everyone needs an editor. Even professional writers and editors miss errors. The important thing is to understand the process and catch as much as you can. Knowing the reasons behind the fixes will make your students much better editors in the long run, and you will also gain the expertise to evaluate your students' papers better when they are older.

The Process: 15 Minutes a Day

This book is intended to provide 33 weeks of grammar instruction and practice. The process should take about fifteen minutes a day, four days a week. If you are using it with an older student, the book might be completed in a semester by doubling up the weeks. The directions from page 3 of the student book are on page 7 of this book.

If you are using this course with a writing class that meets weekly, we recommend having each family purchase the Teacher's Manual. Ask the parents to go over the passages at home with their children. That frees you up to focus on just some of the concepts so it does not take up too much class time.

Get Ready

Follow the instructions on the blue page in the front of this manual to download the student book. Print out one copy per student. You can also purchase a spiral-bound version of the student book at IEW.com/FIX-2-SB.

Student Notebook. If you printed a copy of the student book, each student will need a two-pocket notebook with three-hole fasteners to store the *Fix It* student pages. The lessons and student pages can be added to the middle section while the pockets may be used to house the Grammar Glossary, which students will not usually need at this level, and the Grammar Cards. If you purchased the spiral-bound student book, then all you need is a place to store the grammar cards.

Grammar Cards. At the back of the student book is a collection of grammar cards, which provide students with easy access to grammar terms and rules after the concepts are introduced in *Fix It* instructions. Students may keep the cards in a resealable plastic pouch or tape the cards to a piece of card stock so that they can easily flip the cards to see the back, as illustrated at right.

Spiral Notebook. Each day your student will be invited to record the vocabulary word with its definition and rewrite the passage neatly. The story rewrite can be kept in the front of a single-subject spiral notebook while the vocabulary list can be kept in the back.

Get Started

Begin the program by reading the directions presented on page 3 of the student book (page 7 of this Teacher's Manual). Tell your student that this program works like a puzzle. It is a series of daily games to practice the elements of grammar that they will learn over many weeks.

Your students will likely miss many of the fixes and markings as they work through the program, so stress that "a mistake is an opportunity to learn." They can use their mistakes to learn grammar better. Thus, keep the lessons light and fun, and teach your students to laugh and learn from the elements they miss.

Learn It

Start the week by reading through the "Learn It" section of the student book. Cut out the related grammar cards located near the back of the student book. Your student may keep these cards handy throughout the year and reference them as needed.

Next, show your student how to apply the lesson to the Day 1 passage. Model how to make the editing marks and grammar notations. Since all the markings are illustrated in this Teacher's Manual, you can easily guide your student.

The explanations below the edited text are for the teacher. The discussion notes provide you with the reasons behind each of the fixes as well as some of the other elements of grammar that may come up in your discussion. Notice that they are organized into two sections: Fixes and Grammar Notations. You will likely need to reference the grammar

The Layout

You can teach the information in any order that makes sense to you and your students. To keep things organized, we have arranged the material like this:

Fixes. These notes provide the reasons for each of the corrections. Use them to explain why a fix was needed or to quiz your students on their understanding.

Grammar Notations. These notes explain the grammar markings and suggest questions that can help you guide your student to see how the grammar works.

Style. This deals with dress-ups and typically appears on Day 4 of every week.

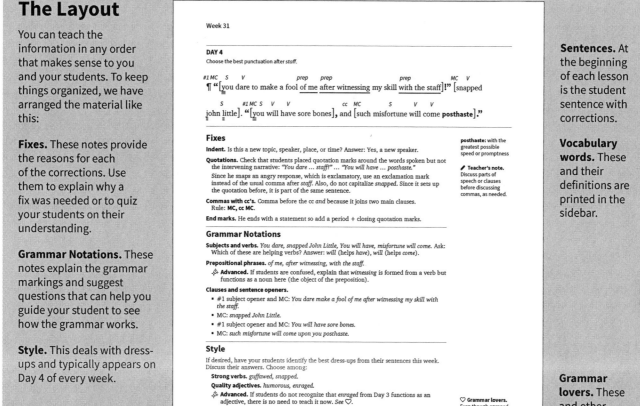

Sentences. At the beginning of each lesson is the student sentence with corrections.

Vocabulary words. These and their definitions are printed in the sidebar.

Grammar lovers. These and other supporting notes can also be found in the sidebar.

notations in order to make the corrections, so do not feel that you have to follow the discussion notes in order. Simply use them as a reference as you work through the passage.

Fix It

On the remaining three days of the week, continue to fix and mark the passage. Review the directions presented on page 7 of this Teacher's Manual and continue to model the process as needed. Students may do some of the lesson on their own, such as looking up the vocabulary word and attempting to fix and mark the passage. However, it can also be done together.

The discussion should not take more than fifteen minutes per day. If you cannot touch on everything in that period of time, that is fine.

Use the discussion notes as needed to explain the fixes and discuss the grammar involved. Use the questions to help your student understand the grammar better, but do not feel compelled to read it all to your student. The principles will be repeated over and over, so there is plenty of time to learn. The daily discussion and practice will bring mastery, so keep this part of the lesson light and fun.

In addition to the regular discussion of grammar, the discussion notes include advanced concepts, teacher's notes, and tidbits for the grammar lovers among you. These additions, set off with icons, are primarily for the teacher's information to explain something that might be confusing in the discussion. If a student is curious, go ahead and discuss those concepts. However, they are generally above the scope of this course and can be just for a teacher's enjoyment and training.

Rewrite

Finally, the rewrite is the key to success. By rewriting the passage and paying careful attention to detail, your student will internalize the corrections. For your convenience, the corrected passage rewrite is printed in the Teacher's Manual at the end of each week's fixes.

Pacing

Adjust the pace of the teaching as needed. If your student is not understanding all the details, then do not require him to add new markings until the previous ones are easy. This mastery learning approach should be fun and low stress. If your students start to groan when you say, "Time for *Fix It!*" something is wrong.

For more on a mastery learning approach to teaching, listen to Andrew Pudewa's "Mastery Learning" talk. It has been included as a free download with your *Fix It!* purchase. See the blue page in the front of this manual for download instructions.

Grammar Glossary

The Grammar Glossary is a tool that can be used for all six *Fix It! Grammar* books. It summarizes most of the information that is taught in the books. Reference it if you want a little more information than was provided with the passage. It will also be a handy grammar guide for your student to use in the future.

Grading

This course is intended to be used as a teaching tool and thus should not be graded. If you must assign a grade, assess the students' rewrite of the passage. You can simply choose one of the passages from the week to evaluate. The passage can be worth ten points. Deduct one point for each error.

Find Help

The scope and sequence for this book is on pages 206–208.

If you would like to see a demonstration of how to do the *Fix It!* lessons, please watch the webinar on the IEW website. It is on the *Fix It!* Overview page. See IEW.com/Fix.

The Institute for Excellence in Writing also provides teacher forums for those using our materials. It is a great place to meet other IEW teachers and find answers to specific writing and grammar questions. To join, see IEW.com/forum.

Instructions

Welcome to *Fix It! Grammar*. This year you can enjoy learning grammar by seeing how it works in a real-life story.

GET READY

To organize your work, you will need a two-pocket notebook with three-hole fasteners and a single-subject spiral notebook. If you have the spiral-bound *Fix It!* student book, then all you need is a single subject spiral notebook.

Use the center of the two-pocket notebook to collect the lesson and *Fix It!* pages as your teacher distributes them each week. Rewrite the passage in the front of the spiral notebook and use the back of the book to write down the vocabulary words and their definitions, working from the back forward.

Grammar cards are located in the back of the student book after page 72 and before the Grammar Glossary section. These may be cut out as they are needed and stored in a resealable plastic pouch or taped to a piece of card stock, as illustrated at right. The cards may be kept in the notebook pocket or tucked into the spiral-bound student book.

LEARN IT

With your teacher, read through the "Learn It" section for the week. This will show you what you will be looking for that week and for weeks to come.

To help you remember and review what you learned, use the grammar card(s) for the week. Keep them handy each time you work on *Fix It!* so that the information is at your fingertips.

FIX IT

Every Day	Read the sentence. Look up the bolded word in a dictionary. Decide which definition best fits the meaning of the word in this sentence. In the vocabulary section of your notebook, write a brief definition (using key words) labeled with the appropriate week. Add to this list every day.
Day 1	Read the instructions for the week with your teacher. Mark and fix the first passage with your teacher's help. Discuss what you missed with your teacher, and then complete the rewrite after fixing.
Days 2–4	Use the abbreviations at the top of the page along with the grammar cards to help you remember how to mark the passage. Your teacher will help you with anything you miss. Remember, a mistake is an opportunity to learn.
Rewrite	After marking, correcting, and discussing the passage with your teacher each day, copy the corrected passage into your notebook so that you end up with a handwritten copy of the complete story. Your teacher can show you an example of the rewrite in the teacher's book.

- Be sure to double-space.
- Do not copy the markings, just the story.
- Be careful to indent where indicated and use capital letters properly.
- Carefully copy the punctuation and use end marks.

Page 3, *Fix It! Grammar:* Robin Hood, Student Book 2

Week 1

Indentation, Capitalization, Articles and Nouns, *Who-Which* Clauses, and End Marks

Be sure to cut out the Week 1 grammar cards located at the back of this book before the Grammar Glossary. Keep them handy so you can reference them as needed. The first card provides the reminders listed on page three of this book.

LEARN IT

Since this is the first day, there are several things you need to know to get started. But do not worry; they are easy! Read through these few things with your teacher, who will use the Day 1 passage to show you how they work.

Indent	In fiction (stories), you should start a new paragraph for these four reasons: new speaker, topic, place, or time. To remember to indent in your rewrite, add the ¶ symbol or an arrow (➜) in front of the sentence that needs an indent.
	In stories, the indentation rules are somewhat flexible, so your choice to indent may be different from what is recommended in the teacher book. That is fine! As long as you can explain why your choice fulfills a rule for indentation, you are good to go.
Capitalization	You will not see any capital letters in your student book sentences. Show where capitals are needed by drawing three short lines directly underneath letters that should be capitalized. In your copy work, be sure to use capital letters where needed instead of those three lines. Rules to remember:

- Always capitalize the first word of a sentence, even a quoted sentence that falls in the middle of a longer sentence.

- Always capitalize proper nouns, which are nouns that name specific persons, places, or things.

- Do not capitalize titles when used alone (like "the king") but do capitalize them when used with a name (King Arthur).

Articles (ar)	Use the grammar cards to review the term *article*. There are only three articles: *a*, *an*, and *the*. Mark them by printing *ar* over each one. Articles are useful because they signal that a noun is coming.
Noun (n)	Use the grammar cards to review the term *noun*. Nouns are things, people, animals, places, and ideas. To determine if a word is a noun, apply the noun test. Print an *n* above each noun in the passage.
Who-Which (w-w)	If you have been doing Excellence in Writing, you have likely heard the term *dress-ups*. Dress-ups are ways of dressing up style in writing by using stronger vocabulary or more complex sentence structure. On Day 4 keep an eye out for the *who-which* clause. Mark it by writing *w-w* above the *who* or *which*.
End Marks	Remember that every sentence must have an end mark. They are missing in this week's sentences. Decide which kind of end mark (period, question mark, or exclamation mark) each sentence needs and add it on.

This week students will focus on indenting to start new paragraphs, adding capital letters when needed, identifying articles, nouns, and *who-which* clauses, and adding the correct end marks.

Indent. The rules for where to indent are more flexible but less clear than they are in academic papers. Determining whether it is a new topic is sometimes open to interpretation, as are the rules for new speakers. Discussion notes will alert you to places where new paragraphs are optional, but do not be too rigid about this. The goal is to teach the basic principles and aim for some consistency. In practice, indentation in papers is far more critical than in fiction, so we can be more flexible in fiction.

Grammar Glossary. Students will not be assigned reading in the Grammar Glossary, which is a tool you may wish to use to learn more about a concept. The same glossary is in all six books, so it includes both "need to know" concepts and extra information for those who wish to learn more.

DAY 1

¶ in the olden days of england, king henry the second **reigned** over the land.

(marked above: ar — n — n — n — n — ar — n — ar — n)

Fixes

reigned: ruled with sole authority

Make corrections as indicated in the passage above. Additional notes below.

Indent. This sentence will start on a new line and include an indent of ½ inch because it is the start of the story and therefore a new topic.

Capitalization.

- *In*—first word of sentence.
- *England*—proper noun because it is a specific place.
- *King Henry the Second*—proper noun with title.
  - ✧ **Advanced.** Do not capitalize articles or prepositions in the middle of titles, so *the* is lowercase.

End marks. This is a statement so add a period.

Grammar Notations

Mark and discuss as indicated above. Additional notes below.

Articles and nouns. *the days, England, King Henry the Second, the land.*

Teach that articles always set up a noun, which follows the article. Ask students to prove this is true with the sentences this week. Sometimes adjectives will come in between them, as in "the olden days." Guide students to find parts of speech they missed.

Rewrite

Show your students how to rewrite the corrected passage on a fresh sheet of paper. A sample of what this week's rewrite should look like is below the Day 4 fixes. Your student can do the rewrite daily or at the end of the week.

DAY 2

¶ there lived within the green **glades** of sherwood forest a famous outlaw whose name was

robin hood.

Fixes

Indent. Tell your students: Look at the last sentence you wrote and the indent card. Do any of the four reasons for starting a new paragraph apply to this sentence? Answer: Yes, the story switches topics from general background information to Robin Hood and switches the setting to Sherwood Forest, so start a new paragraph.

✧ **Advanced.** Starting a new paragraph here is technically correct and easiest for most students to understand. However, when the topics change quickly from sentence to sentence, it is equally fine to keep some sentences in the same paragraph. These opening sentences set the stage for the story so could be seen as treating the same general topic.

Capitalization.

- *There*—first word of sentence.
- *Sherwood Forest*—proper noun. Note that *green glades* is descriptive and just a common noun. It does not name a specific place, as *Sherwood Forest* does.
- *Robin Hood*—proper noun.

End marks. This is a statement so add a period.

Grammar Notations

Articles and nouns. *the glades, Sherwood Forest, a outlaw, name, Robin Hood.*

Ask students to show you that each article is followed by a noun. In one case (*a famous outlaw*), an adjective comes in between.

✧ **Advanced.** *Who-which* clauses. Some students may recognize that *whose* is the possessive form of *who* and *which*, in this case referring back to *outlaw*. If they mark it as a *who-which* clause, great! If not, you do not need to teach it now.

✏ **Teacher's note.** This *whose* clause is correct with no commas because it is essential to the meaning of the rest of the sentence (not any famous outlaw but the one whose name was Robin Hood), but you do not need to teach this advanced concept now.

glades: open spaces in a forest

Remind your students to use the Fix It and Rewrite It card to remember what to do each day.

DAY 3

n .... *ar n* ...... *n* .... *n*

no archer that ever lived could shoot a bow and arrow with such **expertise** as he did.

Fixes

expertise: expert skill or knowledge

Indent. Is this a new topic, speaker, place, or time? Answer: No. The sentence continues to give background information about Robin Hood, so students should not start a new paragraph.

Capitalization. *No*—first word of sentence.

End marks. This is a statement so add a period.

Grammar Notations

Articles and nouns. *archer, a bow … arrow, expertise.*

Ask students to tell you the article-noun pairs: *a bow.*

DAY 4

n   *n*   *w-w*

he was not alone, either, for at his side were blameless, loyal men, who **rambled** with him
≡

ar   *n*

through the greenwood shades**.**

Fixes

Indent. Is this a new topic, speaker, place, or time? Answer: No. The sentence is still about Robin Hood, so no new paragraph.

Capitalization. *He*—first word of sentence.

End marks. This is a statement so add a period.

Grammar Notations

Articles and nouns. *side, men, the shades.* Ask students to show you the article-noun pairs: *the shades.* Explain that it is common for an adjective (*greenwood*) to come between the article and noun.

Who-which clauses.

Check that students labeled *who* and ask them to read the entire clause aloud: *who rambled with him through the greenwood shades.*

Ask: What noun does *who* point back to or describe? Answer: *men.*

✏ **Teacher's note.** This *who* clause is set off with commas because it is nonessential to the meaning of the rest of the sentence. If we remove it, at his side were still blameless, loyal men. This is an advanced concept, however, difficult for most students at this level.

rambled: wandered in a leisurely manner

Explain that **shades** means a place of comparative darkness, in this case, the forest, shaded because of little sunlight.

STUDENT REWRITE

To ensure that the editing sticks, have your student rewrite the passage in a separate section of the notebook. Below is what that rewrite should look like.

In the olden days of England, King Henry the Second reigned over the land.

There lived within the green glades of Sherwood Forest a famous outlaw whose name was Robin Hood. No archer that ever lived could shoot a bow and arrow with such expertise as he did. He was not alone, either, for at his side were blameless, loyal men, who rambled with him through the greenwood shades.

Week 2

Pronouns, Verbs, Coordinating Conjunctions, Its/It's, Comma with Items in a Series

Use the Week 2 grammar cards located in the back of this book to discuss the following concepts. Keep them handy so you can reference them as needed.

LEARN IT

Pronouns (*pr*)
Pronouns refer back to some person or thing previously mentioned. A handy list is printed on the Pronouns grammar card. When you see these listed pronouns in the passages, label them with a *pr*.

Verbs (*vb*)
Review the verb test on the Verbs grammar card. Read through the list of helping verbs on the back of the card. Helping verbs are always followed by an action verb, which they are helping out. The helping verb is like a boy scout who holds the arm of an elderly lady to help her cross the street. One always helps the other along.

Mark all the verbs in this week's fixes with a *vb*.

Coordinating Conjunctions (*cc*)
Coordinating conjunctions are used to connect together two or more of the same types of words, phrases, or clauses. As you find them in these fixes, learn to identify what words the coordinating conjunction is joining.

Using the acronym FANBOYS, review the list of coordinating conjunctions on the grammar card. Label coordinating conjunctions by printing *cc* over each one.

Its versus It's

it's

Some words, like *it's* and *its*, are easily confused. To help you remember the difference between the possessive *its*, which does not have an apostrophe, and the contraction *it's*, which has an apostrophe and means *it is*, think of the apostrophe as a small *i*.

When you see **its/it's** in this week's fixes, circle the correct usage on the student pages and copy the correct version in your copy work.

Commas with Items in a Series

| a and b |
| a, b, and c |

There are many rules for when to use commas; this week you will learn one of them. Items in a series are two or more words or groups of words joined with a cc, usually *and*.

Three or more items in a series take commas. For example, you might be asked to go to the store to buy milk, eggs, and bread. Notice that there are commas after *milk* and *eggs*. Although the comma before the coordinating conjunction *and* is sometimes optional, it is usually needed to avoid confusion. Thus, it is easiest just to include it always.

> ✏ **Teacher's note.** Concepts are cumulative, so each week students will continue to practice concepts from prior weeks. Sometimes the instructions will have them work on those concepts in different ways, so go over their instructions with them weekly.
>
> As you progress through these lessons, you will find many things to address in each passage. You do not need to cover them all! Keep it light and make it a game. Your student does not have to master the elements the first time out. Over time with repetition, mastery will come.

Page 6, *Fix It! Grammar:* **Robin Hood, Student Book 2**

Pronouns. Students are asked to mark only these basic pronouns: *I, me, my, you, your, he, him, his, she, her, it, its, we, they, them, their.*

A few basic pronouns like *us* and *our*, as well as reflexive pronouns, are not listed because they do not appear in Weeks 2 – 6, where students are marking pronouns.

Students do not need to label *who, whom,* or *whose* as pronouns. For a chart of all these pronouns, see **Grammar Glossary** page G-7.

Coordinating conjunctions. Identifying what words cc's join is important because this affects punctuation and grammar. For now, simply help students make that identification.

Commas with items in a series. These must always be the same part of speech or grammatical construction usually connected by *and*. Guide students to see what same part of speech the *and* is connecting.

The comma before the cc with three or more items in a series is known as the *Oxford comma*, which most writers prefer. It is never wrong to include it and may be confusing to leave it out.

Institute for Excellence in Writing

DAY 1

pr   vb   vb   vb   n   vb   ar   n   ar   n
¶ you might be wondering how robin hood fell under the **wrath** of the law.

Fixes

wrath: fierce anger

Indent. Is this a new topic, speaker, place, or time? Answer: Yes, so start a new paragraph. The story goes back in time to explain why Robin Hood is outlawed in Sherwood Forest. See ✎.

✎ **Teacher's note.** A digression into the past is known as a flashback in literature.

Capitalization.

- *You*—first word of sentence.
- *Robin Hood*—proper noun.

End marks. This is a statement so add a period.

Grammar Notations

Articles and nouns. *Robin Hood, the wrath, the law.*

Ask students to show you the article-noun pairs: *the wrath, the law.*

Pronouns. *You.* If students ask, explain that sometimes narrators address the reader directly, as here. *You* is therefore the reader!

Verbs. *might be wondering, fell.*

Ask: Which of these are helping verbs, acting like a boy scout helping someone cross the street? Answer: *might be,* helping out *wondering.*

DAY 2

TIP: Three or more items in a series need commas between them. Find that situation in the passage below and add commas where appropriate.

n   *vb*   *cc*   *ar*   *n*

when robin was eighteen—mature**,** strong**,** and **dauntless**—the sheriff of nottingham

vb   *n*   *ar* *n*   *ar*   *n*

challenged young men in the area to a shooting match**.**

Fixes

dauntless: without fear

Indent. Is this a new topic, speaker, place, or time? Answer: No, it begins the story of how Robin Hood became outlawed.

Capitalization.

- *When*—first word of sentence.
- *Robin*—proper noun.
- *Sheriff of Nottingham*—proper noun. The title is capitalized because it goes with the name.
    - ✧ **Advanced.** Do not capitalize prepositions (*of*) or articles in the middle of titles.

Commas with items in a series.

Ask: What is the series and where do the commas go? Answer: *mature, strong, and dauntless.*

Ask students what part of speech these three words are. Answer: adjectives. Point out that with cc's, all the items must be the same part of speech.

  ✧ **Advanced.** If students ask whether the last comma in a series (the Oxford comma) is needed, tell them not necessarily. Since it is not wrong to include it, however, it is better to include it always.

End marks. This is a statement so add a period.

Grammar Notations

Articles and nouns. *Robin, the Sheriff of Nottingham, men, the area, a shooting match.*

Ask students to show you the article-noun pairs: *the Sheriff of Nottingham, the area, a shooting match.*

  ✧ **Advanced.** *shooting match* is a compound noun meaning *a contest in marksmanship.* See compound nouns under Grammar Glossary: Parts of Speech: Nouns, page G-5. *Sheriff of Nottingham* is the full title, which also counts as a noun.

Verbs. *was, challenged.*

If students overlook *was*, show them a list of the main *be* verbs (*am, is, are, was, were*) and ask them to find the one in this sentence.

  ✧ **Advanced.** *Was* is not a helping verb here because there is no other verb right after for it to connect to. It is not critical that students distinguish helping verbs from action verbs, only that they know these are all verbs. *See* ♡.

♡ **Grammar lovers.** (These notes are for those teachers who enjoy learning more, not for students.) *Was* is a linking verb, linking the subject, *Robin*, to its subject complement, *eighteen*.

DAY 3

TIP: The passage below has another series of the same part of speech. Add commas where appropriate.

   n   *vb*   *ar*   *n*   *vb*   *pr*   *n*   *cc*   *n*   *cc*   *vb*   *n*

robin **readily** accepted the match**,** grabbed his bow and arrow**,** and started off from locksley,

   w-w   *vb*   *ar*   *n*   *pr*   *vb*

which was the town where he lived**.**

Fixes

Indent. Is this a new topic, speaker, place, or time? Answer: No, it continues the story of Robin's outlawry.

Capitalization.

- *Robin*—first word of sentence and proper noun.
- *Locksley*—proper noun because it names a specific place.

Commas with items in a series.

Ask: What does each *and* join? Answer: *bow, arrow* (two nouns); *accepted, grabbed, started* (three verbs.)

Ask: Which one gets commas and where do the commas go? Answer: the three verbs: *accepted the match, grabbed his bow and arrow, and started off from Locksley.*

✦ **Advanced.** This example illustrates why it is important to help students identify what the cc's are joining. If a cc joins only two items in a series, there is no comma before it (unless those two items are main clauses). If it joins three or more, they are separated by commas.

End marks. This is a statement so add a period.

Grammar Notations

Articles, nouns, and pronouns. *Robin, the match, his, bow, arrow, Locksley, the town, he.* Ask students to show you the article-noun pairs: *the match, the town.*

Verbs. *accepted, grabbed, started, was, lived.* Help students find *was* or any missing part of speech as needed.

✦ **Advanced.** *Was* is not a helping verb. See ♡ **1.**

***Who-which* clauses.** Ask students to read the entire *which* clause aloud: *which was the town where he lived.* Ask: What noun does *which* point back to or describe? Answer: *Locksley.* Point out that *which* comes immediately after the noun it describes.

✦ **Advanced.** Older students may be ready to learn the invisible who-which, a sophisticated construction that drops the *who* or *which* and a *be* verb after it. This sentence sounds more elegant without *which was: Robin started off from Locksley, the town where he lived. See* ♡ **2** *and* ✐**.**

---

readily: quickly and easily

♡ **1. Grammar lovers.** *Was* links the subject to the subject complement (*town*), a noun that points back to the subject.

♡ **2. Grammar lovers.** The invisible who-which is also known as an appositive, a noun (*the town*) that renames the noun immediately before it (*Locksley*).

✐ **Teacher's note.** *Who-which* clauses are set off with commas if they are nonessential, which means they can be removed from the sentence without changing the meaning of the rest of the sentence. Ask if the sentence makes sense without this clause. It does, so the clause is nonessential and needs a comma before *which*. See Grammar Glossary: Punctuation: Commas: Rule 15. Essential-Nonessential Elements, page G-24.

DAY 4

pr vb ar   *n   cc   n   vb   vb pr   n*
it was a pleasant, **carefree** day, but circumstances would soon change its ~~it's~~ mood.

Fixes

carefree: without anxiety or worry

Indent. Is this a new topic, speaker, place, or time? Answer: No, it is still on Robin's outlawry.

Capitalization. *It*—first word of sentence.

Homophones and usage.

Ask your students to circle the correct word when given a choice, explain its meaning, and check the spelling when copied. Answer: *its* for the possessive form of *it*.

Ask: What does *it* refer back to? Answer: the day. "Its mood" refers to the mood of that day.

End marks. This is a statement so add a period.

Grammar Notations

Articles and nouns. *a day, circumstances, mood.*

Ask students to show you the article-noun pairs: *a day*.

Adjectives often come in between an article and its noun, as here with *pleasant, carefree*.

Verbs. *was, would change.*

Ask: Which of these is a helping verb? Answer: Only *would*, which helps along *change*. *Was* is not a helping verb here because there is no verb afterward for it to help along.

Coordinating conjunctions. *but.*

✧ **Advanced.** Ask: What grammatical construction does *but* join? Answer: two main clauses (MCs), or complete thoughts. A main clause has a subject and verb and can stand alone as a sentence. Two MCs require a comma with a cc to link them together. Pattern: **MC, cc MC**.

STUDENT REWRITE

You might be wondering how Robin Hood fell under the wrath of the law. When Robin was eighteen—mature, strong, and dauntless—the Sheriff of Nottingham challenged young men in the area to a shooting match. Robin readily accepted the match, grabbed his bow and arrow, and started off from Locksley, which was the town where he lived. It was a pleasant, carefree day, but circumstances would soon change its mood.

Week 3

Quotations, Homophones, Strong Verbs

Use the Week 3 grammar cards located in the back of this book to discuss the following concepts. Keep them handy so you can reference them as needed.

LEARN IT

Quotations

Spoken words should be enclosed with quotation marks. These are the rules:

- Enclose what someone says in quotation marks but not narration that sets up a quotation.
- When the speaker continues with more than one sentence, do not add close quotes until the end of his speech. Sometimes a speech will cover more than one day's assignment.
- Commas and periods go inside closing quotation marks.
- If narration interrupts a speech, use commas on both sides of the interruption. Commas "hug" the word they follow—that is, they come right next to it—not the word after them.

You will need to add quotation marks on Day 4 before and after the spoken words. Place the closing end mark inside the quotation marks.

Homophones and Usage

When sentences offer a choice of words, circle the correct one and then write it in your copy work. Homophones are words that sound alike but are spelled differently and have different meanings. Usage errors occur when one word is written but a different word is intended, like *its* and *it's*.

This week you have two sets of homophones: *there/their/they're* and *to/two/too*. Use the grammar cards to help you remember which is which.

Who-Which

If you have been doing Excellence in Writing, you have likely heard the term dress-ups. Dress-ups are ways of dressing up style in writing by using stronger vocabulary or more complex sentence structures. Keep an eye out for *who-which* clauses, which make sentences more complex. Mark them by writing *w-w* above the *who* or *which*.

Strong Verb

Another dress-up is the strong verb. On Day 4 select the strongest verb from the week's passages. Of the verbs used this week, which one is more colorful, provides a stronger image or feeling, or is more specific?

Students will be given a choice of homophones and some usage errors. As needed, help them circle and use the correct word.

Discuss each fix with your students and help them correctly mark the sentence in their student book. They may then copy it in their notebook, continuing where they left off last week. They should not include parts of speech notations, symbols, or underlining in their copy work.

Optional: If you are doing IEW writing, it is worth using these fixes to reinforce the concept of dress-ups and sentence openers. Now that your student has had a chance to identify verbs, reinforce the concept of strong verbs.

From now on at the end of Day 4, students will be asked to select the strongest verb from the week's sentences. Guide them to choose a word that provides a strong image or feeling or that is more specific.

DAY 1

$$n \qquad\qquad vb \qquad pr \quad vb \qquad\qquad\qquad n \qquad cc \quad pr \qquad n$$

¶ robin **blithely** whistled as he strolled along, thinking of maid marian and her bright eyes,

~~to / two /~~ too.

Fixes

blithely: in a joyous, merry manner

Indent. Is this a new topic, speaker, place, or time? Answer: Yes. Even though it is still the story of how Robin came to be an outlaw, we move to a side topic about his being in love with Maid Marian.

Capitalization.
- *Robin*—first word of sentence.
- *Maid Marian*—proper noun. Capitalize *Maid* because it is a title used with a name.

Homophones and usage. *too,* meaning *also.* It is correct to set off this transition with a comma.

End marks. This is a statement so add a period.

Grammar Notations

Verbs. *whistled, strolled.*

- ✏️ **Teacher's note.** If students mark *thinking* as a verb, decide whether or not they are ready to understand verbals, which are words formed from verbs but not used as verbs. If they are not ready, it is fine to let it go. See Grammar Glossary: Parts of Speech: Verbals, page G-9. *See* ♡ **1.**

Pronouns. *he, her. See* ♡ **2.**

Coordinating conjunctions. Ask: What words does *and* join? Answer: *Maid Marian* and *eyes* (two nouns, so no comma).

♡ **1. Grammar lovers.** This verbal *thinking* is a present participle, functioning as an adjective describing Robin.

♡ **2. Grammar lovers.** *Her* is a possessive pronoun in this passage (the bright eyes belonging to her), but it is sometimes an objective pronoun, as in *he thought of her.*

DAY 2

$$n \quad ar \quad\quad n \quad\quad n \quad\quad\quad vb \quad\quad\quad ar \quad n \quad w\text{-}w \quad pr \quad vb \quad ar \quad n$$

at such times, a young lad's heart **fancifully** turns toward the lass whom he loves the best.

Fixes

Indent. Is this a new topic, speaker, place, or time? Answer: No new paragraph because this is still about Robin's love.

Capitalization. *At*—first word of sentence.

End marks. This is a statement so add a period.

fanciful: led by imagination and feeling rather than reason

Grammar Notations

Articles and nouns. *times, a lad's heart, the lass, the best.*

If students have trouble recognizing *best* as a noun, point out that an article always has a noun after it and there is only one word after this *the. Best* is usually an adjective (as in "the best lass"), which is why this may be confusing.

Who-which clauses. Check that students labeled *whom* and ask them to read the entire clause aloud: *whom he loves the best.*

Ask: What noun does *whom* point back to or describe? Answer: *lass.* Point out that it comes immediately after the noun it describes. Students should follow this pattern in their own writing until they have mastered more advanced *who-which* clauses. *See* ♡.

✐ **Teacher's note.** Do not worry yet about teaching *whom* versus *who.*

✐ **Teacher's note.** This *who* clause is not set off with a comma because it is essential: it specifies or defines which lass is meant. If you remove the clause, does the sentence still makes sense? No (we wonder which lass), so the clause is essential and not set off with a comma. See Grammar Glossary: Punctuation: Commas: Rule 15. Essential-Nonessential Elements, page G-24.

♡ **Grammar lovers.** *Who* is in the subjective case and *whom* is in the objective case. In this sentence, we use *whom* because it is the direct object of *loves.* If students wonder why it is spelled this way, explain that *whom* goes with *her.* Since he loves *her,* we use *whom.*

DAY 3

pr vb n n cc ar
¶ he came suddenly upon fifteen foresters clothed in lincoln green and seated beneath a huge

n cc pr n
oak tree, feasting and drinking **convivially** beneath its ~~it's~~ branches.

Fixes

convivial: fond of feasting and merry company

Indent. Is this a new topic, speaker, place, or time? Answer: Yes, the passage turns from love to his encounter with the foresters.

Capitalization.

- *He*—first word of sentence.
- *Lincoln*—capitalize words derived from proper nouns.
- Do not capitalize types of plants like *oak tree*.

Homophones and usage. *its branches*. Ask: What does *it* refer back to? Answer: the oak tree.

End marks. This is a statement so add a period.

Grammar Notations

Articles and nouns. *foresters, Lincoln green, a oak tree, branches*.

⚝ **Advanced.** *Lincoln green* and *oak tree* are compound nouns. *See* ✐.

Verbs. *came*.

If students wish to mark *clothed* and *seated* or *feasting* and *drinking* as verbs, that is fine.

♡ **Grammar lovers.** Technically, *clothed* and *seated* are past participles and *feasting* and *drinking* are present participles, functioning as adjectives instead of as verbs.

Participles do not function as verbs unless they have a subject and helping verb immediately setting them up. Contrast this: The foresters *were* clothed; they *were* feasting. They still express a verb action, which is why this concept is advanced for this level. For more about verbals, see Grammar Glossary, G-9.

Coordinating conjunctions. Ask: What words does each *and* join? Answer: *clothed, seated* (two -ed words); *feasting, drinking* (two -ing words). Since these are each only two items in a series (not main clauses), they do not take a comma.

✐ **Teacher's note.** Lincoln green is a warm olive green named after the town of Lincoln, famous for its cloth and expert dyers during the Middle Ages. The foresters are employees of the crown. After they become outlaws, Robin Hood and his men also dress in Lincoln green.

DAY 4

pr   ar n   n   vb   n   pr   vb pr vb

¶ one of the men in green **accosted** robin. "you there ~~/their /they're~~, where are you going with

pr   n   n   cc   n

your quick step**,** **shoddy** bow**,** and cheap arrows**?"**

Fixes

Indent. Is this a new topic, speaker, place, or time? Answer: Yes, we have a new speaker. The first sentence sets up his speech so should go in the same paragraph as the actual dialogue.

Capitalization.

- *One, You*—first word of sentences.
- *Robin.*

Homophones and usage. Students should circle *there.* Ask them: What does *there* mean in this context? Answer: in that place. Remind students to check the spelling when they copy it into their notebook.

Quotations. Check that students placed quotation marks around the words spoken.

Commas with items in a series.

Ask: What words does *and* join? Answer: *step, bow, arrows* (three nouns).

Ask: What is the series and how should it be punctuated? Answer: *quick step, shoddy bow, and cheap arrows.* Pattern: **a, b, and** c.

End marks. He is asking a question, so close with a question mark placed inside the quotation marks.

accosted: boldly addressed or confronted

shoddy: of poor quality

Grammar Notations

Articles, nouns, and pronouns. *One, the men, green, Robin, step, bow, arrows.*

✧ **Advanced.** *One* is a pronoun here, acting as the subject of *accosted.* If students do not catch it, just explain briefly and move on. It is not a critical concept at this level.

✧ **Advanced.** If students do not recognize that *green* is a noun instead of an adjective, you can let it go. *See* ✎.

Verbs. *accosted, are going.* Ask: Which of these is a helping verb? Answer: *are,* which helps *going* (you are going).

✎ **Teacher's note.** We know that *green* is a noun because it has to be the object of the preposition *in*.

Style

Discuss the concept of strong verbs. Evaluate the action verbs from this week's sentences and decide which one is the strongest. Which dresses up the sentences best? Discuss their answer. Most likely candidates: *strolled* or *accosted.*

STUDENT REWRITE

Robin blithely whistled as he strolled along, thinking of Maid Marian and her bright eyes, too. At such times, a young lad's heart fancifully turns toward the lass whom he loves the best.

He came suddenly upon fifteen foresters clothed in Lincoln green and seated beneath a huge oak tree, feasting and drinking convivially beneath its branches.

One of the men in green accosted Robin. "You there, where are you going with your quick step, shoddy bow, and cheap arrows?"

Week 4

Teacher's note.
As you discuss each fix with your students and help them correctly mark the sentence in their student book, keep the exercise light and fun. It should be like a game. If your student groans when you say, "Time for Fix It!" something is wrong.

Adjectives, Nouns of Direct Address (NDAs), Usage: Then/Than

Use the Week 4 grammar cards located in the back of this book to discuss the following concepts. Keep them handy so you can reference them as needed.

LEARN IT

Adjectives (adj)
Adjectives describe nouns or pronouns and usually come before the noun. Use the Week 4 grammar card to review the adjective test. Mark adjectives with *adj*.

Commas with NDAs
This week you will learn about another comma rule. Commas are needed to set off nouns of direct address (NDAs). NDAs are usually names where someone is directly addressed by name, but in this story it is more common to see them as terms like *my friend* or *fair maiden* used in place of a name. Look for them in Day 4 and set them off with commas.

Homophones and Usage
This week you will be asked to choose the correct term: *then* (meaning *immediately afterward* or *next*) or *than* (a comparison term). This week's grammar card includes these and other terms that will come up in a few weeks.

Quotations
Sometimes a quotation will continue in another day's fix. Follow the directions for when to close them off and when to wait.

Page 10, Fix It! Grammar: Robin Hood, Student Book 2

DAY 1

¶ then/~~than~~ robin grew angry, for no young sprout likes to be **taunted** with his green years.

(grammar labels above the sentence: n, vb, adj, cc, adj, adj, n, vb, pr, adj, n)

Fixes

Indent. Is this a new topic, speaker, place, or time? Answer: Yes, the sentence pulls out of someone else's speech and turns attention to Robin's response. Pulling out of one character's speech usually counts as a new topic.

Capitalization.

- *Then*—first word of sentence.
- *Robin.*

Homophones and usage. *Then*, meaning *next* or *immediately afterward*.

End marks. This is a statement so add a period.

> **taunted:** ridiculed; provoked by witty insults
>
> Check students' understanding: **green** means young or not fully mature yet; **sprout** usually refers to a plant's new growth, but it can also mean a young person.

Grammar Notations

Verbs. *grew, likes.* See ♡.

- ☼ **Advanced.** If students mark the infinitive *to be* or the past participle *taunted* as a verb, you can point out that these are what we call verbals, words formed from verbs but usually not functioning as one. It is not critical that they distinguish verbals yet, although *Fix It!* will do so by not marking them as verbs. Encourage students to mark action verbs for the strong verb dress-up in their own writing.

Adjectives. *angry, no, young, green.*

- ☼ **Advanced.** Students may have trouble seeing that *angry* is an adjective instead of part of the verb. Point out that it describes the noun *Robin*, so it is an adjective.
- ☼ **Advanced.** If students do not mark *no*, it is not critical. Often *no* is an adverb, but since it describes a noun (*sprout*), it is an adjective.

Coordinating conjunctions. *for.*

Ask: What does this cc join? Answer: two main clauses (MCs): 1) Robin grew angry; 2) no young sprout likes to be taunted with his green years.

- ☼ **Advanced.** When two MCs are joined by a cc, they need a comma in front of the cc to hold them together. Pattern: **MC, cc MC**.

> ♡ **Grammar lovers.** *grew* is a linking verb connecting *Robin* to the subject complement *angry*.

DAY 2

Robin has more to say, so do not close the quotation until he finishes speaking in the next passage.

| pr | vb | | n | cc | n | vb | adj | adj | n | pr | vb | n |

¶ he replied, "my bow and arrows are as respectable as any man's. i am off to nottingham to

| pr | ar | adj | n |

prove it in a **champion** match.

Fixes

Indent. Is this a new topic, speaker, place, or time? Answer: Yes, we have a new speaker.

Capitalization.
- *He, My, I*—first word of sentences.
- *I, Nottingham*—proper nouns. *Nottingham* is a city.

Quotations. Check that students placed quotation marks before *My* but not at the end of the passage since Robin continues speaking in the Day 3 sentence.

Explain that there is a comma after *replied* because any narrative with a subject and speaking verb (*He replied*) that sets up a quotation takes a comma.

End marks. This is a statement so add a period.

> **champion:**
> first among all contestants, so the match that will determine the best archer

---

Grammar Notations

Verbs. *replied, are, am.* If students do not catch *are* or *am*, give them a list of basic *be* verbs (*am, is, are, was, were*) and ask them to find as many as they can.

  ✧ **Advanced.** *to prove* is a verbal known as an infinitive, which is *to* plus the verb. Infinitives do not function as verbs.

Adjectives. *respectable, any, champion.*

  ✧ **Advanced.** Students may have trouble identifying *respectable* as an adjective because it comes after the noun. Point out that it describes a noun (*bow and arrows*), so it must be an adjective.

Coordinating conjunctions. Ask: What does *and* join? Answer: *bow, arrows* (two nouns, so no comma).

> ✐ **Teacher's note.**
> The construction "as … as" is an idiom, and idioms do not easily lend themselves to parts of speech breakdown.

DAY 3

Robin is still speaking, so continue writing where you left off with no quotation marks until the end of this speech.

pr   vb   vb   adj   adj   n   ar adj   n   ar   n

there~~/their/they're~~ i will shoot with other worthy archers for the grand prize: a barrel of

adj   n   cc ar adj   n

top-notch ale and a new bow, ~~to/two/~~too."

Fixes

top-notch: outstanding; superior

Indent. Is this a new topic, speaker, place, or time? Answer: No, Robin is still speaking and on the same topic.

Capitalization.

- *There*—first word of sentence.
- *I*—proper noun.

Homophones and usage.

Students should circle *there*. Ask them: What does *there* mean in this context? Answer: *in that place.*

Students should circle *too*. Ask: What does the word mean in this context? Answer: *also.*

Quotations. Check that students continued writing where they left off without using quotation marks since Robin is still speaking. Also check that they placed quotation marks after *too*.

End marks. This is a statement so add a period. Check that it is placed inside closing quotation marks.

Grammar Notations

Verbs. *will shoot*. Ask: Which of these is a helping verb? Answer: *will* because it helps out *shoot*.

Coordinating conjunctions. Ask what words *and* connects. Answer: *barrel, bow* (two nouns).

- ✧ **Advanced.** If students mark *ale* and *bow*, explain that *ale* is part of a prepositional phrase describing *barrel*. Technically, *and* connects *barrel* and *bow*.
- ✧ **Advanced.** *For* is a preposition in this sentence, not a cc. If students are confused, remind them that words can function as more than one part of speech depending on how they are used.

DAY 4

TIP: In the passage below, can you find where to add the missing comma?

	vb	*cc*	*vb*		*adj*	*n*	*pr*	*vb*	*vb*	*vb*	*n*

¶ at this, all laughed aloud and **retorted**, "well boasted, fair infant! he will be taking ale with

pr   n

his milk next!"

🖉 **Teacher's note.** You may wish to discuss why the characters in this story drink ale instead of water. In the Middle Ages, the poor drank ale or cider because water was generally unclean. In the woods, cider would have been harder to make than ale. Plus, the original Robin Hood tales depict the woodsmen as carefree, bold, brave, and compassionate men who also enjoy feasting and drinking their ale.

> **retorted:** replied in similar manner back to the speaker, in this case mockingly
>
> Explain to students that the woodsmen are mocking Robin Hood by calling him "fair infant." **Fair** is a general term simply meaning *good*.

Fixes

Indent. Is this a new topic, speaker, place, or time? Answer: Yes, a new speaker.

Capitalization. *At, Well, He*—first word of sentences, including quoted sentences.

Quotations. Check that students placed quotation marks around the words spoken.

Commas with NDAs. Ask students if they can find where to add the missing comma. If they have trouble finding the noun of direct address, point out that it is not always someone's name. Answer: *fair infant*, which should be set off with a comma after *boasted*.

End marks. His mockery is exclamatory, so students can use a period or an exclamation mark inside the closing quotation marks.

Grammar Notations

Pronouns. *he, his*.

⚝ **Advanced.** *all* is an indefinite pronoun because there is no specific noun it is replacing, but you do not need to teach indefinite pronouns now.

Verbs. *laughed, retorted, will be taking*.

Ask: Which of these are helping verbs? Answer: *will be*, which help along *taking*.

🖉 **Teacher's note.** *boasted* is a past participle, another verbal not functioning as a verb because there is no subject and helping verb in front of it. However, if students mark it as a verb, that is fine. They do not need to understand this advanced concept yet.

Coordinating conjunctions. *and*. Ask what words *and* connects. Answer: *laughed, retorted* (two verbs, so no comma).

Style

Review the concept of strong verbs. Evaluate the action verbs from this week's sentences and decide which one is the strongest. Which dresses up the sentences best? Discuss their answer. Most likely candidate: *retorted*.

STUDENT REWRITE

Then Robin grew angry, for no young sprout likes to be taunted with his green years.

He replied, "My bow and arrows are as respectable as any man's. I am off to Nottingham to prove it in a champion match. There I will shoot with other worthy archers for the grand prize: a barrel of top-notch ale and a new bow, too."

At this, all laughed aloud and retorted, "Well boasted, fair infant! He will be taking ale with his milk next!"

Week 5

-ly Adverbs, Prepositions, Your/You're

Use the Week 5 grammar cards located in the back of this book to discuss the following concepts. Keep them handy so you can reference them as needed.

LEARN IT

-ly Adverbs (ly)

Many adverbs end in -ly. Look for them this week and mark them with an *ly*. The -ly word is another Excellence in Writing dress-up.

Notice the -ly adverbs in this sentence: "The *strikingly* tall stranger *vigorously* walked toward Robin." The first one (*strikingly*) modifies an adjective, and the second one (*vigorously*) modifies a verb.

Prepositions (prep)

Prepositional phrases are words that tell the position of something. For example, *under the table, near the door,* and *over the mantle* are all prepositional phrases.

Prepositional phrases always begin with a preposition and end with a noun. Use the list of prepositions on the Week 5 grammar card to help you find them.

Notice that the prepositional phrase includes both a preposition and a noun, but no verb. To help you remember this, think "preposition + noun, no verb."

Thus, whenever you see a preposition in the passage, write *prep* above it. In order to see the prepositional phrase better, underline the entire phrase like this:

In the morning the dog barked. The cat slept under the table.

Identifying prepositional phrases can be challenging, so if you find this difficult, your teacher can help you.

Your/You're

This week you have another homophone: the possessive *your* and the contraction *you're*. Use the grammar card from Weeks 3 and 5 to help you remember which is which.

This program uses mastery learning to teach grammar concepts. Thus, your student will have many opportunities to practice each of the markings. To understand how this works, listen to the talks "Mastery Learning" and "But, But, But … What About Grammar?" See the blue page of this book for free download instructions.

Continue to have your student copy the corrected text into their notebook. Be sure they are not including the markings or underlines. Although this step may seem like a waste of time, it is actually a great exercise to ensure the transfer of learning.

DAY 1

Choose end marks to follow *away* and *leader*. Think about where to place the last mark of punctuation in relation to the closing quotation marks.

                prep   *pr*   *n*   *n*   *vb*   *ar*   *n*   *vb* *adj* *n* *prep*

¶ **affronted** by ~~there~~/their/~~they're~~ mockery, robin challenged the foresters. "see that herd of

n

deer over there/~~their~~/~~they're~~ more ~~then~~/than sixty yards away? i bet you twenty pounds i

                                      adj   *n*   *pr vb pr*   *adj*   *n*   *pr*

vb vb ar   *n*

can hit the leader!"

Fixes

Indent. Is this a new topic, speaker, place, or time? Answer: Yes, a new speaker. These sentences can go in the same paragraph since the first sets up the speech.

Capitalization.

- *Affronted, See*—first word of sentences.
- *Robin, I*—proper nouns.

Homophones and usage.

The first is the possessive *their* (the mockery of the foresters); the second is the adverb *there* meaning *in that place* (the deer over in that place).

Than implicitly compares one distance to one greater than sixty yards.

Quotations. Check that students placed quotation marks around the words spoken.

End marks.

Question mark after *away* since he is asking a question.

Robin's claim is bold so could use either an exclamation mark or a period, placed inside the closing quotation marks.

Grammar Notations

Verbs. *challenged, See, bet, can hit.* Ask: Which of these are helping verbs? Answer: *can,* which helps out *hit.*

  ✦ **Advanced.** Some students may mark *affronted* as a verb. Explain that it functions as an adjective describing *Robin. See* ♡.

Adjectives. *that, sixty, twenty.* Explain that numbers are adjectives when they describe a noun (*sixty yards, twenty pounds*) but nouns if they stand alone. *See* ✎.

Prepositional phrases. *by their mockery, of deer. See* ✎.

- Check that your students underline each phrase starting with a preposition and ending with a noun.
- Using the parts of speech notations and preposition grammar card, show your student how each phrase fits the prepositional phrase pattern (**preposition + noun/pronoun**) and has no verb in it. For example, *by their mockery* begins with a word from the preposition list and ends with a noun, and *their* is not a verb.

affronted: offended; embarrassed

Explain that a **pound** is a British unit of money.

♡ **Grammar lovers.** For more information about participles and when they function as verbs or adjectives, see the Grammar Glossary: Sentence Openers: #4 -ing Participial Phrase Opener: Advanced #4 Opener, page G-41.

✎ **Teacher's note.** The goal is to flag most of the common parts of speech. When their identification is especially difficult, the words are not labeled in the passage. Advanced students may catch these: *Over there* is an adverb phrase answering the adverb question "See where?" It is not a prepositional phrase because *there* as a pronoun means *that place*, and it does not make sense to say "over that place."

DAY 2

¶ then/~~than~~ robin **composedly** took his bow in his hand, grabbed an arrow, and drew the

> *n* · *ly* · *vb* · *pr* · *n* · *prep* · *pr* · *n* · *vb* · *ar* · *n* · *cc* · *vb* · *ar*

feather to his ear. the next moment an arrow sped down the glade and shot the noblest **buck**

> *n* · *prep* · *pr* · *n* · *ar* · *adj* · *n* · *ar* · *n* · *vb* · *prep* · *ar* · *n* · *cc* · *vb* · *ar* · *adj* · *n*

of the herd.

> *prep* · *ar* · *n*

Fixes

composedly: calmly

buck: a male deer

Indent. Is this a new topic, speaker, place, or time? Answer: Yes, it pulls out of Robin's speech and turns attention to his actions.

Capitalization.
- *Then, The*—first word of sentences.
- *Robin*—proper noun.

Homophones and usage. *Then*, meaning *next* or *immediately afterward*.

Commas with items in a series.

Ask: What words do the cc's connect and how they should be punctuated? Answer: *took, grabbed,* and *drew* (three verbs, so commas: **a, b, and c**); *sped* and *shot* (two verbs, so no comma: **a and b**).

End marks. This is a statement so add a period.

Grammar Notations

Adjectives. *next, noblest*. Explain that *noblest* is the superlative (*-est*) form of the adjective *noble* and is also an adjective.

-ly Adverbs. *composedly*. Ask: What part of speech does this adverb describe? Answer: a verb, *took*.

Prepositional phrases. *in his hand, to his ear, down the glade, of the herd*. Check that your students underlined each phrase.

Using the students' parts of speech notations on today's passage and the Preposition grammar card, show that each phrase fits the prepositional phrase pattern (**preposition + noun/pronoun**) and has no verb in it. For example, *in, to, down,* and *of* are all on the preposition list; *hand, ear, glade,* and *herd* are all nouns; *his* and *the* are not verbs.

Institute for Excellence in Writing

DAY 3

ar   n   vb   vb   prep   n   cc   ar   pr w-w vb   ar   n   vb   ar   n

¶ all the foresters were filled <u>with rage</u>, but the one who lost the **wager seethed** the most.

Fixes

Indent. Is this a new topic, speaker, place, or time? Answer: Yes, a new topic, turning attention to the foresters' reaction.

Capitalization. *All*—first word of sentence.

End marks. This is a statement so add a period.

wager: bet; something staked on an uncertain event

seethed: burned with anger

Grammar Notations

Verbs. *were filled, lost, seethed.*

> Ask: Which of these are helping verbs? Answer: *were*, which helps out *filled*.

Prepositional phrases. *with rage.*

> Check for underlines. Have students show you how the phrase fits the pattern of **preposition + noun (and no verb).**

Coordinating conjunctions. *but.*

> Ask what the cc's connect. Answer: two main clauses.

> ✧ **Advanced.** Two main clauses joined by a coordinating conjunction need a comma before the cc. Pattern: **MC, cc MC.**

Pronouns. *One* is a pronoun here acting as the subject of *seethed.*

***Who-which* clauses.** Check that students marked *who* and ask them to read the entire clause aloud: *who lost the wager.*

> Ask: What noun or pronoun does this clause describe? Answer: *one.* Show that *who* comes immediately after *one.*

> ✎ **Teacher's note.** Most *who-which* clauses take commas, but not if they are essential. This clause defines which *one* is meant, the one who lost the wager, so it is needed or essential to the meaning of the main clause and therefore not set off with commas. Another grammatical term for essential elements is restrictive because they restrict the information to that particular one.

DAY 4

Hint: In the passage below look for the NDA (noun of direct address).

| ar   n   ly   vb   n pr vb vb ar   n   n   w-w vb ar adj |

¶ the loser heatedly responded, "fool, you have killed the king's deer, which is a **capital**

| n   prep n   pr   n   vb   vb   vb |

offense. by law, your ~~you're~~ ears should be shaven."

Fixes

Indent. Is this a new topic, speaker, place, or time? Answer: Yes, a new speaker.

Capitalization.

- *The, Fool, By*—first word of sentences.

    When a quoted sentence comes after narrative that sets it up, we still capitalize the first word in the quotation even though it comes after other words in the complete sentence: *The loser responded, "You … ."*

    The rule is to capitalize first words of sentences and first words of quoted sentences.

- Do not capitalize *king's* because the title is not used with a name.

Homophones and usage. *your*, the possessive.

Quotations. Check that students placed quotation marks around the words spoken. Show again that commas are used with direct quotations when a speaking verb (*responded*) sets up the quote.

Commas with NDAs. Ask students to find the noun of direct address. Point out that it is not always someone's name. Answer: *Fool*, which should be set off with a comma.

End marks. This is a statement so add a period inside the closing quotation marks.

Grammar Notations

Nouns. *loser, Fool, king's deer, offense, law, ears.* See ✎ **1**.

Verbs. *responded, have killed, is, should be shaven.*

Ask: Which of these are helping verbs? Answer: *have, should be*. If students missed *is*, show them a list of *be* verbs (*am, is, are, was, were*) and have them search for it.

☼ **Advanced.** *is* is not a helping verb here because it is not followed by another verb.

-ly Adverbs. *heatedly*. Ask: What part of speech does this adverb describe? Answer: a verb, *responded*.

Who-which clauses. Check that students marked *which* and ask them to read the entire clause aloud: *which is a capital offense*.

☼ **Advanced.** Usually *who-which* clauses describe the noun that comes immediately before them. Sometimes they describe the idea of the preceding clause instead. It is not the deer that is a capital offense but the idea of killing one. Encourage young and struggling students to form *who-which* clauses immediately after the noun they describe. See ✎ **2**.

Prepositional phrases. *By law*. Check for underlines. Have students show how the phrase fits the pattern: **preposition + noun (no verb)**.

Continued on next page ▸

capital: punishable by death

Check that students understand the forester is addressing Robin with the offensive term *fool*.

✎ **1. Teacher's note.** *King's* is a possessive noun. Some grammar books teach these as adjectives since they modify the noun after them. Technically, they are nouns in the possessive (genitive) case, meaning *of the king*. However, the only important thing to understand is that *king's* is possessive, which is why it needs an apostrophe to show possession. If students mark this as an adjective or do not label it at all, you can let it go.

✎ **2. Teacher's note.** This clause adds information to the main clause but does not specify which deer or change the meaning of the main clause, so it is nonessential and is set off with a comma.

Style

Review the concept of strong verbs. Evaluate the action verbs from this week's sentences and decide which one is the strongest. Which dresses up the sentences best? Discuss their answer. Best possibilities: *sped, seethed.*

STUDENT REWRITE

Affronted by their mockery, Robin challenged the foresters. "See that herd of deer over there more than sixty yards away? I bet you twenty pounds I can hit the leader!"

Then Robin composedly took his bow in his hand, grabbed an arrow, and drew the feather to his ear. The next moment an arrow sped down the glade and shot the noblest buck of the herd.

All the foresters were filled with rage, but the one who lost the wager seethed the most.

The loser heatedly responded, "Fool, you have killed the king's deer, which is a capital offense. By law, your ears should be shaven."

Week 6

Dress-Ups: Quality Adjectives and -ly Adverbs

LEARN IT

This week you will have an opportunity to practice what you have learned so far. Keep your grammar cards handy to help you remember the rules.

Continue to use the abbreviations at the top of the next page and the grammar cards to help you remember how to mark and correct the passage. Your teacher will help you with anything you miss. Remember, a mistake is an opportunity to learn.

Dress-Ups So far you have reviewed three of the Excellence in Writing dress-ups: strong verb, quality adjective, and -ly adverb. If you are taking an IEW writing course, the -ly adverb list your teacher provides for you to select words from will help expand your vocabulary. (For more information on Excellence in Writing programs, see IEW.com/start.)

To practice identifying the dress-ups, on Day 4 review the passages from the week and choose the strongest verb, adjective, and -ly adverb from this week's fixes. Remember that the words you count as dress-ups in your own writing should be strong ones.

Once the sentence has been marked, have your student copy it in their notebook without all the grammar notations, continuing where they left off last week. This rewrite cements the fixes in a student's mind.

Page 14, *Fix It! Grammar:* **Robin Hood, Student Book 2**

DAY 1

<pre>
         ly   ar   n   vb   prep pr n   vb   pr n   prep ar   n   cc vb pr
¶ impulsively the forester sprang to his feet, armed his bow with an arrow, and sent it
</pre>

<pre>
            prep   n
whistling after robin.
</pre>

Fixes

Indent. Is this a new topic, speaker, place, or time? Answer: Yes, because of a new topic, leaving speech and turning to his actions.

Capitalization.

- *Impulsively*—first word of sentence.
- *Robin*—proper noun.

Commas with items in a series.

Ask: Which words does this coordinating conjunction *and* join? Answer: *sprang, armed, sent.*

Ask: What part of speech are they? Answer: verbs.

Ask: What punctuation? Answer: commas in the pattern **a, b, and c.**

End marks. This is a statement so add a period.

Grammar Notations

Verbs. *sprang, armed, sent.*

  ✏ **Teacher's note.** If students mark *whistling* as a verb, praise them even though technically it is not a verb. *See* ♡.

-ly Adverbs. Ask: What part of speech does *impulsively* describe? Answer: a verb, *sprang* (*the forester impulsively sprang to his feet*).

Prepositional phrases. *to his feet, with an arrow, after Robin.* Check for underlines. Have students use their parts of speech notations to show the pattern in each of these phrases: **preposition + noun (no verb).**

> ✏ **Teacher's note.** Remember that you do not need to complete all the discussion notes with your student. They are there if you need them, but if your student has mastered a skill you do not need to reinforce it daily. Use the grammar notations to help your student gain mastery, but do not let this become a drudgery. Continue to make the entire process a game. Let your student tell you what he or she knows and laugh when something is missed or mismarked: a mistake is an opportunity to learn.

impulsively: quickly and rashly

♡ **Grammar lovers.** The -ing participle *whistling* is a verbal formed from a verb but functioning as an adjective describing *it*.

DAY 2

n   vb   adj   ar   n   vb   adj prep n   ar   n   ly

robin hood was fortunate that the forester was drunk <u>with ale</u> because the arrow narrowly

vb   pr   cc   pr   adj   n   ly   vb   prep ar adj   n

missed him, but his **hot-blooded opponent** immediately reached <u>for a second arrow</u>.

Fixes

Indent. Is this a new topic, speaker, place, or time? Answer: No, this continues the account of the forester's attempt to punish Robin.

Capitalization. *Robin Hood*—first word of sentence and proper noun.

End marks. This is a statement so add a period.

hot-blooded: excitable and quick to act

opponent: adversary; person on the opposing side

Grammar Notations

Verbs. *was, was, missed, reached.*

  ✎ **Teacher's note.** If students miss either *was*, show them a list of *be* verbs (*am, is, are, was, were*) and ask them to search for any of them. *See* ♡.

Adjectives. *fortunate, drunk, hot-blooded, second.*

  ❅ **Advanced.** *fortunate* and *drunk* are adjectives describing the noun that comes before them: fortunate Robin Hood; the drunk forester.

-ly Adverbs. *narrowly, immediately*. Ask: What part of speech do these adverbs describe? Answer: verbs, *missed* and *reached*.

Prepositional phrases. *with ale, for a second arrow*. Check for underlines. Ask: With each of these phrases, show the pattern: **preposition + noun (no verb)**.

Coordinating conjunctions. Ask: What does the cc *but* connect? Answer: two main clauses with a comma (*Robin Hood was fortunate that the forester was drunk with ale; his hot-blooded opponent immediately reached for a second arrow*).

  ❅ **Advanced.** This is the comma rule **MC, cc MC** (two main clauses may be joined by a comma plus cc).

♡ **Grammar lovers.** Both *was*'s are linking verbs, not helping verbs, linking the subject to the subject complement (adjective) that follows.

DAY 3

prep   *n*   *adj*   *n*   *vb*   *ar*   *n*   *prep*   *ar*   *n*   *pr*   *vb*   *pr*   *cc*   *pr*   *vb*

in self-defense young robin returned an arrow to the forester. it struck him, and he **toppled**

         prep   *ar*   *n*

forward with a cry**.**

Fixes

Indent. Is this a new topic, speaker, place, or time? Answer: No. It is still on the topic of what happened as an immediate result of Robin's killing the deer.

Capitalization.

- *In, It*—first word of sentences.
- *Robin.*

End marks. This is a statement so add a period.

> **toppled:** fell or tumbled down, as from too heavy a top

Grammar Notations

Prepositional phrases. *In self-defense, to the forester, with a cry*. Check for underlines.

Ask: With each of these phrases, show the pattern: **preposition + noun (no verb)**.

Coordinating conjunctions. *and*.

Ask: What does the cc connect? Answer: two main clauses with a comma (*It struck him; he toppled forward with a cry*).

✧ **Advanced.** This is the comma rule for two main clauses joined by a coordinating conjunction: **MC, cc MC**.

DAY 4

n   *vb*   *pr*   *n*   *vb*   *adj*   *prep*   *pr*   *cc*   *pr*   *vb*   *vb*   *prep*   *pr*

robin hood **hastened** away. his heart was sick within him, for it was now borne upon him

pr   *vb*   *vb*   *ar*   *n*

that he had killed a man.

Fixes

Indent. Is this a new topic, speaker, place, or time? Answer: No, the topic is the same.

Capitalization. *Robin Hood, His*—first word of sentences.

Spelling. Check that students spell *borne* correctly. This has nothing to do with giving birth but is the past participle of the verb *to bear*. *To bear upon someone* is to press or weigh heavily upon him.

End marks. This is a statement so add a period.

> **hastened:** hurried; moved with haste

Grammar Notations

Verbs. *hastened, was, was borne, had killed.*

Ask: Which of these are helping verbs? Answer: the second *was*, which helps out *borne*, and *had*, which helps out *killed*. The first *was* is a linking verb connecting the subject (*heart*) to an adjective.

Adjectives. *sick.* See ♡.

Prepositional phrases. *within him, upon him.* Check for underlines.

Ask: With each of these phrases, show the pattern: **preposition + noun (no verb)**.

   ✧ **Advanced.** If students mark *for* as a preposition, remind them that words can be more than one part of speech depending on how they are used. Sometimes *for* is a preposition, but only when it fits the pattern. See coordinating conjunctions, below.

Coordinating conjunctions. *for.*

   ✧ **Advanced.** When a cc connects two main clauses, the sentence needs a comma (Rule: **MC, cc MC**): *His heart was sick within him, for it was now borne upon him that he had killed a man.*

> ♡ **Grammar lovers.** The adjective *sick* is a subject complement, which follows a linking verb. See the Grammar Glossary: Parts of Speech: Nouns: Other Noun Functions (Advanced), page G-6.

Style

Have your students identify the best dress-ups from this week's sentences. These should be words that provide a powerful image or feeling or that are more specific. Discuss their answers. Best possibilities:

Strong verbs. *sprang, slung, toppled, hastened.*

Quality adjectives. *hot-blooded.*

-ly adverbs. *impulsively, narrowly.*

STUDENT REWRITE

Impulsively the forester sprang to his feet, armed his bow with an arrow, and sent it whistling after Robin. Robin Hood was fortunate that the forester was drunk with ale because the arrow narrowly missed him, but his hot-blooded opponent immediately reached for a second arrow. In self-defense young Robin returned an arrow to the forester. It struck him, and he toppled forward with a cry. Robin Hood hastened away. His heart was sick within him, for it was now borne upon him that he had killed a man.

Week 7

Subjects and Clause Identification

To help you remember these things for future lessons, add the Week 7 grammar card to your collection. Keep the remaining cards handy for review.

LEARN IT

Subject (*S*)
Verbs (*V*)

Now that you have gotten good at finding nouns and verbs, it is time to learn about subjects, which are nouns or pronouns that perform a verb action. However, not all nouns and pronouns function as a subject.

A subject is not a part of speech. It is actually the function or job of some nouns and pronouns. Thus, saying that a noun is a subject identifies how it functions in that sentence.

The easiest way to identify subjects is to find the verb first and then ask, "Who or what is doing this action?" That is the subject. Since you are now identifying subject-verb pairs (*S-V*), mark subjects with a capital *S* and verbs with a capital *V* instead of *vb*.

The only nouns or pronouns you need to mark now are those that are the subject. Do not mark any noun or pronoun that is not a subject. Also, you do not need to mark the articles anymore.

Clauses

Since you will be identifying subjects, you can also find the clauses. A clause is a group of words that hang together and have a subject and a verb.

Some clauses are independent or main (MC for main clause) and can stand alone as sentences, whereas others are dependent and must be connected to a MC to be a sentence. A sentence can have more than one clause and thus more than one subject-verb pair.

To help you see the clauses in a sentence, place each clause within brackets [ ]. You will find that almost all the words in a sentence will end up in one of the clauses, even many prepositional phrases!

Your teacher can help guide you as long as you need help. Be patient. After a time, this will get easier, and it will make the upcoming comma rules much easier to understand if you can easily see the clauses in a sentence.

Who-Which
(*S/w-w*)

Interestingly, the *who* or *which* is usually the subject of its clause, so label that word as both a subject and *who-which* (*S/w-w*). Add that label to your *Who-which* grammar card to remember this marking.

> ✏ **Teacher's note.** Keep these lessons short and fun. Make these notations more of a game than an exercise. You cannot help too much! The goal is daily repetition to gently move your students toward mastery.
>
> ◀ **Listen.** For more on the process of mastery learning, see the blue page of this book for a free mp3 download entitled "Mastery Learning."

Students will no longer mark articles and nouns or pronouns. Instead, they should identify subjects by finding the verb first and then asking, "Who or what is doing this action?" That is the subject. They will mark subjects with *S* and verbs with *V*.

Explain what a **clause** is: a group of words that hang together and have a subject and a verb. Ask students to enclose them in brackets in their student pages.

Discuss each fix with your students and help them correctly mark the sentence in their student book. Help your student as much as he needs, even if it takes all year.

✏ **Teacher's note.** Students often have trouble seeing what words to include in front of the subject-verb of a dependent clause. The most common dependent clause starters are *who, which, that,* and what IEW calls the www words: *when, while, where, as, since, if, although, because.* Show your students this list to choose from if they do not include one of these words with the rest of the dependent clause.

> who, which, that, when, while, where, as, since, if, although, because

DAY 1

¶ [robin hood escaped to sherwood forest], for [he was now an outlaw on ~~to~~ / two / ~~too~~

accounts].

S V prep cc S V prep adj

Fixes

accounts: reasons

Indent. Is this a new topic, speaker, place, or time? Answer: Yes, a new place.

Capitalization.
- *Robin Hood*—first word of sentence.
- *Sherwood Forest*—proper noun.

Homophones and usage. *two*, the number.

End marks. This is a statement so add a period.

Grammar Notations

Subjects and verbs. *Robin Hood (S) escaped (vb), he (S) was (vb).* If students wonder, explain that *was* is not a helping verb since it is not followed by another verb. *See* ♡.

Prepositional phrases. *to Sherwood Forest, on two accounts.* Check for underlines. With each of these phrases, ask students to show the pattern: **preposition + noun (no verb)**.

Coordinating conjunctions. *for.*

  ✨ **Advanced.** When a cc connects two main clauses, the sentence needs a comma (Rule: **MC, cc MC**): *Robin Hood escaped to Sherwood Forest, for he was now an outlaw on two accounts.*

Clauses. After students have marked everything else, work them through questions like the following to help them identify the clauses. Keep this light and fun; make it a game. As you help them identify the clauses, check that they put brackets around each clause. *See* ✏.

- What is the first verb? *escaped.* Who or what is doing this action? *Robin Hood.* What is the clause? *Robin Hood escaped to Sherwood Forest.* (Include related prepositional phrases within the clauses.)
- What is the next verb? *was.* Who or what is doing this action? *he.* What is the clause? *He was now an outlaw on two accounts.*

♡ **Grammar lovers.** *was* is a linking verb, linking the subject (*he*) to a subject complement (*outlaw*).

✏ **Teacher's note.** End the clause at a logical place after the S-V pair. Students should pick up prepositional phrases that go with the clause, but keep it simple. The ending is not as critical as the beginning.

DAY 2

S V V   S   V   prep   adj   cc   S   V   V
[he had shot a deer] [that the king **reserved** for his own table], and, worse, [he had slain a

man, ~~to two~~ too].

Fixes

Indent. Is this a new topic, speaker, place, or time? Answer: No, this continues to explain
why he was outlawed.

Capitalization.

- *He*—first word of sentence.
- Do not capitalize *king*, which is a common noun here since there is no name.

Homophones and usage. *too*, meaning *also*.

End marks. This is a statement so add a period.

Grammar Notations

Subjects and verbs. *He had shot, king reserved, he had slain.* Ask: Identify the helping
verbs. Answer: *had* (twice), which helps along *shot* and *slain*.

Prepositional phrases. *for his own table.* Check for underline. Ask students to show the
pattern: **preposition + noun (no verb).**

Coordinating conjunctions. *and.*

☆ **Advanced.** What does the cc connect? Answer: two main clauses with a comma
(Rule: **MC, cc MC**): *He had shot a deer,* and *he had slain a man.*

Clauses. Guide your students to place brackets around each clause. To find the clauses,
remind them to look for the verbs.

- What is the first verb? *had shot.* Who is doing this action? *He.*
  What is the clause? *He had shot a deer.*
- What is the next verb? *reserved.* Who is doing this action? *the king.*
  What is the clause? *that the king reserved for his own table. See ✏.*
- What is the last verb? *had slain.* Who is doing the action? *he.*
  What is the clause? *He had slain a man.*

reserved: saved for
future use

It was a common
practice for royalty
and the aristocracy
in England to have
exclusive rights to
hunt in the forests of
their domain. This
encouraged illegal
poaching among the
poorest classes.

✏ **Teacher's note.** If
your students do not
include *that* at the
start of this clause,
show them the list
of common clause
starters on page 44
and ask them to find
one of them in the
passage.

DAY 3

adj			S	V	V	ly		V	prep		S/w-w	V		prep

[two hundred pounds would be **lavishly** rewarded to the man] [who delivered robin hood to

the king].

Fixes

Indent. Is this a new topic, speaker, place, or time? Answer: No, the topic is the same.

Capitalization.
- *Two*—first word of sentence.
- *Robin Hood.*
- Lowercase: *king.*

End marks. This is a statement so add a period.

Grammar Notations

Subjects and verbs. *pounds would be rewarded, who delivered.*

Ask: Which of these are helping verbs? Answer: *would be,* which helps along *rewarded.*

Prepositional phrases. *to the man, to the king.* Check for underlines. Ask students to show the pattern: **preposition + noun (no verb).**

Who-which **clauses.** Ask: What noun does this clause describe and where is it? Answer: *man,* which comes immediately before the *who* clause. See ✎.

- ✿ **Advanced.** The *who-which* clause defines what man is meant, the man who delivered Robin, so it is essential to the meaning of the main clause and therefore not set off with a comma.

Clauses. Guide your students to place square brackets around each clause. To find the clauses look for the verbs.

- What is the first verb? *would be rewarded.* Help students to see that *pounds* is the subject.
  What is the clause? *Two hundred pounds would be lavishly rewarded to the man.* See ♡.
- What is the next verb? *delivered.* Who is doing this action? *who.* This is advanced, so decide if your students are ready to understand it.
  What is the clause? *who delivered Robin Hood to the king.*

---

lavishly: abundantly.

Two hundred pounds would have been a huge sum of money — literally 200 pounds of silver!

✎ **Teacher's note.** The subject of any *who-which* clause is usually *who* or *which.* It follows the noun it describes and needs its own verb in the clause.

♡ **Grammar lovers.** The first clause is in passive voice, so the subject of the sentence (pounds) is being acted upon by someone else (the king). In passive voice, the person or thing doing the action is not the subject of the sentence. However, this is too advanced to teach at this level. See Grammar Glossary: Additional Rules and Concepts: Passive versus Active Voice, page G-33.

DAY 4

S   prep   V   V   S   V
[because the sheriff of <u>nottingham</u> was related to ~~two / too~~ the slain forester], [he had a

vendetta to ~~two / too~~ catch <u>robin hood</u>.

Fixes

Indent. Is this a new topic, speaker, place, or time? Answer: Students may wish to start a new paragraph because attention turns to the sheriff's desire for revenge. Next week's passages show that there is only one sentence on this subject, however, which could equally well be seen as the same topic of Robin's outlawry. Let your students choose!

Capitalization.

- *Because*—first word of sentence.
- *Sheriff of Nottingham, Robin Hood*—proper nouns.

Homophones and usage.

- *to*, the adverb.
- the *to* in an infinitive that goes with a verb form: *to catch*.

End marks. This is a statement so add a period.

Grammar Notations

Subjects and verbs. *Sheriff of Nottingham was related, he had.*

Ask: Which of these are helping verbs? Answer: *was*, which helps along *related*.

✧ **Advanced.** If students mark the infinitive *to catch* as a verb, decide whether to let it go. It is another verbal (an infinitive), which does not function as a verb because it has no subject.

Prepositional phrases. *of Nottingham; to the slain forester.* Check for underlines. If students did not mark the first one, that is fine since it is part of a title. The goal is to distinguish the main prepositional phrases from other structural elements in the sentences to help later on with punctuation.

✧ **Advanced.** If students marked *to catch*, praise them because the *to* in infinitives is a preposition. However, since infinitives work a little differently from regular prepositional phrases, we will not flag them as prepositions in this book.

Clauses. Guide your students to place brackets around each clause.

- What is the first verb? *was related.* Who is doing the action? *Sheriff of Nottingham.* What word begins this clause (not the subject this time)? *Because.* What is the clause? *Because the Sheriff of Nottingham was related to the slain forester.* See ✎.
- What is the next verb? *had.* What is the subject? *he.* What is the clause? *he had a vendetta to catch Robin Hood.*

Continued on next page ▶

vendetta: a private feud where someone seeks to avenge the death of a family member

✎ **Teacher's note.** Your student might notice that this clause cannot stand alone at a sentence. That is right! This is a dependent clause because it has a subject and a verb but it cannot stand alone. It needs to be attached to a main clause to be a complete sentence. This will be addressed next week when you introduce the adverb clause.

Style

Have your students evaluate this week's sentences for the best of the following dress-ups. Discuss their answers. Best possibilities:

Strong verbs. *reserved, slain.*
Quality adjectives. *slain. See ✎.*
-ly adverbs. *lavishly.*

✎ **Teacher's note.**
Point out that the same word functions as a verb in one sentence and an adjective in another.

STUDENT REWRITE

Robin Hood escaped to Sherwood Forest, for he was now an outlaw on two accounts. He had shot a deer that the king reserved for his own table, and, worse, he had slain a man, too. Two hundred pounds would be lavishly rewarded to the man who delivered Robin Hood to the king. Because the Sheriff of Nottingham was related to the slain forester, he had a vendetta to catch Robin Hood.

Week 8

Main and Dependent Clauses, Clause Starters, Lie versus Lay

Cut out the Week 8 grammar cards to help you remember these concepts.

___

LEARN IT

Last week you learned how to identify the subject of a sentence by finding the verb, and you put square brackets around the clauses. This week you will learn how to tell the difference between two types of clauses: main and dependent. For each subject-verb pair, you will need to determine if it belongs to a main clause or a dependent clause. Use brackets [ ] to surround main clauses and parentheses ( ) to surround dependent clauses. Here is how you can tell.

Main Clause (MC)	A main clause is a clause that can stand alone as a sentence. Like all clauses, it must have a subject and a verb. Examples: [*Robin Hood stood alone*]. [*His courageous men stood with him*].
	Main clauses usually start with a subject or with an article (*a, an, the*) and/or adjectives plus subject. Sometimes the subject-verb will be switched. Examples: [*There gathered around him displaced countrymen*]. [*Up rose his Merry Men*].
	If there is a prepositional phrase in the middle or at the end of the clause, include it in the clause. However, if the prepositional phrase comes at the beginning, do not include it. Examples: [*Robin perched in the sycamore tree*]. <u>*In the tree*</u> [*Robin was safe*].
	To help you see the main clauses, label them *MC*.
Dependent Clause (DC)	A dependent clause cannot stand alone as a sentence. It looks like a main clause, but one or more words in front of it turn the main clause into something that leaves us hanging. Place the dependent clause in parentheses ( ) and label it *DC*.
	A *who-which* clause is one example of a dependent clause. It cannot stand alone. Examples: (*which displayed great courage*) or (*who sang like a bird*).
Clause Starters (cl)	There is another list of words that can be used to start a dependent clause. The words are *when, while, where, as, since, if, although, because*. To help you remember the list, use the acronym www.asia.b.
www.asia.b	Officially, these words are called subordinating conjunctions because they begin a subordinate clause, but you do not have to worry about the terminology. For now, just learn the list of words. There are more words that can be added to that list, but this is a good start.
	Mark the www.asia.b word with a *cl* and put parentheses around the clause. Label the clause *DC*.
Usage: lie/lay	It is important to learn when to use *lay* and when to use *lie* (in the sense of lying down, not telling a lie). You lie yourself down; you lay down an object. Thus, a character might lie down, but he will lay down his weapons. You can lie on the couch but lay your book on the table. It is tricky because the past tense of *lie* is *lay*, but the past tense of *lay* is *laid*. Keep the grammar card for this handy, and practice in the Fix Its.

Teacher's note. Discuss each fix with your students and help them correctly mark the sentence in their student book. They may then copy it in their notebook.

MC. Teach the difference between main and dependent clauses, recognizing that the difference is critical to being able to punctuate sentences properly.

Teacher's note. Clause starters (www.asia.b words) are both a dress-up and a sentence opener in IEW's style system because they add complexity to the sentence structure. However, that distinction will not be addressed until Week 12.

DAY 1

MC   S   V   prep   prep   prep adj   DC cl S   ly   V

¶ [robin hood lay, ~~laid~~ in hiding in sherwood forest for one year] (as he **adroitly** prepared his

adj
new life).

Fixes *See ✐.*

Indent. Is this a new topic, speaker, place, or time? Answer: Yes, a new scene and time.

Capitalization. The capitalized words will no longer be specifically addressed in the Fix It! notes unless there is a special situation to discuss. Simply use the three underlines above to check for words that need capitalizing and refer to the grammar card or Grammar Glossary for the rules.

Homophones and usage. *lay*, the past tense of *lie*. Robin Hood is lying himself in hiding.

End marks. This is a statement so add a period.

Grammar Notations

Subjects and verbs. *Robin Hood lay, he prepared.*

Prepositional phrases. *in hiding, in Sherwood Forest, for one year.* Check for underlines. Ask students to show the pattern: **preposition + noun (no verb).**

  ✧ **Advanced.** If students have trouble explaining how *in hiding* fits the pattern, just tell them that *-ing* words sometimes function as nouns. *See ♡.*

Clauses. Check for brackets and parentheses and MC or DC identification.

- *Robin Hood lay in hiding in Sherwood Forest for one year.*

    Ask: What kind of clause is this? Answer: MC. It has a subject (*Robin Hood*) and verb (*lay*) and can stand alone as a sentence.

- *as he adroitly prepared his new life.*

    Ask: What kind of clause is this? Answer: DC. It begins with a subordinating conjunction (*as*), it has a subject and a verb so is a clause, and it cannot stand alone as a sentence.

    Read the clause aloud to your students to help them hear that it is incomplete by itself and needs to be attached to a main clause to be a legal sentence.

Sidebar:

adroitly: skillfully and nimbly, using both his body and his mind well

✐ **Teacher's note.** Explanations for clause labels are with parts of speech under Grammar Notations.

♡ **Grammar lovers.** We call -ing words *gerunds* when they function as nouns. *Hiding* is the object of the preposition, which is a noun function.

DAY 2

DC cl   S   V   V   adj   adj   MC   V   prep   adj

(while he was gaining valuable hunting skills), [there ~~/their /they're~~ gathered <u>around him</u> many

DC
S   S/w-w   V   V

others] (who were **displaced**, ~~to /two /~~too).

Fixes

Indent. Is this a new topic, speaker, place, or time? Answer: Arguably a new topic—turning attention from Robin Hood alone to others displaced like him. However, it could be seen as the same topic about all who were escaping from the law. Let students choose!

Homophones and usage. *there* (in that place), *too* (also).

End marks. This is a statement so add a period.

Grammar Notations

Subjects and verbs. *he was gaining, others gathered, who* (referring back to *others*) *were displaced*.

Ask: Which of these are helping verbs? Answer: *was*, which helps *gaining*; *were*, which helps *displaced*.

✧ **Advanced.** Students may be confused by *there*, which is a pronoun used to introduce the clause, not the subject. The true subject comes after *gathered*, which students may hear more clearly if you revise the sentence: *many others gathered around him.*

Adjectives. *valuable hunting, many.*

If students do not mark *hunting*, point out that it describes the noun *skills* so must be an adjective because only adjectives can describe nouns. See ✏ **1.**

Prepositional phrases. *around him.*

Check for underline. Ask students to show the pattern: **preposition** (*around*) **+ noun/pronoun** (*him*).

***Who-which* clauses.** Ask: What noun does this clause describe and where is it? Answer: *others*, which comes immediately before the *who* clause. See ✏ **2.**

Clauses. Check for brackets and parentheses and MC and DC identification.

- DC: *While he was gaining valuable hunting skills.* Ask students to read this aloud. Help them hear how the thought is incomplete; it cannot stand alone as a sentence.
- MC: *there gathered around him many others.*
- DC: *who were displaced.* Explain that all *who-which* clauses are dependent.

displaced: lacking a home; removed from their proper place

✏ **1. Teacher's note.** *Hunting* is an easy example to show that *-ing* words (present participles) sometimes function as adjectives.

✏ **2. Teacher's note.** This *who-which* clause defines which *others* is meant, *those who were also displaced*, so it is essential and therefore not set off with a comma.

DAY 3

DC
MC adj   S   S/w-w   V   adj   V   V   prep   DC cl   S   V   V
[some men (who were **famished**) had shot deer in wintertime], (when they could obtain

            adj   prep
~~to/two/~~too little food for ~~there/~~their~~/they're~~ families).

Fixes

Indent. Is this a new topic, speaker, place, or time? Answer: No, it is the same topic about the men escaping from the law.

Homophones and usage. *too, their.*

Ask: What does *too* mean here? Answer: *to an excessive amount* (that is, too small an amount).

their families, possessive, meaning the families belonging to the men.

End marks. This is a statement so add a period.

famished: extremely hungry

Grammar Notations

Subjects and verbs. *who were, men had shot, they could obtain.*

Ask: Which of these are helping verbs? Answer: *had*, which helps *shot*; *could*, which helps *obtain*.

Students may have trouble understanding that *who*, not *men*, is the subject of *were*, but this is an important concept so introduce it. The *who* clause should not steal the main verb but needs its own verb. Guiding students to understand this and see the separate clauses will help them avoid writing sentence fragments like "Men who were famished." See ♡.

Prepositional phrases. *in wintertime, for their families.*

Check for underlines. Ask students to show the pattern: **preposition + noun/pronoun (no verb).**

***Who-which* clauses.** Ask: What noun does this clause describe and where is it? Answer: *men*, which comes immediately before the *who* clause.

✎ **Teacher's note.** This *who* clause is essential (no commas) because it explains which men: some who were famished.

Clauses. Check: brackets and parentheses; MC and DC identification.

- MC: *Some men … had shot deer in wintertime.* This is a complete thought that can stand alone. Inside of this main clause is the dependent w-w clause.
- DC: *who were famished.*
- DC: *when they could obtain too little food for their families.* Ask students to read this aloud. Help them hear how the thought is incomplete; it cannot stand alone as a sentence.
- ♡ **Grammar lovers.** When *where* or *when* follows a noun it also describes, it starts an adjective clause, not an adverb clause (what *when* clauses usually are). When it does, the adjective clause will be either essential (no commas) or nonessential (commas), as here. The *when* clause merely adds information but does not affect the meaning of the rest of the sentence. This is too advanced to teach this level but helps explain why there is a comma before this www.asia.b word.

♡ **Grammar lovers.** *Were* is not a helping verb but a linking verb connecting the subject to the subject complement *famished.* If a sentence is *not* in passive voice, an *-ed* word after a linking verb is likely an adjective instead of part of the verb. Contrast *men who were welcomed into the forest* where *were welcomed* is the verb because someone did that action (*welcomed them*).

See Grammar Glossary: Parts of Speech: Verbs: Linking Verbs, page G-8; Parts of Speech: Adjectives, page G-10; Additional Rules and Concepts: Passive versus Active Voice, page G-33.

DAY 4

DC   *cl*   *S*   *V*   *V*   *prep*   MC *S* *V*   *ly*   *V*

(although the foresters had discovered them <u>in the act</u>), [they had **narrowly** escaped], thus

saving themselves.

Fixes

Indent. Is this a new topic, speaker, place, or time? Answer: No.

End marks. This is a statement so add a period.

Grammar Notations

Subjects and verbs. *foresters had discovered, they had escaped.*

Ask: Which of these are helping verbs? Answer: both *had*'s, helping out *discovered* and *escaped*.

Prepositional phrases. *in the act.*

Check for underline. Ask students to show the pattern: **preposition + noun/pronoun (no verb).**

Clauses. Check for brackets and parentheses and MC and DC identification.

- DC: *Although the foresters had discovered them in the act.* Ask students to read this aloud to hear that the thought is incomplete.
- MC: *they had narrowly escaped.* This has a subject and a verb and could stand alone as a sentence.
- ✧ **Advanced.** If students are confused, explain that *saving themselves* is not a clause because it has no subject or helping verb. Clauses must have a subject and a verb. Contrast this clause: *They were saving themselves. See* ♡.

Style

Have your students identify the best dress-ups from this week's sentences. Discuss their answers. Best possibilities:

Strong verbs. *gathered, displaced.*

Quality adjectives. *famished.*

-ly adverbs. *adroitly, narrowly.*

narrowly: with little room to spare

♡ **Grammar lovers.** *saving* functions as an adjective in this sentence, but this is too advanced to teach students yet.

STUDENT REWRITE

Robin Hood lay in hiding in Sherwood Forest for one year as he adroitly prepared his new life. While he was gaining valuable hunting skills, there gathered around him many others who were displaced, too. Some men who were famished had shot deer in wintertime, when they could obtain too little food for their families. Although the foresters had discovered them in the act, they had narrowly escaped, thus saving themselves.

Week 9

No New Concepts

LEARN IT

Last week you learned the difference between a main clause (MC) and a dependent clause (DC). This week you will have the opportunity to practice what you have already learned, which is quite a bit! So far we have covered these concepts:

- When to indent
- Capitalization rules
- Parts of speech, subjects, and clauses
  - subjects of clauses (S)
  - verbs and helping verbs (vb)
  - coordinating conjunctions (cc)
  - adjectives (adj)
  - prepositions (prep) with the phrases underlined
  - main clauses (MC) with brackets around the MCs
  - dependent clauses (DC) with parentheses around the dependent clauses
    - who-which (S/w-w)
    - clause starters or www.asia.b words (cl)
- End marks
- Punctuation
  - Commas with items in a series.
  - Commas with nouns of direct address (NDAs).
  - Quotation marks around speech.

That is quite an accomplishment! You might want to thin out your grammar cards and remove those that you have mastered.

Discuss each fix with your students and help them correctly mark the sentence in their student book. This is not easy, so continue to help your students as much as they need. Continue to make it a game, and do not get discouraged if they cannot identify all the pieces without help. This skill comes with extended practice, so give yourself and your students grace as you make and discuss the notations each day.

🔊 **Listen.** To help you keep grammar in perspective, listen to Andrew Pudewa's talk "But, But, But ... What About Grammar?" Instructions to download the mp3 can be found on the blue page in the front of this book.

Page 20, *Fix It! Grammar:* **Robin Hood, Student Book 2**

Institute for Excellence in Writing

DAY 1

MC adj S   V   V   V   prep   DC cl

[other men had been forced out of ~~there/~~their ~~/they're~~ inheritance] (because ~~there/~~their ~~/they're~~

adj   S   V

insatiable king wanted ~~there/~~their ~~/they're~~ lands).

Fixes

Indent. Is this a new topic, speaker, place, or time? Answer: No, same topic about other outlaws like Robin.

Homophones and usage. All possessive: *their* inheritance, *their* king, *their* lands.

End marks. This is a statement so add a period.

Grammar Notations

Subjects and verbs. *men had been forced, king wanted.*

Prepositional phrases. *of their inheritance.*

Check for underlines. Ask students to show the pattern: **preposition + noun/pronoun (no verb).** *See ✏.*

Clauses. Check for brackets and parentheses and MC and DC identification.

- MC: *Other men had been forced out of their inheritance.*
  This is a complete thought and could stand alone as a sentence.

- DC: *because their insatiable king wanted their lands.*
  Ask students to read this aloud to hear that the thought is incomplete.

insatiable: not able to be satisfied or appeased

✏ Teacher's note.
out is an adverb here (*forced out*), not a preposition. See Grammar Glossary: Parts of Speech: Verbs: Verb + Adverb, page G-8.

DAY 2

MC S   V   V   V   prep   adj   adj   cc   adj

[some had been **despoiled** by a great baron, rich abbot, or powerful squire].

Fixes

Indent. Is this a new topic, speaker, place, or time? Answer: No, same topic.

Capitalization.

- *Some*—first word of sentence.
- Lowercase—*baron, abbot, squire*. These are titles without proper names following them, so they are common nouns.

Commas with items in a series.

Ask: What does the cc *or* connect? Answer: three nouns (*baron, abbot, squire*).

Ask: What is the series and how should it be punctuated? Answer: *baron, abbot, or squire*. Pattern: **a, b, or c**. The comma rule for items in a series works with any coordinating conjunction, not just *and*.

End marks. This is a statement so add a period.

Grammar Notations

Subjects and verbs. *Some had been deposited.*

Ask: Which of these are helping verbs? Answer: *had been*, which helps along *despoiled*.

Prepositional phrases. *by a great baron, rich abbot, or powerful squire.*

Check for underlines. Ask students to show the pattern: **preposition + noun/pronoun (no verb)**.

Clauses. Check for brackets and parentheses and MC and DC identification.

- MC: *Some had been despoiled by a great baron, rich abbot, or powerful squire.*

despoiled: robbed of possessions

An abbot was the head of a monastery; barons and squires were different ranks among the nobility. In the Middle Ages, there was a great deal of corruption in the church and among the nobility, who ought to have been protecting those under their care rather than robbing them.

DAY 3

prep adj   *cc*   *MC S*   *V*   *V prep*   *DC*
                                                   S/w-w   *V*   *adj*   *adj*

for one cause or another, [all had come to sherwood forest], (which was a vast, uncharted

                DC cl   *S*   *V*   *V*

wood), (where they might escape **oppression**).

Fixes

Indent. Is this a new topic, speaker, place, or time? Answer: No, same topic.

End marks. This is a statement so add a period.

Grammar Notations

Subjects and verbs. *all had come, which was, they might escape*. Ask: Which of these are helping verbs? Answer: *had*, which helps along *come*; *might*, which helps *escape*.

If students have trouble recognizing that *was* is a verb, show them a list of *be* verbs (*am, is, are, was, were*) and ask them to find one. Remind them that *which* is the subject of a *which* clause.

Prepositional phrases. *For one cause or another, to Sherwood Forest*. Check for underlines. Ask students to show the pattern: **preposition + noun/pronoun (no verb)**.

  ⚡ **Advanced.** The first prepositional phrase has two objects of the same preposition (*cause, another*). See 🖊.

Coordinating conjunctions. Ask: What does the cc *or* connect? Answer: two nouns (*cause, another*).

Who-which clauses. Have students read the clause aloud: *which was a vast, uncharted wood*. Ask: What noun does this clause describe and where is it? Answer: *Sherwood Forest*, which comes immediately before *which*.

  ⚡ **Advanced.** The invisible who-which works well here: *all had come to Sherwood Forest, a vast, uncharted wood*.

Clauses. Check for brackets and parentheses and MC and DC identification.

- MC: *all had come to Sherwood Forest*. It is a complete thought that can stand alone.
- DC (w-w clause): *which was a vast, uncharted wood*.
- DC: *where they might escape oppression*. Ask students to read this aloud to hear that the thought is incomplete. See ♡.

oppression: the cruel or unjust abuse of power or authority

Check that your students understand **uncharted**, which refers to an area that has not been mapped or surveyed.

🖊 **Teacher's note.** *another* is a pronoun, but it functions like any noun so can be linked with a noun in a series.

♡ **Grammar lovers.** Most of the time a www.asia.b word will begin an adverb clause. However, this one begins an adjective clause because it describes a noun (Sherwood Forest). This distinction between adverb and adjective clauses with www words like *where* and *when* is too advanced for this level. See Adjective clauses in the Sentence, Clauses, and Phrases section of the Grammar Glossary (page G-17).

DAY 4

prep adj adj   MC S prep adj   cc   adj   V

thus, in all that year, [a band of strong and goodhearted **yeomen** gathered about robin hood

cc   V

and chose him to be ~~there~~/their ~~they're~~ leader].

Fixes

Indent. Is this a new topic, speaker, place, or time? Answer: No, same topic.

Homophones and usage. *their leader*, possessive, the leader of the yeomen.

End marks. This is a statement so add a period.

Grammar Notations

Subjects and verbs. *band gathered … chose.*

Prepositional phrases. *in all that year, of strong and goodhearted yeomen.*

Check for underlines. Ask students to show the pattern: **preposition + noun/pronoun (no verb)**.

✏ **Teacher's note.** Although the *to* in infinitives (*to be*) is a preposition, we are not marking infinitives since they follow a slightly different pattern.

✦ **Advanced.** *about* is an adverb here meaning *on every side* or *in every direction* rather than a preposition, but if students mark *about Robin Hood* as a prepositional phrase, it is fine.

Coordinating conjunctions. Ask: What do the cc's *and* connect? Answer: The first connects two adjectives (*strong, goodhearted*); the second connects two verbs (*gathered, chose*) that have the same subject (*band*).

✏ **Teacher's note.** It is correct not to have a comma before either of these cc's since both join only two items in a series that are not main clauses. Pattern: **a and b**.

Clauses. Check for square brackets and parentheses and MC and DC identification.

- MC: *a band of strong and goodhearted yeomen gathered about Robin Hood and chose him to be their leader.* This is a complete thought and could stand alone as a sentence.

Style

Have your students choose the strongest of this week's dress-ups. Discuss their answers. Best possibilities:

Strong verbs. *despoiled, gathered.*

Quality adjectives. *insatiable, vast, uncharted, goodhearted.*

yeomen (pronounced with a long *o* sound: *yoh - men*): landowners who cultivate their own land

Even though yeomen in the Middle Ages were not of the nobility, they were property owners, not tenants on someone else's land. This was important in England during this time because yeomen had certain political rights denied to peasants. In the story, the nobles are robbing yeomen of the rights they are entitled to.

STUDENT REWRITE

Since this passage continues without another indentation, be sure students continue writing where last week's passage left off.

Other men had been forced out of their inheritance because their insatiable king wanted their lands. Some had been despoiled by a great baron, rich abbot, or powerful squire. For one cause or another, all had come to Sherwood Forest, which was a vast, uncharted wood, where they might escape oppression. Thus, in all that year, a band of strong and goodhearted yeomen gathered about Robin Hood and chose him to be their leader.

Week 10

Sentence Openers: #1 Subject, #2 Prepositional Phrase

LEARN IT

The dress-ups are one part of IEW style. The five dress-ups are -ly adverb, *who-which* clause, strong verb, quality adjective, and www.asia.b words (clause starters). The dress-ups help you use stronger vocabulary and more complex sentence structure.

Now that you are familiar with all the dress-ups, you can learn some sentence openers. Since you have learned about clauses and phrases, these will be easy. There is a grammar card that you can use to remember these openers.

#1 Subject Opener
In week 8 you learned that main clauses usually start with a subject or with an article (*a, an, the*) and/or adjectives plus subject. You also learned that sometimes the subject-verb will be switched. Examples: [*There gathered around him displaced countrymen*]. [*Up rose his Merry Men*].

We call the sentences that start with this pattern subject openers and we label them with a #1. When you see a sentence starting with a main clause, label it #1 MC.

#2 Prepositional
This is the second sentence opener. When a sentence begins with a prepositional phrase, mark it a #2 prep.

Be sure the #2 follows this pattern: preposition + noun/pronoun (no verb). These openers are not clauses; they are phrases. A clause must have a subject and a verb. Prepositional phrases have no verb.

Continue to underline all prepositional phrases, including #2 openers. Do not include #2 openers with the main clauses after them when adding brackets. Example: *In the tree* [*Robin safely hid*].

If you are doing IEW writing and have introduced sentence openers to your students, you can reinforce them here. Have students mark the sentence openers they have learned by writing the appropriate number in the space above the beginning of each sentence. They should do this last after identifying clauses and phrases.

If you are not doing IEW writing, it is still well worth the effort to learn the sentence opener system. Identifying the openers helps determine whether or not to use commas.

For a refresher on sentence openers, see the Stylistic Techniques section of the Grammar Glossary (page G-35).

Remember, you do not need to cover all these notations with your student. Limit the teaching to fifteen minutes, knowing that you will review the concepts many times. Keep these lessons light and fun.

DAY 1

#1 *MC   S   V DC S V prep   V   DC cl S*

¶ [the yeomen **vowed**] (that they would in return rob ~~there~~/their~~/they're~~ oppressors) (as they

       V V V

themselves had been robbed).

Fixes

vowed: made a solemn promise

Indent. Is this a new topic, speaker, place, or time? Answer: Yes. Attention turns to a new topic, the goal to return to the poor what had been taken from them.

Homophones and usage. *their oppressors*, possessive.

End marks. This is a statement so add a period.

Grammar Notations

Subject-verb pairs. *yeomen vowed, they would rob, they had been robbed.*

Prepositional phrases. *in return.*

Check for underline. Ask students to show the pattern: **preposition + noun/pronoun (no verb)**.

Clauses and sentence openers.

- #1 subject opener and MC: *The yeomen vowed.*
  With subject openers, it is common to see articles and/or adjectives in front of the subject of the main clause.

- DC: *that they would in return rob their oppressors. See ♡.*

- DC (www.asia.b clause): *as they themselves had been robbed.*
  Ask students to read this aloud to hear that the thought is incomplete. This dependent clause needs to be attached to a main clause for a legal sentence.

♡ **Grammar lovers.** This first DC is a noun clause, which starts with *that* and follows a verb.

DAY 2

DC cl S   V   V   prep   adj   cc

(if possessions were **plundered** by even the most powerful baron, abbot, knight, or squire),

MC S V   V   cc V   prep

[the yeomen would recapture the goods and return them to the poor].

Fixes

Indent. Is this a new topic, speaker, place, or time? Answer: No, same topic.

Commas with items in a series.

 Ask: Which words does the coordinating conjunction *or* join? Answer: *baron, abbot, knight, squire*.

 Ask: What part of speech are they? Answer: nouns.

 Ask: What pattern? Answer: **a, b, c, and d**.

End marks. This is a statement so add a period.

Grammar Notations

Subject-verb pairs. *possessions were plundered, yeomen would recapture … return. See* ✐.

 Ask: Which of these are helping verbs? Answer: *were*, which helps out *plundered*, and *would*, which helps *recapture*.

Prepositional phrases. *by even the most powerful baron, abbot, knight, or squire; to the poor.*

 Check for underlines. Ask students to show the pattern: **preposition + noun/pronoun (no verb)**.

 Point out that the first phrase has more than one object of the preposition (the noun ending the phrase): *baron, abbot, knight, squire.*

Clauses and sentence openers (no openers to mark this time).

- DC (www.asia.b clause): *If possessions were plundered by even the most powerful baron, abbot, knight, or squire*. Ask students to read this aloud to hear that the thought is incomplete.
- MC: *the yeomen would recapture the goods and return them to the poor*. Ask if students can hear that this is a complete thought and could stand alone as a sentence.

plundered: robbed; taken wrongfully

✎ **Teacher's note.** When two verbs have the same subject (*yeomen*), there is no comma to separate them. Pattern: **MC cc 2nd verb**.

DAY 3

#2 *prep*   *prep*   *MC*   *adj*   *cc*   *adj*   *S*   *V*   *V*

to those in need, [these brave and upright men would offer **succor**].

succor: help; relief; aid

Fixes

Indent. Is this a new topic, speaker, place, or time? Answer: No, same topic.

End marks. This is a statement so add a period.

Grammar Notations

Subjects and verbs. *men would offer.*

Prepositional phrases. *To those, in need.*

Check for underlines. Ask students to show the pattern: **preposition + noun/pronoun (no verb).**

Coordinating conjunctions. Ask: What does the cc *and* connect? Answer: two adjectives (*brave, upright*), so no comma.

Clauses and sentence openers.

- #2 prepositional phrase opener: *To those in need.*

   Ask students to explain why this is a phrase and not a clause. Answer: It does not have a verb so cannot be a clause.

   Explain that openers can have more than one thing in them. In this case, two prepositional phrases open the sentence. Except for #1 subject openers, it helps to think of sentence openers as everything that comes before the main clause.

- MC: *these brave and upright men would offer succor.*

DAY 4

#2 prep   MC S ly V   cc   DC cl S

besides this, [they **earnestly** swore never to harm a child or to wrong a woman] (whether she

V   cc

was a maid, wife, or widow).

Fixes

Indent. Is this a new topic, speaker, place, or time? Answer: No, same topic.

Comma with items in a series.

Ask: What do the cc's *or* connect? Answer: two infinitive phrases (*to harm or to wrong*); three nouns (*maid, wife, or widow*).

Ask: Which requires commas? Answer: the three nouns.

End marks. This is a statement so add a period.

Grammar Notations

Subjects and verbs. *they swore, she was.* See ♡.

Prepositional phrases. *Besides this.* Check for underline.

Clauses and sentence openers.

- #2 prepositional phrase opener: *Besides this.* Ask students to explain why this is a phrase and not a clause. Answer: It does not have a verb so cannot be a clause.
- MC: *they earnestly swore never to harm a child or to wrong a woman.* Can students hear that this is a complete thought that could stand alone as a sentence?
- DC (www.asia.b clause): *whether she was a maid, wife, or widow.* Ask students to read this aloud to hear that the thought is incomplete. See ✎.

Style

If desired, have your students identify the best dress-ups from this week's sentences. Discuss their answers. Best possibilities:

Strong verbs. *vowed, plundered, recapture.*

Quality adjectives. *upright.*

-ly adverbs. *earnestly.*

earnestly: sincerely and seriously

In the Middle Ages, a maid meant an unmarried woman.

♡ **Grammar lovers.** *Was* in this sentence is a linking verb, not a helping verb, because it links the subject (*she*) to the subject complements *maid*, *wife*, and *widow*.

✎ **Teacher's note.** *Whether* is not one of the www words, but it starts an adverb clause. If students do not mark it, simply point it out, show the subject and verb, and help them put parentheses around the clause. Invite students to add *whether* to the list on the back of the week 8 adverb clause starters card.

STUDENT REWRITE

The yeomen vowed that they would in return rob their oppressors as they themselves had been robbed. If possessions were plundered by even the most powerful baron, abbot, knight, or squire, the yeomen would recapture the goods and return them to the poor. To those in need, these brave and upright men would offer succor. Besides this, they earnestly swore never to harm a child or to wrong a woman whether she was a maid, wife, or widow.

Week 11

Sentence Openers: #3 -ly Adverb, Combining Sentences with a Who-Which

LEARN IT

This week you will learn the next sentence opener.

#3 -ly Adverb Opener

The difference between an -ly adverb dress-up and an -ly adverb sentence opener is simply where the word appears: It will be the first word in the sentence if it is an opener; it will be later than the first word if it is a dress-up.

Continue to label all the -ly adverbs with an *ly*. If it is the first word of a sentence, mark it with a *#3 ly*.

Do not include the #3 opener in the MC brackets. It is just tacked onto the front of the sentence. Example: *Regularly,* [*the common folk came to praise Robin and his Merry Men*].

On Day 4 when you decide on the strongest dress-ups, choose from one of the -ly dress-ups if there are any that week, not an opener.

Combining Sentences

Who-which clauses are handy because they can often be used to combine sentences. On Day 2 this week and on occasion in the future, you will be asked to create your own sentence by combining the two provided with a *who-which*. Your teacher can help you if needed. Combine the sentences as instructed. Complete the labeling and brackets using the new sentence.

If you are evaluating dress-ups on Day 4, remind students to choose a dress-up -ly adverb, not an opener, if there are any that week.

This week students also will be asked to combine two sentences into one by creating a *who-which* clause. This will change the structure of the sentence and what they need to fix and label. Have them revise the sentence first in their student book and then label the revised sentence instead of the original.

Page 24, *Fix It! Grammar:* **Robin Hood, Student Book 2**

DAY 1

#2 *prep*   *prep*   *MC*   *S*   *V*   *cc*   *prep*   *prep*

in times of desperation, [these yeomen transferred money or food from the pockets of the

    adj   *prep*   *prep*   *adj*

corrupt nobility into the hands of **impoverished** families].

Fixes

impoverished: poor; reduced to poverty

Indent. Is this a new topic, speaker, place, or time? Answer: No, same topic.

End marks. This is a statement so add a period.

Grammar Notations

Subjects and verbs. *yeomen transferred.*

Prepositional phrases. *In times, of desperation, from the pockets, of the corrupt nobility, into the hands, of impoverished families.*

Check for underlines. Ask students to show how these fit the prepositional phrase pattern.

Coordinating conjunctions. Ask: What does *or* connect? Answer: two nouns (*money or food*), so no comma.

Clauses and sentence openers.

- #2 prepositional phrase opener: *In times of desperation.*

    Notice that again there are two prepositional phrases in the opener.
    Ask: Why is this a phrase and not a clause? Answer: There is no verb.

- MC: *these yeomen transferred money or food from the pockets of the corrupt nobility into the hands of impoverished families.*

    Ask: Is this a complete thought that could stand alone as a sentence? Answer: Yes!

DAY 2

First, combine the two sentences by starting a new *who* clause after *folk*. The new sentence should have two verbs, one that goes with *who* and one that goes with *folk*. Use the new sentence for the rest of your Fix It work.

audacious escapades: recklessly brave and bold adventures

```
                                        DC S/w-w
#3 ly        MC        adj      S   who  V                    cc           V    adj
¶ regularly, [the common folk, (came to praise robin and his merry men), they related many
```

```
   prep        adj
tales of his audacious escapades].
```

Combine sentences with a who

Check that students combined the sentences correctly and put commas on both sides of the new *who* clause. If students combine the sentences differently, that is perfectly fine so long as it makes sense and creates a legal *who* clause. Here is one example: *Regularly, the common folk, who related many tales of his audacious escapades, came to praise Robin and his Merry Men.* See ✎.

If students struggle with this, guide them through it until they can do it on their own. They will continue to practice writing *who-which* clauses in later weeks.

✎ **Teacher's note.** The *who-which* clause is set off with commas because it is nonessential. It adds information but does not affect the meaning of the main clause, which states that the common folk related many tales.

Fixes

Indent. Is this a new topic, speaker, place, or time? Answer: Start a new paragraph for a new topic, the people's reaction to their help.

Capitalization.

- *Regularly*—first word of sentence.
- *Robin, Merry Men.* The original tales about Robin Hood refer to his band of men with the specific term *Merry Men*, so it is considered proper and always capitalized. However, if students interpret *merry* as descriptive only, it is fine if they do not capitalize *merry men*. Just aim for consistency.

End marks. This is a statement so add a period.

Grammar Notations

Subjects and verbs. *folk related, who came.* Remind students to mark the revised sentence rather than the original.

Remind students that *who-which* clauses need their own verb that usually goes with the *who* or *which*. It is easiest to see which verb goes with *folk* by removing the *who* clause from the sentence: *The common folk … related many tales.* Who related? *The common folk.*

Adjectives. *common, many, audacious.* Note: *Merry* is technically an adjective but counts here as part of a compound noun.

Prepositional phrases. *of his audacious escapades.* Check for underline. Ask how this fits the prepositional phrase pattern and emphasize no verb.

Coordinating conjunctions. Ask: What does the cc *and* connect? Answer: two nouns, *Robin* and *Merry Men*, so no comma.

Continued on next page ▶

Clauses and sentence openers.

- #3 -ly adverb opener: *Regularly*. This is an opener and not a dress-up because *regularly* is the first word in the sentence. It would count as a dress-up if it came later.
- MC: *the common folk ... related many tales of his audacious escapades*. Point out that this main clause has inside of it a dependent clause.

    Ask: Is this a complete thought that could stand alone as a sentence? Answer: Yes.

- DC (w-w clause): *who came to praise Robin and his Merry Men*.

DAY 3

#3 ly   prep   adj   prep   MC S   V   DC
naturally, because of robin hood's **magnanimous** work in sherwood forest, [people felt] (that

S   V   prep
he was like them).

Fixes

magnanimous:
generous and noble

Indent. Is this a new topic, speaker, place, or time? Answer: No, same topic.

End marks. This is a statement so add a period.

Grammar Notations

Subjects and verbs. *people felt, he was.*

Prepositional phrases. *because of Robin Hood's magnanimous work, in Sherwood Forest, like them.*

  ✧ **Advanced.** *Because of* confuses many students. Explain that *because* always starts an adverb clause except when it is followed by *of*. *Because of* is always a preposition.

Challenge students to show how this phrase fits the prepositional phrase pattern: *because of* is on the preposition list; the phrase ends with a noun, *work*; and none of these words is a verb. Emphasize that there is no verb, so it cannot be a clause because all clauses must have a subject and a verb.

Clauses and sentence openers.

- #3 -ly adverb opener: *Naturally*.
- MC: *people felt*. Ask: Is this a complete thought that could stand alone as a sentence? Answer: Yes.
- DC: *that he was like them*. See ♡.

  ✎ **Teacher's note.** If students do not mark this as a DC, first check that they know *was* is a verb. If not, show them the list of *be* verbs on their Week 2 verbs card and ask them to find one in this passage. If they do not include *that* as the clause starter, remind them that *who, which,* and *that* are common clause starters in addition to the www.asia.b words.

♡ **Grammar lovers.** This dependent clause is a noun clause, which begins with *that* and follows a verb. The concept is too advanced for this level.

DAY 4

#2 *prep*   *MC S*   *V*   *V*   *prep*   *DC / S/w-w V V*   *ly*   *prep*

in a sense, [robin had therefore returned to the town] (he had left), living **vicariously** through

DC w-w S V V

the town folk (whom he was forced to leave).

Fixes

Indent. Is this a new topic, speaker, place, or time? Answer: No, same topic.

End marks. This is a statement so add a period.

Grammar Notations

Subjects and verbs. *Robin had returned, he had left, he was forced.*

Ask: Which of these are helping verbs? Answer: *had* (both times), which helps out *returned* and *left*; *was*, which helps out *forced*.

Prepositional phrases. *In a sense, to the town, through the town folk.*

Check for underlines. Ask how these fit the prepositional phrase pattern and emphasize no verbs in any of them.

Who-which clauses. Have students read the second clause aloud: *whom he was forced to leave.* See ✎.

Ask: What noun does this clause describe and where is it? Answer: *town folk*, which comes immediately before *whom*.

✧ **Advanced.** Students may think *he had left* is a main clause, but it is actually dependent. *Which* or *that* is implied (*which he had left*) but hidden for a more stylish construction. In IEW writing we call this an invisible which. The clause is still dependent. Like most *who-which* clauses, it describes the noun that comes before it, *the town*.

Clauses and sentence openers.

- #2 prepositional phrase opener: *In a sense.*

    Ask: Why is this a phrase and not a clause? Answer: There is no verb.

- MC: *Robin had therefore returned to the town.*

    Ask: Is this a complete thought that could stand alone as a sentence? Answer: Yes.

- DC (w-w clause): (invisible *which*) *he had left.*

- DC (w-w clause): *whom he was forced to leave.* See ♡.

Style

If desired, have your students identify the best dress-ups from this week's sentences. Discuss their answers. Best possibilities:

Strong verbs. *transferred.*

Quality adjectives. *impoverished, audacious, magnanimous.*

-ly adverbs (not the first word of any sentence). *vicariously.*

vicariously: as if enjoyed through the experiences of others

✎ **Teacher's note.**
This *who-which* clause is not set off with a comma because it is essential: it specifies or defines which town folk are meant—not just any town folk, but those he had to leave.

♡ **Grammar lovers.**
Who or *which* is usually the subject of a *who-which* clause, but not *whom*. Do not worry if students do not understand this.

Whom is in the objective case (the object of *to leave*), so it cannot be the subject of the clause.

STUDENT REWRITE

Since this passage continues without another indentation, be sure students continue writing where last week's passage left off.

In times of desperation, these yeomen transferred money or food from the pockets of the corrupt nobility into the hands of impoverished families.

Regularly, the common folk, who came to praise Robin and his Merry Men, related many tales of his audacious escapades. Naturally, because of Robin Hood's magnanimous work in Sherwood Forest, people felt that he was like them. In a sense, Robin had therefore returned to the town he had left, living vicariously through the town folk whom he was forced to leave.

Week 12

Commas with Quotations, Commas with Adjectives before a Noun, Sentence Opener #5

LEARN IT

This week you will learn two more comma rules and sentence opener #5.

Commas with Quotation
You have likely noticed in your rewrites that when quotations are set up by a speaking verb either before or after the quotation, they need a comma to separate the narrative from the quotation. From now on, you will have to add the punctuation needed for quotations. To help you remember the rules, refer to the Week 3 grammar card entitled "Quotations."

These are the patterns:

speaking verb + comma + " "

> Robin **told** his men**,** "Let's seek adventure."

" " + comma + speaking verb

> "Let's seek adventure**,**" Robin **suggested**.

Remember: commas and periods go *inside* closing quotation marks. You will need to add the punctuation for quotations in the Day 4 passage.

Commas with Adjectives Before a Noun
This rule is a little more complicated and will require some practice before you really get it. It has to do with two or more adjectives before a noun. Here are the rules:

Coordinate adjectives need commas. Usually two or more adjectives before a noun are separated by commas, as in *dewy, silent leaves*. When the adjectives describe the noun independently, they need commas and are known as coordinate adjectives. Note that since there is no coordinating conjunction (it is not *dewy and silent leaves*), this is not the same as items in a series.

There are two tricks to tell if the two adjectives might be coordinate adjectives.

- Can you reverse their order and they sound right?
- Can you add *and* between them?

If both tests work, the adjectives are likely coordinate and will need a comma between them. If they fail the test, they are likely cumulative adjectives.

Cumulative adjectives do not take commas. Sometimes the last adjective before the noun pairs with the noun as a unit; the adjective before that describes the last adjective-noun pair, not the noun separately, as in *one fair morn*. These are called cumulative adjectives and do not take commas. Notice that *fair, one morn* and *one and fair morn* both sound odd, so these are not coordinate adjectives.

#5 Clausal Opener
We are skipping the #4 opener and moving on to #5. Just like the #3 -ly adverb opener, the main difference between the #5 clausal opener and the www.asia.b word dress-up is that the opener starts the sentence and the dress-up comes later in the sentence.

The #5 clausal opener also takes a comma after the clause.

Page 26, *Fix It! Grammar: Robin Hood*, Student Book 2

Reminder: If you are not doing IEW writing, it is still well worth the effort to learn the sentence opener system. Identifying the openers helps determine whether or not to use commas.

✏ **Teacher's note.** Remember to keep the exercise light and fun. It should be like a game.

✏ **Teacher's note.** These tricks are not a rule and depend on our not overthinking them. If students do not hear them correctly, just tell them these are helpful tricks but not hard-and-fast rules.

Use the grammar card for this week to remember the tricks.

When needed, remind students never to put a comma between the last adjective and noun.

DAY 1

Look for two adjectives before a noun (twice). Ask if you could switch their order or add *and* between them. If so, they need a comma between them.

#5 DC cl   S   V   *ly*   V   *prep*   *adj adj*   *prep*

¶ (when birds were **melodiously** singing in the oak one fair morn hidden among its ~~it's~~

adj   *adj*   *MC*   *S*   *V*

dewy, silent leaves), [robin hood rose], needing a change.

Fixes

Indent. Is this a new topic, speaker, place, or time? Answer: Yes, a new time.

Homophones and usage. *its leaves.* Ask: What does *its* refer back to? Answer: *the oak.*

Commas with adjectives.

Original: *one fair morn.* Ask: Do these two adjectives before the noun need a comma? Short answer: No.

> Tricks to tell: a) Can you reverse their order and they still sound right? No, *fair one morn* sounds awkward. b) Can you add *and* between them? Answer: No, *one and fair morn* does not make sense. Since both tests fail, these adjectives are cumulative—*one* describes *fair morn*—and do not take a comma between them.

Original: *dewy silent leaves.* Ask: Do these two adjectives before the noun need a comma? Short answer: Yes, so check that students add the comma in their copy work.

> Tricks to tell: a) Can you reverse their order and they still sound right? Answer: Yes, *dewy, silent leaves* and *silent, dewy leaves* both sound right. b) Can you add *and* between them? Answer: Yes, *dewy and silent leaves* also works. Since both tests work, these adjectives are coordinate and need a comma between them.

End marks. This is a statement so add a period.

Grammar Notations

Subjects and verbs. *birds were singing, Robin Hood rose.*

Ask: Which of these are helping verbs? Answer: *were*, which helps out *singing.*

Prepositional phrases. *in the oak; among its dewy, silent leaves.*

Check underlines. Ask students to explain the pattern and emphasize that there are no verbs in these phrases. Clauses have verbs; prepositional phrases do not.

Clauses and sentence openers.

- DC and #5 clausal opener: *When birds were melodiously singing in the oak one fair morn hidden among its dewy, silent leaves.* See ✏ **1.**

  Ask: Why is this a dependent clause? Answer: It has a subject and verb but cannot stand alone. Legal sentences need at least one main clause. Ask students to read this aloud to hear that the thought is incomplete. See ✏ **2.**

- MC: *Robin Hood rose.* Ask: Is this a complete thought that could stand alone as a sentence? Answer: Yes. See ✏ **3.**

melodiously: tunefully; in a sweet-sounding way

✏ **1. Teacher's note.** Also, it is OK if students end the clause after *singing*, which picks up the subject-verb pair (the main thing to recognize), after *in the oak one fair morn*, or after *hidden among its dewy, silent leaves.*

✏ **2. Teacher's note.** DCs usually begin with subordinating conjunctions (www. asia.b words) or *that, who,* or *which.*

✏ **3. Teacher's note.** It may help to explain that dependent clauses will not start with a subject (including article + adjectives + subject), as main clauses do.

DAY 2

#5 DC cl S   V   adj   MC   V   S   adj   cc
(as he considered his next move), [up rose his merry men], each fellow washing his head and

prep   adj   adj
hands in the cold, **gurgling** brook.

Fixes

Indent. Is this a new topic, speaker, place, or time? Answer: No, same topic.

Commas with adjectives. Original: *cold gurgling brook*. Ask: Do these two adjectives before the noun need a comma? Short answer: Yes.

Tricks to tell: a) Can you reverse their order and they still sound right? Answer: Yes, *cold, gurgling brook* and *gurgling, cold brook* both sound right. b) Can you add *and* between them? Answer: Yes, *cold and gurgling brook* also works.

Since both tests work, these adjectives are coordinate and need a comma between them.

End marks. This is a statement so add a period.

gurgling: flowing in an irregular, noisy current

Grammar Notations

Subjects and verbs. *he considered, rose Merry Men*.

⁂ **Advanced.** *up* is an adverb here connected to the verb (*rose up*), not a preposition. You can tell because it does not have an object or fit the prepositional phrase pattern.

✏ **Teacher's note.** If students mark *washing* or *gurgling* as a verb, decide whether or not to let it go. They are both verbals that do not function as verbs.

Prepositional phrases. *in the cold, gurgling brook.* Check underline.

Ask students to explain the pattern.

Ask: Why is this a phrase and not a clause? Answer: There is no verb. If students are confused, explain that *gurgling* is an adjective describing *brook*. See ✏ **1.**

Coordinating conjunctions. Ask: What does the cc *and* connect? Answer: two nouns (*head and hands*), so no comma.

Clauses and sentence openers.

- #5 clausal opener and DC: *As he considered his next move.* Show that a comma follows #5 openers.

  Ask students to read this aloud to hear that the thought is incomplete. See ✏ **2.**

- MC: *up rose his Merry Men.*

  Ask: Is this a complete thought that could stand alone as a sentence? Answer: Yes.

  Students may see this more clearly if you revise the sentence with the subject first: *His Merry Men rose up.*

✏ **1. Teacher's note.** If students mark *washing* or *gurgling* as a verb, decide whether or not to let it go. They are both verbals that do not function as verbs.

✏ **2. Teacher's note.** DCs usually begin with subordinating conjunctions (www. asia words) or *that, who,* or *which.*

DAY 3

#2 prep   prep   MC S   V   cc

from stone to stone [they **cavorted** about], laughing and enjoying themselves.

Fixes

Indent. Is this a new topic, speaker, place, or time? Answer: No, same topic.

End marks. This is a statement so add a period.

cavorted: behaved in a high-spirited, festive manner

Grammar Notations

Subjects and verbs. *they cavorted about.*

✦ **Advanced.** *about* is part of this verb phrase.

Prepositional phrases. *From stone, to stone.*

In checking underlines, check that students realize these are actually two separate prepositional phrases. Ask them to explain the pattern.

Coordinating conjunctions. Ask: What does the cc *and* connect? Answer: two *-ing* words. See ♡.

Clauses and sentence openers.

- #2 prepositional phrase opener: *From stone to stone.*
  Ask: Why is this a phrase and not a clause? Answer: There is no verb.

- MC: *they cavorted about.*
  Ask: Is this a complete thought that could stand alone as a sentence? Answer: Yes.

♡ **Grammar lovers.** *Laughing* and *enjoying* are not verbs but present participles, functioning as adjectives describing *they.*

DAY 4

#3 *ly*   MC S   V   V   *prep*   DC cl V   *adj*   *adj*   *prep*

clearly, [robin was not **captivated** by the brook] (as were his carefree, festive men). ¶ "for

adj   MC S   V   V   *adj*   MC S   V

fourteen days [we have enjoyed no **sport**], my friends," [he complained].

> 🖉 **Teacher's note.** You do not need to go through all the discussion points. Focus on areas where your student needs more help. If he needs help in all of them, simply reduce what he has to mark and address it again later.

captivated: attracted or enchanted

sport: pleasant pastime

Remind students to think about the context when choosing definitions; *sport* is not an athletic activity in this context.

Fixes

Indent. Is this a new topic, speaker, place, or time? Answer: The first sentence continues the same topic, but the second sentence starts a new paragraph because of a new speaker.

Students may not catch this. Remind them to think about whether or not to start a new paragraph with every sentence, not just at the start of each day's passage.

Capitalization. Do not capitalize *he* because *he complained* sets up the quotation that comes before it and is therefore part of the same sentence. It does not start a new sentence.

Quotations. Check that students placed quotation marks around the words spoken.

Also, check that students added a comma after *friends* inside the closing quotation marks to separate the subject and speaking verb (*he complained*) from the quotation it sets up. The pattern is **quotation + comma + speaking verb**.

Commas with adjectives. Work students through the two tests to tell if these are coordinate adjectives and need the comma or if they are cumulative and do not. 1) Does it sound right to say *festive, carefree men*? Yes. 2) Could we say *carefree and festive men*? Yes, on both counts, so these are coordinate and need a comma.

Commas with NDAs. Ask: What is the noun of direct address and how should it be punctuated? Answer: *my friends*, which should be set off with commas.

End marks. This is a statement so add a period.

Grammar Notations

Subjects and verbs. *Robin was ... captivated, men were* (this reverses the usual subject-verb order), *we have enjoyed, he complained.*

Ask: Which of these are helping verbs? Answer: *was*, which helps out *captivated*; *have*, which helps out *enjoyed*.

Prepositional phrases. *by the brook; For fourteen days.* Check underlines, and ask students to explain the pattern.

Continued on next page ▶

Clauses and sentence openers.

- #3 -ly adverb opener: *Clearly*. *Clearly* takes a comma after it because it modifies the whole clause: it was clear that Robin was not captivated by the brook.
- MC: *Robin was not captivated by the brook.* Ask: Is this a complete thought that could stand alone as a sentence? Answer: Yes.
- DC (www.asia.b clause): *as were his carefree, festive men.* Ask students to read this aloud to hear that the thought is incomplete.
- #2 prepositional phrase opener: *For fourteen days.*
- MC: *we have enjoyed no sport.* Students should understand that this is a complete thought.
- MC: *he complained.* Note: Have students mark MCs that set up speech separately from the speech even though the complete thought usually includes the quoted words.

Style

If desired, have your students identify the best dress-ups from this week's sentences. Discuss their answers. Choose among:

Strong verbs. *cavorted, captivated.*

Quality adjectives. *gurgling.*

-ly adverbs (not the first word of any sentence). *melodiously.*

STUDENT REWRITE

When birds were melodiously singing in the oak one fair morn hidden among its dewy, silent leaves, Robin Hood rose, needing a change. As he considered his next move, up rose his Merry Men, each fellow washing his head and hands in the cold, gurgling brook. From stone to stone they cavorted about, laughing and enjoying themselves. Clearly, Robin was not captivated by the brook as were his carefree, festive men.

"For fourteen days we have enjoyed no sport, my friends," he complained.

Week 13

Sentence Openers: #6 vss

LEARN IT

This week you will learn one more sentence opener.

#6 vss   These openers are designed to pack a punch or add variation to the flow of writing. They should be at least two words long and no more than five, and they must be legal sentences (subject + verb and be able to stand alone).

This opener should also be strong. *Robin sat down* or *Robin was happy* are not strong sentences. *Robin sank onto a bench* or *Robin leaped with joy* are stronger.

The new grammar card for this week includes all the sentence openers learned thus far for easier reference.

If you are teaching the sentence openers, stress that the #6 vss needs a subject and a verb and must be able to stand alone as a sentence.

Page 28, *Fix It! Grammar:* **Robin Hood, Student Book 2**

DAY 1

Robin will continue speaking, so do not put closing quotation marks at the end.

```
#2 prep          MC S  V      V                                      MC S        V    #6 MC V   prep
```
"without delay [i will journey abroad to seek adventures]," [robin added]. "[tarry for me

here].

Fixes

tarry: stay in a place

Indent. Is this a new topic, speaker, place, or time? Answer: No. Continue writing in the same paragraph because Robin is still talking about his desire to find adventure.

Quotations.

- Check that students put quotation marks around his two sentences but not the interrupter, the narrative words that interrupt his speech. Since Robin is not yet finished speaking, students should not use closing quotation marks yet.

- Insert a comma after *adventures* to separate the interrupter (*Robin added*) from his spoken words. Remind students that commas and periods go inside closing quotation marks. The pattern is **quotation + comma + speaking verb**.

- ✧ **Advanced.** Robin's first statement is a complete thought, so the period after *added* is correct.

End marks. This is a statement so add a period but no closing quotation marks until Robin finishes speaking in the next passage.

Grammar Notations

Subjects and verbs. *I will journey, Robin added, Tarry.*

Ask: What is the subject of *tarry*? Answer: *you,* which is implied. This is in the imperative voice, directed to someone and issuing a command.

Prepositional phrases. *Without delay, for me.* Check underlines. Ask students to explain the pattern.

Clauses and sentence openers.

- #2 prepositional phrase opener: *Without delay.*
- MC: *I will journey abroad to seek adventures.* Ask: Is this a complete thought that could stand alone as a sentence? Answer: Yes.
- MC: *Robin added.* Ask: Is this a legal sentence? Answer: Yes.
- #6 and MC: *Tarry for me here.*

  Ask: Is this a legal sentence? Answer: Yes. Does it fit the rules for #6 openers? Yes. Why? It has five words so is short; it is a legal sentence. *See* ✎.

✎ **Teacher's note.** Perceptive students may enjoy challenging this designation as a vss on the basis that it is not strong. Feel free to agree and move on! The goal right now is accurate understanding of what makes a sentence and what counts as short.

DAY 2

In your rewrite, combine the two sentences with a *which* clause and remember to label *which*. Also, this ends Robin's speech. What punctuation should come after *aid*?

DC S/w-w
#3 ly   MC V   DC   S   V   **which**   V   V *prep*
only [make certain] (that ~~your~~/you're ready to **heed** my call), (~~the call~~ will sound as

adj   *adj*   *prep*   DC cl S   V
three short blasts upon the bugle horn) (if i require your~~/you're~~ aid)."

Combine sentences with a which

Check that students combined the sentences correctly and put a comma in front of the new *which* clause. See 🖋.

heed: give great attention to

Fixes

Indent. Is this a new topic, speaker, place, or time? Answer: No, since Robin is still speaking.

Homophones and usage.

- *you're ready*, the contraction meaning *you are ready*.

  🖋 **Teacher's note.** You may wish to mention that contractions work well in dialogue but are usually considered too casual for academic papers.

- *your aid*, the possessive.

Quotations. Students should continue writing where they left off without quotation marks since it is the same person speaking. Since Robin ends his speech here, check that they close his speech with quotation marks after *aid*.

Comma with adjectives before a noun. Ask: Should there be a comma between these two adjectives before a noun? Apply the two tests:

- Can you reverse their order: *short three blasts*? No.
- Can you put *and* in between them: *three and short blasts*? No.

This fails on both counts, so *three short blasts* uses cumulative adjectives. *Three* modifies *short blasts* and therefore should not have a comma.

End marks. Period at the end inside the closing quotation marks.

🖋 **Teacher's note.**
This *who-which* clause is another nonessential *which* clause. It adds information but does not affect the meaning of the rest of the sentence. The clause is set off with only one comma because it completes the sentence. It includes the idea in the *if* clause, which does not take a comma before it, but students may keep the two clauses separate in marking parentheses around them.

Grammar Notations

Subjects and verbs. *make (certain), you're, which will sound, I require.* See ♡.

Ask: What is the subject of *make*? Answer: *you*, which is implied, another instance of the imperative voice.

If students have trouble seeing that *you're* has a subject and verb, remind them that this is a contraction formed from two words, *you are*. *You* is the subject and *are* is the verb.

Prepositional phrases. *as three short blasts, upon the bugle horn.* Check underlines.

♡ **Grammar lovers.**
Although *certain* is an adjective, it functions here as part of the idiom *make certain*.

Continued on next page ▶

✦ **Advanced.** *As* is one of the www words (a subordinating conjunction), but it is also in the preposition list. To tell which it is, follow the pattern tests. In this case, since there is no verb, *as three short blasts* cannot be a clause. It begins with a word that can be a preposition, it ends with a noun (*blasts*), and it has two adjectives but no verbs in between—so it fits the prepositional phrase pattern.

Clauses and sentence openers.

- #3 -ly adverb: *Only.*
- MC: *make certain* (with the subject, *you*, implied).
- DC: *that you're ready to heed my call.* Ask: Is this a legal sentence? Answer: Yes. *See* ♡.
- DC (w-w clause): *which will sound as three short blasts upon the bugle horn.* Students may put parentheses here or at the end of the sentence. *See* ✎.
- DC (www.asia.b clause): *if I require your aid.*

♡ **Grammar lovers.** The first DC is a noun clause, which begins with *that* and follows a verb.

✎ **Teacher's note.** Technically, the second DC, a *which* clause, includes *if I require your aid* since the adverb clause is essential. The w-w clause is shown here without the adverb clause for clarity.

DAY 3

#6 MC   S   V   #3 ly   MC S   V   prep   prep   prep   adj

¶ [robin hood set off]. widely [he **ranged** through the forest in search of glorious adventure].

Fixes

Indent. Is this a new topic, speaker, place, or time? Answer: Yes, a new topic because we pull out of Robin's speech and turn to his actions.

End marks. This is a statement so add a period.

ranged: passed through (an area), exploring and searching

Grammar Notations

Subjects and verbs. *Robin Hood set off* (*off* is an adverb, but *to set off* has a different meaning from *to set.* See Grammar Glossary, page G-8), *he ranged.*

Prepositional phrases. *through the forest, in search, of glorious adventure.*

Check underlines. Ask students to show how these fit the pattern: **preposition + noun (no verb)**.

If students are confused by *search*, point out that it can be a noun (as here) as well as a verb.

Clauses and sentence openers.

- #6 vss and MC: *Robin Hood set off.*
- #3 -ly adverb: *Widely.*
- MC: *he ranged through the forest in search of glorious adventure.*

DAY 4

#5 DC cl   S   DC S   V   ly   V   MC S   V   prep   adj   adj

(when the path (he took) sharply curved), [it brought him to a broad, pebbly stream], **spanned**

prep   adj   adj

by a narrow wooden bridge.

Fixes

Indent. Is this a new topic, speaker, place, or time? Answer: No, because the passage continues the topic of Robin's search for adventure. If students argue for a new paragraph based on a new place, praise them! The prior sentence is short enough and on topic enough to stay in the same paragraph, but it could go either way.

Commas with adjectives.

Original: *broad pebbly stream*. Ask: Do these two adjectives before the noun need a comma? Short answer: Yes.

> Tricks to tell: a) Can you reverse their order and they still sound right? Answer: Yes, *broad, pebbly stream* and *pebbly, broad stream* both sound right. b) Can you add *and* between them? Answer: Yes, *broad and pebbly stream* also works.

> Since both tests work, these adjectives are coordinate and need a comma between them. *See* ✏ **1.**

Original: *narrow wooden bridge*. Ask: Do these two adjectives before the noun need a comma? Short answer: No, *narrow wooden bridge* is correct.

> Tricks to tell: a) Can you reverse their order and they still sound right? Answer: No, *wooden narrow bridge* sounds strange. b) Can you add *and* between them? Answer: No, *narrow and wooden bridge* sounds strange also.

> Neither test works because *narrow* describes *wooden bridge*. These adjectives are cumulative and should not have a comma between them. *See* ✏ **1.**

End marks. This is a statement so add a period.

Grammar Notations

Subjects and verbs. *path curved, he took, it brought.*

> ✦ **Advanced.** Guide students to match the correct verbs to their subjects: *curved* goes with *path*; *took* goes with *he*.

Adjectives. *broad, pebbly, narrow, wooden. See* ♡.

> ✦ **Advanced.** Ask students to explain why *pebbly* is an adjective and not an -ly adverb. Answer: It describes a noun. Adverbs never describe nouns, only adjectives or verbs (or sometimes other adverbs). *See* ✏ **2.**

Prepositional phrases. *to a broad, pebbly stream; by a narrow wooden bridge.*

> Check underlines. Ask students to show how these fit the pattern: **preposition + noun (no verb)**.

Continued on next page ▶

---

spanned: extended over and across

✏ **1. Teacher's note.** When adjectives are coordinate, each adjective independently modifies the noun: it is a broad stream and a pebbly stream. When adjectives are cumulative, the first adjective describes the second adjective plus noun together. It is a narrow bridge that is wooden (a narrow wooden-bridge).

♡ **Grammar lovers.** *spanned* functions as an adjective here, describing *stream*, but this is too advanced for this level.

✏ **2. Teacher's note.** In IEW's system, *pebbly* is known as an imposter -ly: it looks like an -ly adverb but is not since it describes a noun.

Clauses and sentence openers.

- #5 clausal opener and DC: *When the path … sharply curved.*

    Point out that a comma follows #5 openers. Ask students to read this aloud to hear that the thought is incomplete.

- DC: *he took.*

    ✿ **Advanced.** Students may not recognize that this is a dependent clause or even that it is a clause by itself since it falls in the middle of another clause. It is actually a hidden w-w clause with an implied *that. See* ♡ **1.**

- MC: *it brought him to a broad, pebbly stream. See* ♡ **2.**

♡ **1. Grammar lovers.** *that* replaces *which* in restrictive w-w clauses.

♡ **2. Grammar lovers.** *Spanned by a narrow wooden bridge* is not a clause but a phrase because the past participle *spanned* needs a subject and helping verb for it to count as a verb, as in *it was spanned.*

Style

If desired, have your students identify the best dress-ups from this week's sentences. Discuss their answers. Choose among:

Strong verbs. *tarry, ranged.*

Quality adjectives. *glorious, broad, pebbly.*

-ly adverbs (not the first word of any sentence). *sharply.*

STUDENT REWRITE

Since this passage continues without another indentation, be sure students continue writing where last week's passage left off.

"Without delay I will journey abroad to seek adventures," Robin added. "Tarry for me here. Only make certain that you're ready to heed my call, which will sound as three short blasts upon the bugle horn if I require your aid."

    Robin Hood set off. Widely he ranged through the forest in search of glorious adventure. When the path he took sharply curved, it brought him to a broad, pebbly stream, spanned by a narrow wooden bridge.

Week 14

Commas with Adverb Clauses

LEARN IT

Commas with Adverb Clauses

When a clause begins with a www.asia.b word, it usually starts an adverb clause. To help you see this in your notations, mark the clauses that begin with a www.asia.b word *AC* instead of *DC*. There are a few exceptions, but you do not need to worry about that now.

There are three comma rules to remember when it comes to adverb clauses:

- Always use commas after #5 clausal openers, even if they are short.
- The comma goes after the clause, not after the www.asia.b word.
- If the www word is a dress-up (not at the first word of a sentence), a comma is usually not needed. Simply watch the patterns: .
  - ➤ Main Clause Adverb Clause (MC AC)
  - ➤ Adverb Clause comma Main Clause (AC, MC)

AC, MC examples:

- *Although the foresters discovered them in the act, they narrowly escaped.*
- *Since the problem was obvious, he continued after a pause.*
- *When he finished, they thanked their old friend heartily for his kindness.*
- *Because the Sheriff of Nottingham was related to the slain forester, he had a vendetta to catch Robin Hood.*

MC AC examples:

- *"Meet me if you dare."*
- *"Your name, Little John, fits you ill because you are far from little!"*
- *Robin Hood and his band guffawed loudly as the stranger grew enraged.*
- *Remain on the other side while I quickly make a staff.*

You may stop marking adjectives and -ly adverbs in this lesson.

Use the Week 14 grammar card to remember these rules.

Commas are where all the labeling will have practical benefit. This week guide students to punctuate adverb clauses properly.

This week guide students to punctuate adverb clauses properly.

The exceptions to the rules are for contrasting elements and adjective clauses, but you do not need to teach this now. See comma rules 13 and 15 for more details (Grammar Glossary pages G-24 to G-25).

Students will no longer need to label adjectives or -ly adverbs, but continue asking students to mark them if they need more practice.

Page 30, *Fix It! Grammar:* Robin Hood, Student Book 2

Institute for Excellence in Writing

DAY 1

```
                                                              DC
#5 AC cl  S      V       MC S    V              S/w-w   V              V      prep
(as he approached), [he noticed a tall stranger], (who was resolutely striding toward the other
```

```
        prep
side of the bridge).
```

Fixes

Indent. Is this a new topic, speaker, place, or time? Answer: Some students will choose the same paragraph because the topic is still about Robin's first adventure, but some will argue it is a new paragraph because we turn attention to what happens at the bridge. Let your students decide!

Commas with adverb clauses. Ask: Does the adverb clause *As he approached* take a comma or not? What is the rule? Answer: Yes, because it is a #5 opener. Rule: **AC, MC.** The comma goes at the end of the introductory adverb clause after *approached*. See ✐.

End marks. This is a statement so add a period.

Grammar Notations

✐ **Teacher's note.** Remember that the additional notes below are for your reference. You do not need to discuss them all if it is overwhelming for your student. Keep the discussion light and fun—make it a game.

Subjects and verbs. *he approached, he noticed, who was striding.* Ask: Which are helping verbs? Answer: *was,* which helps out *striding.*

Prepositional phrases. *toward the other side, of the bridge.* Check underlines. Ask students to show how these fit the pattern: **preposition + noun (no verb).**

Who-which clauses. Have students read the clause aloud: *who was resolutely striding toward the other side of the bridge.*

Ask: What noun does this clause describe and where is it? Answer: *stranger,* which the *who* clause immediately follows.

Clauses and sentence openers. Check parentheses and brackets.

- #5 opener and AC (adverb clause): *As he approached.*
- MC: *he noticed a tall stranger.*
- DC (w-w clause): *who was resolutely striding toward the other side of the bridge.*

resolutely: in a determined manner

✐ **Teacher's note.** Many comma rules depend on the kinds and placement of the clauses. **Encourage your student to identify and mark the clauses before working on the commas.**

Notice that clauses beginning with a www.asia.b word are now marked with AC instead of DC.

Sometimes a www.asia.b word will start a different kind of clause, but students do not need to differentiate them at this level. In these cases the markings will show DC. If your students use AC, you can let it go for now.

DAY 2

#1 MC S   *V*   *AC cl*   *S*   *V*   *AC cl*   *S*   *V*

[robin **quickened** his pace] (when the stranger did ~~to / two /~~ too) (since each imagined to cross

first).

Fixes

Indent. Is this a new topic, speaker, place, or time? Answer: No, same topic.

Homophones and usage. *too,* meaning *also.*

Commas with adverb clauses. Ask: How should we punctuate these adverb clauses? Answer: No commas with mid-sentence adverb clauses, so no comma before *when* or *since*. Rule: **MC AC**. *See ✐.*

End marks. This is a statement so add a period.

> **quickened:** hastened; made more rapid

> ✐ **Teacher's note.** Remind students to identify clauses before working on commas.

Grammar Notations

Subjects and verbs. *Robin quickened, stranger did, each imagined.*

Clauses and sentence openers.

- #1 MC: *Robin quickened his pace.*
- AC (adverb clause): *when the stranger did too.*
- AC (adverb clause): *since each imagined to cross first.*

DAY 3

#5   *AC cl*   *S*   *V*   *MC V*   *MC*   *V*   *S*

¶ "(if you know your ~~you're~~ best interest), [stand back], sir," [demanded robin **brusquely**],

   AC   *cl*   *S*   *V*   *V*

"(because the better man should cross first)."

Fixes

Indent. Is this a new topic, speaker, place, or time? Answer: Yes, a new speaker.

Quotation marks. Check for quotation marks around the words spoken but not the narration that interrupts his sentence: *"If … sir," demanded Robin brusquely, "because … first."*

Capitalization. Use lowercase for *sir*. See ✏ **1.**

Homophones and usage. *your best interest,* the possessive.

Commas. Ask students to explain the reason for each comma. Guide them to understand those they missed by referencing the Grammar Notations.

- *"If you know your best interest, … "* Comma after *interest* because of the #5 sentence opener: **AC, MC.**
- *" … stand back, sir, … "* Commas around *sir* to set off NDA. Check that the comma after *sir* is inside the closing quotation marks.
- *" … sir," demanded Robin brusquely, "because … "* Commas around narrative interrupting Robin's speech because he continues the same sentence after the narrative. Also, *demanded* is a speaking verb, which sets up quotations with a comma. See ✏ **2.**

End marks. This is a statement so add a period inside the closing quotation marks.

Grammar Notations

Subjects and verbs. *you know, stand back* (*you* is the implied subject; *back* is part of the verb phrase), *demanded Robin, man should cross.*

Ask: Which are helping verbs? Answer: *should,* which helps out *cross.*

Clauses and sentence openers.

- #5 opener and AC (adverb clause): *If you know your best interest.* Ask students to read the clause aloud to hear that it cannot stand alone but needs a main clause to be a legal sentence.
- MC: *stand back.*
  - ✧ **Advanced.** *You* is the subject because this is in the imperative (command) voice; *sir* is not the subject but a NDA.
- MC: *demanded Robin brusquely.* If students are confused, explain that sometimes the verb comes before its subject. It is more common to say *Robin brusquely demanded,* but both are correct.
- AC (adverb clause): *because the better man should cross first.* Ask students to read the clause aloud to hear that it cannot stand alone.

brusquely: in an abrupt, blunt manner

✏ **1. Teacher's note.** In NDAs, titles are usually capitalized if they substitute for someone's name; two exceptions are *sir* and *madam.*

✏ **2. Teacher's note.** Note that normally a www dress-up (*because*) would not be set off with a comma, but the comma is there because of the narrative interrupting, not because of the dress-up.

DAY 4

¶ "no," [responded the confident **interloper**], "[you stand back yourself] (since i am the better man)."

Labels above the sentence: MC V ... S MC S V ... AC cl S V

Fixes

Indent. Is this a new topic, speaker, place, or time? Answer: Yes, a new speaker so a new paragraph.

Quotation marks. Check that students placed quotation marks around the words spoken: *"No," … "you … man."*

Commas.

- Check that students placed commas around the interrupter (after *no* and after *interloper*) because it has a speaking verb setting up the quotation and because his sentence continues.

  Like periods, commas go inside closing quotation marks: *"No," responded the interloper.*

- No comma before *since*. Rule: **MC AC**. It helps to check clauses first.

End marks. This is a statement so add a period inside the closing quotation marks.

Grammar Notations

Subjects and verbs. *interloper responded, you stand back* (*back* is part of a verb phrase), *I am.*

Clauses and sentence openers.

- MC: *responded the confident interloper.* Either count this as a #1 subject opener since it effectively begins with the main clause even though the subject is later, or do not label the opener at all.
- MC: *you stand back yourself.*
- AC (adverb clause): *since I am the better man.*

Style

If desired, have your students identify the best dress-ups from this week's sentences. Discuss their answers. Choose among:

Strong verbs. *striding, quickened.*

Quality adjectives. *confident.*

-ly adverbs (not the first word of any sentence). *resolutely, brusquely.*

---

interloper: a person who interferes or meddles in the affairs of others.

Note that the stranger is an interloper only from Robin Hood's perspective!

STUDENT REWRITE

Since this passage continues without another indentation, be sure students continue writing where last week's passage left off.

As he approached, he noticed a tall stranger, who was resolutely striding toward the other side of the bridge. Robin quickened his pace when the stranger did too since each imagined to cross first.

"If you know your best interest, stand back, sir," demanded Robin brusquely, "because the better man should cross first."

"No," responded the confident interloper, "you stand back yourself since I am the better man."

Week 15

More Homophones, Additional Clause Starters

LEARN IT

Homophones This week you have another homophone: the possessive *whose* and the contraction *who's*. Use the grammar card from Weeks 2 and 15 to help you remember which is which.

Clause Starters In Week 8 you learned about the www word dress-up and the list of typical starters: *when, while, where, as, since, if, although, because* (www. asia.b).

Other words can also start a dependent clause. You will find one in this week's fixes: *until*. Begin to collect other words to add to the www.asia.b list on the back of the *cl* (Clause Starters) grammar card. Here are a few to get you started:

- *until*
- *whereas*
- *unless*
- *before*
- *after*
- *as if*
- *wherever*
- *whenever*

Three of those words (*until, before, after*) can also serve as prepositions. You can think of them as double agents. The key to identifying them as clauses starters is to look for a verb. If the word is followed by a subject and a verb, it is likely a clause starter. If there is no subject-verb pair, it is likely a preposition.

Do you remember the technical term for these words? They are subordinating conjunctions, but you can call them clause starters for now.

Review Now for some more review. See if you can answer the questions below. If not, check your grammar cards for the answers.

1. In stories, what four reasons do we follow to begin a new paragraph?

2. When is a word capitalized?

Do you remember what these vocabulary words mean? If not, look them up in your vocabulary list in the back of your notebook.

- reigned
- glades
- expertise
- rambled
- wrath
- dauntless
- readily
- carefree

> **Teacher's answers**
>
> **1.** new topic, speaker, time, or place
>
> **2.** when it starts a sentence or quoted sentence; when it is a proper noun

A new clause starter will appear in this week's fixes: *until*. Explain to your students that the www.asia.b list is not all-inclusive. Have your students copy the additional words listed onto the back of their Week 8 clause starters card.

These exercises should be a game that is fun to play. The detailed discussion notes are mainly for the teacher's benefit. You do not need to discuss them all for your student to succeed.

◆ **Listen.** If your student is struggling, reduce the number of things to look for. If you have not listened to Andrew Pudewa's Mastery Learning talk, now would be a good time. See the blue page at the front of this book for download instructions.

DAY 1

#5 *AC cl   S   V   V   DC   S/w-w V   MC V   S   prep   MC V*

¶ "(since time will tell) (~~whose~~/who's the better man)," [asserted robin], "for now [bide]

AC cl   S   V   cc   MC S V   V   prep

(where you are), or else [i will fire an arrow at you]."

Fixes

bide: wait; remain

Indent. Is this a new topic, speaker, place, or time? Answer: Yes, a new speaker and a new paragraph.

Quotation marks. Check that students placed quotation marks around the words spoken: *"Since … man," asserted Robin, "for now … at you."*

Ask students to explain why commas are needed after *man* (inside the quotations) and *Robin*. Answer: Robin's speech is interrupted by narrative (*asserted Robin*), which needs commas on both sides of it. See ✎.

Homophones and usage. *who's,* the contraction for *who is*.

End marks. This is a statement so add a period inside the closing quotation marks.

Grammar Notations

Subjects and verbs. *time will tell, who's (who is), asserted Robin, bide, you are, I will fire.*

Ask: Which are helping verbs? Answer: *will* (helps *tell*); *will* (helps *fire*).

✧ **Advanced.** Ask students to explain how *bide* could be a complete thought. Answer: It is in the imperative voice, a command, and the subject, *you,* is understood.

Prepositional phrases. *for now, at you.* Check underlines. Ask students to show how these fit the pattern: **preposition + noun (no verb).** See ♡.

Coordinating conjunctions. *or.*

✧ **Advanced.** Ask what the cc connects. Answer: Two main clauses. The first is a single word (*bide*) with the subject (*you*) understood. See under clauses, below.

Clauses and sentence openers.

- #5 opener and AC (adverb clause): *Since time will tell.*
- DC (w-w clause): *who's the better man.*
- MC: *asserted Robin.*
- MC: *bide.* Note: The full main clause includes the adverb clause that follows (*bide where you are*), but *bide* alone has the subject (an implied *you*) and verb of this main clause.
- AC (adverb clause): *where you are.* Check that students understand why this is an adverb clause (begins with a www word) and why it is dependent (cannot stand alone).
- MC: *I will fire an arrow at you.*

✎ **Teacher's note.** If your students ask why there is no comma after the first AC (*since time will tell*), explain that the w-w clause that follows completes the thought, so save the #5 opener comma for the end of both clauses.

♡ **Grammar lovers.** Students may be confused about *for,* which sometimes is a coordinating conjunction. In this sentence it fits the preposition pattern and does not join two or more items in a series, so it has to be a preposition and not a conjunction.

DAY 2

#6 MC   S   V   #1 MC S V V   AC cl   S V

¶ ["hah!" the other exclaimed]. " [i will **tan your ~~you're~~ hide**] (until ~~its~~ it's as many colors as

                               AC cl S   V   prep

a beggar's cloak) (if you even touch a string on your ~~you're~~ bow)."

Fixes

Indent. Is this a new topic, speaker, place, or time? Answer: Yes, a new speaker and a new paragraph.

Homophones and usage.

- *your hide*, the possessive.
- *it's as many colors as a beggar's cloak*. Ask: What does *it's* mean? Answer: *it is*. Remind students of the mnemonic device: *it's* with the apostrophe replaced by a superscripted *i*.

it^{i}s

- *your bow*, the possessive.

Quotation marks. Check that students placed quotation marks around the words spoken: *"Hah!" the other exclaimed. "I will ... bow."*

> ✧ **Advanced.** Exclamatory expressions like *"Hah!"* can stand alone with an exclamation mark, which means we need the period after the interrupter and before the complete sentence that follows.

Commas with adverb clauses. Check that students did not put commas before *until* or *if*. Rule: **MC AC**. It helps to work through the clause construction before addressing these commas.

> ✧ **Advanced.** The www words are the most common, but there are many more subordinating conjunctions, including *until*. The instructions on page 32 of the student book invite students to add a few common ones, such as *until*, to their clause starter list.

End marks. This is a statement so add a period inside the closing quotation marks.

Grammar Notations

Subjects and verbs. *other exclaimed, I will tan, it's, you touch.*

> ✧ **Advanced.** Guide students to see that the contraction *it's* has both a subject (*it*) and a verb (*is*).

Prepositional phrases. *on your bow*. Check underlines. Ask students to show how this fits the pattern: **preposition + noun (no verb)**.

Clauses and sentence openers.

- #6 vss and MC: *"Hah!" the other exclaimed.*
- #1 subject opener and MC: *I will tan your hide.*
- AC (adverb clause): *until it's as many colors as a beggar's cloak. See* ✏.
- AC (adverb clause): *if you even touch a string on your bow*. Ask students to read this aloud to hear that it cannot stand alone. It needs an MC to be legal.

---

tan one's hide: beat one soundly. This idiom, an expression that cannot be understood literally, comes from hitting an animal's hide to turn it into leather.

A **beggar's cloak** would be many colors from being patched numerous times.

✏ **Teacher's note.** The construction "as ... as" is an idiom, and idioms do not easily lend themselves to parts of speech breakdown—dictionaries do not list their parts of speech at all. The second *as* in the "as ... as" construction sometimes starts a prepositional phrase and sometimes starts a clause, which is the important part to grasp. However, it is simpler to just call this construction an idiom and be done with it!

DAY 3

#1 MC S   V   prep   *MC   V   S   cc S   V   V*
                                                                    MC

¶ " [you joke like a **numskull**]," [returned robin], "for [i could swiftly fire this arrow clean

prep

through your ~~you're~~ arrogant heart]."

Fixes

numskull: a dull-witted person

Indent. Is this a new topic, speaker, place, or time? Answer: Yes, a new speaker and paragraph.

Capitalization. We do not capitalize *for* because it is not the first word of a quoted sentence. Students may see this better if you remove the interrupter: *"You joke like a numskull, for I could swiftly fire this arrow clean through your arrogant heart."*

Homophones and usage. *your heart*, the possessive.

Quotation marks. Check that students placed quotation marks around the words spoken and commas around the interrupter: *"You ... numskull," returned Robin, "for heart."*

Ask: What is the speaking verb in the interrupter? Answer: *returned*. Check that students added commas around the interrupter.

End marks. This is a statement so add a period inside the closing quotation marks.

Grammar Notations

Subjects and verbs. *You joke, returned Robin, I could fire.*

Prepositional phrases. *like a numskull, through your arrogant heart.*

Check underlines. Ask students to show how these fit the pattern: **preposition + noun (no verb)**.

Coordinating conjunctions. Ask what the cc *for* connects. Answer: the two main clauses in his speech: a) *You joke like a numskull*; b) *I could swiftly fire this arrow clean through your arrogant heart.*

Clauses and sentence openers.

- #1 subject opener and MC: *You joke like a numskull.*
- MC: *returned Robin.*
- MC: *I could swiftly fire this arrow clean through your arrogant heart.*

DAY 4

#3 ly   *MC*   *S*   *V*   *prep*   *MC S*   *V* *prep*

¶ resentfully [the stranger answered back to him], "[you joke like a **faintheart**]."

Fixes

faintheart: a coward; one who lacks courage or is faint of heart

Indent. Is this a new topic, speaker, place, or time? Answer: Yes, a new speaker and paragraph.

Quotations. Check that students placed quotation marks around the words spoken: *"You joke … faintheart."*

Check that students added a comma after *him* to set up the quotation with the speaking verb. Ask: What is the speaking verb? Answer: *answered back*.

End marks. This is a statement so add a period.

Grammar Notations

Subjects and verbs. *stranger answered back, you joke.*

Prepositional phrases. *to him, like a faintheart.* Check underlines. Ask students to show how these fit the pattern: **preposition + noun (no verb)**.

Clauses and sentence openers.

- #3 -ly adverb opener: *Resentfully.*
- MC: *the stranger answered back to him.*
- MC: *You joke like a faintheart.*

Style

If desired, have your students identify the best dress-ups from this week's sentences. Discuss their answers. Best possibilities:

Strong verbs. *asserted, bide, tan … hide.*

Quality adjectives. *arrogant.*

-ly adverbs (not the first word of any sentence). *swiftly.*

STUDENT REWRITE

"Since time will tell who's the better man," asserted Robin, "for now bide where you are, or else I will fire an arrow at you."

"Hah!" the other exclaimed. "I will tan your hide until it's as many colors as a beggar's cloak if you even touch a string on your bow."

"You joke like a numskull," returned Robin, "for I could swiftly fire this arrow clean through your arrogant heart."

Resentfully the stranger answered back to him, "You joke like a faintheart."

Week 16

No New Concepts

LEARN IT

There are no new concepts this week. See if you can answer the questions below. If not, check your grammar cards for the answers.

1. Name the three articles.
2. What do articles do?
3. Describe a noun.
4. What is the noun test?

Do you remember what these vocabulary words mean? If not, look them up in your vocabulary list in the back of your notebook.

- blithely
- fancifully
- convivially
- accosted
- shoddy
- taunted
- champion
- top-notch
- retorted

> **Teacher's answers**
>
> 1. *the, a, an*
> 2. introduce a noun
> 3. person, place, thing, or idea
> 4. countable? two _____
>   article? the/a/an _____

This week students will practice the concepts they have already learned. Continue to make it a game.

If certain concepts, such as prepositional phrases, are easy, then you do not need to address them in your conversation.

Page 34, *Fix It! Grammar:* **Robin Hood, Student Book 2**

DAY 1

#1 *MC*   *S*   *V*   *MC S*   *V*   *prep*   *prep*

[the tall stranger continued], "[you stand there ~~/their /they're~~ with a **lethal** bow to shoot at my

         DC cl   *S*   *V*

heart], (while i have only a plain blackthorn staff to meet you with)."

Fixes

Indent. Is this a new topic, speaker, place, or time? Answer: No. It continues the topic of the stranger's complaint of an unfair fight.

Capitalization. Remind students that first words of quoted sentences (in this case, *You*) should be capitalized even when those sentences appear in the middle of a longer sentence.

Homophones and usage. Ask: What does *there* mean? Answer: *in that place.*

Quotations. Check for quotation marks around the speech: *"You stand … meet you with."*

Check that students added a comma after *continued* because a speaking verb sets up the quotation. Ask: What is the speaking verb? Answer: *continued.*

Commas with adjectives. If students did not catch this, ask them to find two adjacent adjectives. Answer: *plain blackthorn.*

Ask students to identify these as coordinate or cumulative. Answer: The two tricks show up negative: 1) *blackthorn, plain staff* sounds awkward; 2) *plain and blackthorn staff* sounds awkward. They are therefore cumulative and do not take a comma.

End marks. This is a statement so add a period inside the closing quotation marks.

Grammar Notations

Subjects and verbs. *stranger continued, You stand, I have.*

Prepositional phrases. *with a lethal bow, at my heart.* Check underlines. *See ♡ .*

> **Prepositions at the end of sentences.** Some people have been taught that sentences should not end with prepositions. This is a carryover from Latin and not a true rule in English. Andrew Pudewa says Winston Churchill gave the definitive answer to this problem when he said, "That is a rule up with which I will not put!"
>
> The point: If the sentence is more awkward to revise with the preposition placed earlier, it is better to have it at the end. In this case, the alternative is a more awkward construction: *"a plain blackthorn staff with which to meet you."* Go with the original!

Clauses and sentence openers.

- MC: *The tall stranger continued.*
- MC: *You stand there with a lethal bow to shoot at my heart.*
- DC (www clause): *while I have only a plain blackthorn staff to meet you with.* Have students read this aloud to hear that it is incomplete by itself.
  - ✦ **Advanced.** If students wonder about the comma before *while*, you could explain that *while* takes a comma when setting up a strong contrast with the clause before it. In such a case, it actually functions as a coordinating conjunction, but this is too advanced for most students even in high school. *While* starts an adverb clause when it means "at the same time."

lethal: causing death

Explain that his staff would have been a large walking stick, which doubles as a weapon in times of need but is no match for an arrow from across a bridge.

♡ **Grammar lovers.** The object of the preposition *with* is *staff: I will meet you with a staff.*

DAY 2

At the end of this passage, Robin is not finished speaking. How does this affect the quotation marks?

#2 prep   prep   MC V   S   MC   V   S   V   V   prep
¶ "by the faith of my heart," [cried robin], "[never have i been called a **craven** in my life]!

Fixes

craven: a coward

Indent. Is this a new topic, speaker, place, or time? Answer: Yes, a new speaker and paragraph.

Capitalization. Do not capitalize *never* because it is not the first word of a quoted sentence. His full sentence begins with *By*.

Quotations. Check that students placed quotation marks around the words spoken but not at the end of his speech since he is not finished: *"By ... heart," cried Robin, "never ... life!*

If students missed the first quotation marks, explain that *"by the faith of my heart"* must be his words because of the word *my*. If this was narrative, it would say, *By the faith of his heart.*

Check that students placed commas around the interrupter (*cried Robin*). Ask them to identify the speaking verb: *cried.*

End marks. Robin is quite excited, so his words should end with an exclamation mark, which needs to go inside the closing quotation marks.

Grammar Notations

Subjects and verbs. *cried Robin, have I been called.*

Ask: What are the helping verbs? Answer: *have been,* which helps out *called* (*I have been called*).

Prepositional phrases. *by the faith, of my heart, in my life.*

Check underlines. Ask students to show how these fit the pattern: **preposition + noun (no verb).**

Clauses and sentence openers.

- #2 prepositional phrase opener: *By the faith of my heart.* Ask: How many prepositional phrases open this sentence? Answer: two.
- MC: *cried Robin.*
- MC: *never have I been called a craven in my life.* If students have trouble realizing that this is a MC, explain that *never* is an adverb (like *not*) and does not affect the clause. It may help to recast the sentence: *I have never been called a craven in my life.*

DAY 3

#5 *AC cl   S   V   V   prep*   *AC cl   S   V   MC S V   V*

(if you will remain on the other side) (while i̲ quickly make a staff), [i̲ will l̶i̶e̶/lay aside my

cc   V

trusty arrows and test your /y̶o̶u̶'̶r̶e̶ **sparring** skills]**."**

Fixes

Indent. Is this a new topic, speaker, place, or time? Answer: No, Robin is still responding to the charge that he is not playing fair.

Homophones and usage.

- *will lay*, the future tense of *to lay*. Robin Hood is *laying down* an object, not *lying himself down*.

- *your sparring skills*, the possessive.

Quotations. Robin continues to speak, so students should continue writing where they left off and not use opening quotation marks, only closing ones: *If ... skills."*

Commas with adverb clauses. It helps to work through the clause construction before addressing these commas. See Grammar Notations.

Ask: What punctuation did you place before *while*? Answer: No comma before mid-sentence adverb clauses: **MC AC**.

Ask: What punctuation did you place after *staff*? Answer: Comma at the end of #5 clausal openers: **AC, MC**. *See* ✎.

End marks. This is a statement so add a period inside the closing quotation marks.

Grammar Notations

Subjects and verbs. *you will remain, I make, I will lay aside ... test.* Note: *aside* is in the verb phrase.

Adjectives. *other, trusty, sparring.* Students may have trouble recognizing that *sparring* is an adjective here since it is formed from a verb. Point out that it describes a noun, *skills*. Since only adjectives can describe nouns, it has to be an adjective.

Prepositional phrases. *on the other side.* Check underlines. Ask students to show how this fits the pattern: **preposition + noun (no verb)**.

Coordinating conjunctions. Ask what the cc *and* connects. Answer: two verbs, *will lay aside* and *test*. Ask: How many subjects go with these two verbs? Answer: one.

Point out that there is no comma before coordinating conjunctions when they join only two verbs. Show in this sentence that *"I will lay aside ... and test"* has no comma. Pattern: **MC cc 2nd verb**.

Clauses and sentence openers.

- #5 opener and AC (adverb clause): *If you will remain on the other side.*
- AC (adverb clause): *while I quickly make a staff.* Ask students to read aloud the two dependent clauses to hear that they cannot stand alone.
- MC: *I will lay aside my trusty arrows and test your sparring skills.*

sparring: boxing, especially with light blows, used more loosely here to suggest physical combat but with staffs instead of fists

✎ **Teacher's note.** With multiple openers, usually save the comma for the end of all of them.

DAY 4

#1 MC S   V   MC   V   S   prep   prep   #3 ly MC   V   S

¶ "[i̲ welcome you to try]," [**countered** the stranger <u>with a twinkle</u> <u>in his eye</u>]. "[gladly will i̲

V

tarry here a while longer].″

countered: made an opposing move or response

Fixes

Indent. Is this a new topic, speaker, place, or time? Answer: Yes, a new speaker and paragraph.

Quotations. Check that students placed quotation marks around the words spoken: *"I welcome … try," countered the stranger with a twinkle in his eye. "Gladly … longer."*

> **quotation + comma + speaking verb.** Check that students added a comma after *try* inside the closing quotation marks because a speaking verb (*countered*) sets up this quotation.

> ✧ **Advanced.** The period after *eye* is correct because the stranger has complete sentences before and after the interrupter; sentences need a period to separate them.

End marks. This is a statement so add a period inside the closing quotation marks.

Grammar Notations

Subjects and verbs. *I welcome, countered … stranger, will I tarry* (*will* = helping verb).

> ✧ **Advanced.** Students may mark *you to try*, but these do not count as a subject or verb. See ♡.

Prepositional phrases. *with a twinkle, in his eye.* Check underlines. Ask students to show how these fit the pattern: **preposition + noun (no verb)**.

Clauses and sentence openers.

- #1 subject opener and MC: *I welcome you to try.*
- MC: *countered the stranger with a twinkle in his eye.* If students have trouble with this, recast the sentence to show better that it is a main clause: *The stranger countered with a twinkle in his eye.*
- #3 -ly adverb opener: *Gladly will I tarry here a while longer.*

♡ **Grammar lovers.** *You* is the direct object of *welcome* and *to try* is an infinitive, which is formed from a verb but does not function as one.

Style

If desired, have your students identify the best dress-ups from this week's sentences. Discuss their answers. Choose among:

Strong verbs. *countered.*

Quality adjectives. *lethal, trusty.*

-ly adverbs (not the first word of any sentence). *quickly.*

STUDENT REWRITE

Since this passage continues without another indentation, be sure students continue writing where last week's passage left off.

The tall stranger continued, "You stand there with a lethal bow to shoot at my heart, while I have only a plain blackthorn staff to meet you with."

"By the faith of my heart," cried Robin, "never have I been called a craven in my life! If you will remain on the other side while I quickly make a staff, I will lay aside my trusty arrows and test your sparring skills."

"I welcome you to try," countered the stranger with a twinkle in his eye. "Gladly will I tarry here a while longer."

Week 17

No New Concepts

LEARN IT

There are no new concepts this week. See if you can answer the questions below. If not, check your grammar cards for the answers.

1. What does FANBOYS stand for?

2. What part of speech are those?

3. What is a main clause (MC)?

Do you remember what these vocabulary words mean? If not, look them up in your vocabulary list in the back of your notebook.

- affronted
- composedly
- buck
- wager
- seethed
- capital
- impulsively
- hot-blooded
- opponent

Have your students continue practicing the concepts they have already learned.

✎ **Teacher's note.** Remember to keep the exercise light and fun. It should be like a game. If your student groans when you say, "Time for Fix It!" something is wrong.

DAY 1

#1 *MC*   *S*   *V*   *prep*

¶ [the calm, mysterious giant then ~~then~~ leaned **sturdily** upon his staff to await robin].

Fixes

sturdily: in a strong and determined way

Indent. Is this a new topic, speaker, place, or time? Answer: Yes, we leave his speech and focus on their actions.

Homophones and usage. *Then*, meaning *next* or *immediately afterward*.

Commas with adjectives. Check if students put a comma after *calm*, and then guide them to see why it is needed by applying the two tests:

- Does *mysterious, calm giant* sound normal? Yes.
- Can we say *calm and mysterious giant*? Yes.

Since both tests work, these are coordinate adjectives and take a comma between them.

End marks. This is a statement so add a period.

Grammar Notations

Subjects and verbs. *giant leaned.*

  ✧ **Advanced.** *to await* is not a verb but an infinitive, which is formed from a verb but does not function as one.

Prepositional phrases. *upon his staff.*

  Check underlines. Ask students to show how this fits the pattern: **preposition + noun (no verb)**.

Clauses and sentence openers.

- #1 subject opener and MC: *The calm, mysterious giant then leaned sturdily upon his staff to await Robin.*

DAY 2

In your rewrite, combine the two sentences with a *which* clause set off with a comma. To determine how, look for a word that repeats in both sentences and that you can replace with *which*.

#1 MC   S   V   *prep*   *prep*   V   cc

[robin hood stepped lightly to the side of the bridge, found a tall oak there ~~, their/they're~~, and

                                              DC S/w-w

V   **which** V   *prep*

cut straight a **hefty** staff], ~~the staff~~ (measured six feet in length).

Combine sentences with a which

Check that students combined the sentences correctly and put a comma in front of the new *which* clause. *See* ✐.

Fixes

Indent. Is this a new topic, speaker, place, or time? Answer: No. This paragraph flips back and forth between Robin preparing his staff and the stranger watching him, but it is all on the same topic.

Homophones and usage. Ask: What does *there* mean? Answer: *in that place*.

Commas with items in a series. Remind students that coordinating conjunctions must join the same parts of speech in a series.

Ask: Which words does the cc *and* join? Answer: *stepped, found, cut*. Ask: What part of speech are they? Answer: verbs. Ask: What pattern? Answer: **a, b, and c**.

End marks. This is a statement so add a period.

Grammar Notations

Subjects and verbs. *Robin Hood stepped, found, cut; which measured*.

Prepositional phrases. *to the side, of the bridge, in length*. Check underlines and ask students to show how these fit the pattern: **preposition + noun (no verb)**.

Clauses and sentence openers.

- #1 subject opener and MC: *Robin Hood stepped to the side of the bridge, found a tall oak there, and cut straight a hefty staff.*

  Guide students to see that this is only one main clause. The subject (*Robin Hood*) is performing three distinct verb actions, but there is only one subject so only one main clause.

- DC (w-w clause): *which measured six feet in length*.

  ✧ **Advanced.** Can your students explain why this is a clause and not a phrase? Answer: It has a subject (*which*) and verb (*measured*). It cannot stand alone, which makes it a dependent clause instead of a main clause.

hefty: impressively large and substantial

✐ **Teacher's note.** This *who-which* clause takes a comma because it is nonessential. It adds information but does not affect the meaning of the main clause.

DAY 3

$$\overset{cc}{\text{relaxed and untroubled,}}\ \overset{MC}{[}\text{the }\overset{S}{\text{stranger }}\textbf{genially}\ \overset{V}{\text{waited }}\underline{\overset{prep}{\text{for him}}}],\ \text{leaning }\underline{\overset{prep}{\text{upon his staff}}}\ \overset{cc}{\text{and}}$$

$$\text{whistling }\overset{AC\ cl\ \ S\ \ \ \ V}{\big(\text{as he gazed about}\big)}.$$

Fixes

Indent. Is this a new topic, speaker, place, or time? Answer: No, it still talks about Robin and the stranger preparing for the bout.

Commas with adverb clauses (check clauses first). Ask: What punctuation did you place before *as*? Answer: No comma before mid-sentence adverb clauses. Rule: **MC AC**.

End marks. This is a statement so add a period.

> **genially:** pleasantly and cheerfully

Grammar Notations

Subjects and verbs. *stranger waited, he gazed about* (*about* is in the verb phrase).

✧ **Advanced.** The verbals in this sentence (*relaxed, untroubled, leaning, whistling*) do not function as verbs because they are not paired with a subject and helping verb. If students mark any of them as verbs, choose whether or not to discuss it since this is a difficult concept for this level. It may help to contrast the same words used as verbs: *He was relaxed; he was untroubled; he was leaning; he was whistling.*

Adjectives. *relaxed, untroubled.*

✧ **Advanced.** Students may have trouble seeing that these are adjectives because they are verbals and do not come immediately before the noun they describe. It may help students to hear the sentence recast this way: *The relaxed and untroubled stranger waited for him.* See ♡.

Prepositional phrases. *for him, upon his staff.* Check underlines and ask students to show how these fit the pattern: **preposition + noun (no verb)**.

✧ **Advanced.** *About* is an adverb meaning *on every side.* You can tell it is not a preposition because it does not have an object. If students object that one cannot end a sentence with a preposition, remind them that that is not a rule of English grammar—and this is not a preposition anyway.

Coordinating conjunctions. *and* (joining two adjectives), *and* (joining two *-ing* words).

✐ **Teacher's note.** When a cc joins only two items in a series that are not main clauses, there is not a comma before the cc. Pattern: **a and b**.

Clauses and sentence openers.

✐ **Teacher's note.** *Relaxed and untroubled* is an invisible #4 opener, too advanced for this level. For now, leave it unmarked. See the Invisible #4s section under Advanced #4 Opener in the Stylistic Techniques section of the Grammar Glossary (page G-42).

- MC: *the stranger genially waited for him.*
- AC (adverb clause): *as he gazed about.*

> ♡ **Grammar lovers.** *Relaxed* and *untroubled* are past participles functioning as adjectives and a great example of an invisible #4 opener. *Leaning* and *whistling* are present participles doing the same thing, functioning as adjectives modifying *stranger*, but they are not marked here because they are too advanced for this level.

DAY 4

#3 ly   MC S   V   AC cl S   V   prep   prep

¶ **furtively** [robin observed him] (as he trimmed his staff), measuring him from top to toe.

Fixes

furtively: slyly and secretively

Indent. Is this a new topic, speaker, place, or time? Answer: Arguably yes. The topic switches to the stranger's size, which it will focus on for a few sentences.

Commas with adverb clauses. Ask: What punctuation did you place before *as*? Answer: No comma. Rule: **MC AC.**

End marks. This is a statement so add a period.

Grammar Notations

Subjects and verbs. *Robin observed, he trimmed.*

✧ **Advanced.** If students wonder, *measuring* is not a verb here because there is no subject and helping verb with it.

Prepositional phrases. *from top, to toe.* Check underlines and ask students to show how these fit the pattern: **preposition + noun (no verb).**

Clauses and sentence openers.

- #3 -ly adverb opener: *Furtively.*
- MC: *Robin observed him.* Ask students if they can hear that this could be a sentence by itself.
- AC (adverb clause): *as he trimmed his staff.* Ask students if they can hear that this cannot stand alone as a sentence.

Style

If desired, have your students identify the best dress-ups from this week's sentences. Discuss their answers. Choose among:

Strong verbs. *gazed, trimmed.*

Quality adjectives. *mysterious, hefty, relaxed, untroubled.*

-ly adverbs (not the first word of any sentence). *sturdily, genially.*

STUDENT REWRITE

The calm, mysterious giant then leaned sturdily upon his staff to await Robin. Robin Hood stepped to the side of the bridge, found a tall oak there, and cut straight a hefty staff, which measured six feet in length. Relaxed and untroubled, the stranger genially waited for him, leaning upon his staff and whistling as he gazed about.

Furtively Robin observed him as he trimmed his staff, measuring him from top to toe.

Week 18

Comma Rule MC, cc MC

LEARN IT

MC, cc MC

Commas are where all the labeling starts to have practical benefit. You have learned that coordinating conjunctions (cc) connect parts of speech: two or more nouns, two or more dependent clauses, two or more main clauses, and so forth.

When a cc joins two main clauses, you need to add a comma right before the coordinating conjunction. You will see a subject and verb after the coordinating conjunction.

The pattern is this: **MC, cc MC.**

Examples:

- [He is of diminished princely stature], *and* [he doesn't care for polo].
- [They had fought well in the wars], *but* [now they were out of work and destitute].

Remember that commas are also needed if the coordinating conjunction is used to combine three or more items in a series. That pattern is **a, b, and c.**

Cut out the grammar card for this week. It includes an additional rule that will be explored next week.

Teach the shorthand for this rule: **MC, cc MC.** Two main clauses joined with a coordinating conjunction need a comma before the cc.

DAY 1

Choose whether *he* or *him* is the correct pronoun.

#1 *MC S*　　　　　*V*　　　*DC*　　*S*　*V*　　　　　*V*　　　　*CC*

[robin **deemed**] (that he had never eyed a taller or more thickset man ~~then~~/than he ~~/him~~).

Fixes

Indent. Is this a new topic, speaker, place, or time? Answer: No.

Homophones and usage.

- *Than* for the comparison.
- *Than he.* The word *than* does not determine which pronoun; you have to look at how it is used in the sentence. The easiest way to figure this out is to finish the construction: *he had never seen a taller man than he was,* so *he,* not *him.*

End marks. This is a statement so add a period.

Grammar Notations

Subjects and verbs. *Robin deemed, he had eyed.* Ask: Which are helping verbs? Answer: *had,* which helps out *eyed.*

Clauses and sentence openers.

- #1 subject opener and MC: *Robin deemed.* Ask students if they can hear that this could be a sentence by itself.
- DC: *that he had never eyed a taller or more thickset man than he.* See ♡.

deemed: formed an opinion; judged

♡ **Grammar lovers.**
This DC is a noun clause, which begins with *that* and follows a verb. See the Grammar Glossary: Sentences, Clauses, and Phrases: Noun Clauses, page G-18.

DAY 2

```
                                          DC   S/w-w   V
                                     (who stood a full seven feet tall),
#3 ly         MC S        V       prep        cc  MC      S      V        prep         cc
usually, [robin towered over others], but [the stranger, was taller by a head and a neck

then/than he/him]. the stranger stood a full seven feet tall
```

Combine sentences with a who

Students were asked to combine the sentences with a *who* clause. Check that they combined the sentences correctly and put commas around the new *who* clause. This version also works: [*the stranger, (who was taller by a head and a neck than he), stood a full seven feet tall*]. See ✎.

Fixes

Indent. Is this a new topic, speaker, place, or time? Answer: No.

Homophones and usage.

- *than* compares Robin to the tall stranger.
- To tell which pronoun is correct, finish the construction: *was taller than he (was)*.

Commas with cc's. Check if students placed commas before the cc's. Guide them to see how the sentence construction determines whether or not a cc needs a comma before it (never after).

Ask: What does the cc *but* connect? Answer: Two main clauses.

Ask: Is a cc alone strong enough to hold two MCs together? Answer: No, it also needs a comma. The rule is **MC, cc MC**. [*Robin towered over others*], *but* [*the stranger … was taller by a head and a neck than he*].

Ask: What does the cc *and* connect? Answer: two nouns (*head and neck*), which do not need a comma because they are only two items in a series, not three or more.

End marks. This is a statement so add a period.

Grammar Notations

Subjects and verbs. *Robin towered, stranger was, who stood.*

Guide students to connect the right subjects and verbs together. Remind them that *who* and *which* clauses must have a verb of their own. *Stood* goes with *who. Stranger* is separated from its verb by the *who* clause.

Prepositional phrases. *over others, by a head and a neck.* Check underlines and ask students to show how these fit the pattern: **preposition + noun/pronoun (no verb)**.

Clauses and sentence openers.

- #3 -ly adverb opener: *Usually.*
- MC: *Robin towered over others.*
- MC: *the stranger … was taller by a head and a neck than he.*
- DC (w-w clause): *who stood a full seven feet tall.*

---

towered: rose above others; was taller than others

✎ **Teacher's note.** This *who* clause takes commas because it is nonessential. It adds information but does not affect the meaning of the main clause. If we removed it from the sentence, the sentence would still make sense.

DAY 3

#5 AC   cl   S   V   MC   S   V   *prep*

(although robin had broad shoulders), [the stranger's **husky** shoulders were broader by twice

the size].

Fixes

husky: big and strong

Indent. Is this a new topic, speaker, place, or time? Answer: No.

Commas with adverb clauses. Ask: What is the punctuation rule with #5 openers? Answer: They always take commas at the end of them: **AC, MC**. Ask: Where should this comma go? Answer: After *shoulders*.

End marks. This is a statement so add a period.

Grammar Notations

Subjects and verbs. *Robin had, shoulders were.*

If students mark *stranger's* as the subject, explain that it is his shoulders that are broader, not the stranger himself, so *shoulders* is the true subject. *Stranger's* is possessive.

Prepositional phrases. *by twice the size.*

Check underlines and ask students to show how this fits the pattern: **preposition** (*by*) **+ noun** (*size*); *twice* is an adverb, not a verb.

Clauses and sentence openers.

- #5 opener and AC (adverb clause): *Although Robin had broad shoulders.*
- MC: *the stranger's husky shoulders were broader by twice the size.*

DAY 4

MC · V · S · prep · MC · S · V · V

¶ "nevertheless," [**muttered** robin to himself], "[i will defeat you readily], my good fellow."

Fixes

muttered: uttered words in a low tone or indistinctly

Indent. Is this a new topic, speaker, place, or time? Answer: Yes, a new speaker and paragraph.

Quotations. Check that students placed quotation marks around the words spoken: *"Nevertheless," muttered Robin to himself, "I ... fellow."*

Ask: What is the speaking verb in the interrupter? Answer: *muttered.*

Commas.

Commas around *muttered Robin to himself* to set off narrative that interrupts a speech.

Commas around the noun of direct address, *my good fellow.*

End marks. This is a statement so add a period inside the closing quotation marks.

Grammar Notations

Subjects and verbs. *muttered Robin, I will defeat.*

Ask: Which of these are helping verbs? Answer: *will,* which helps *defeat.*

Prepositional phrases. *to himself.*

Check underlines and ask students to show how this fits the pattern: **preposition** (*to*) **+ noun or pronoun** (*himself*).

Clauses and sentence openers.

- MC: *muttered Robin to himself.*
- MC: *I will defeat you readily.*

Style

If desired, have your students identify the best dress-ups from this week's sentences. Discuss their answers. Choose among:

Strong verbs. *deemed, towered, muttered.*

Quality adjectives. *thickset, husky.*

-ly adverbs (not the first word of any sentence). *readily.*

STUDENT REWRITE

Since this passage continues without another indentation, be sure students continue writing where last week's passage left off.

Robin deemed that he had never eyed a taller or more thickset man than he. Usually, Robin towered over others, but the stranger, who stood a full seven feet tall, was taller by a head and a neck than he. Although Robin had broad shoulders, the stranger's husky shoulders were broader by twice the size.

"Nevertheless," muttered Robin to himself, "I will defeat you readily, my good fellow."

Week 19

Comma Rule MC cc 2nd Verb

LEARN IT

MC cc 2nd Verb Sometimes coordinating conjunctions need a comma before them and sometimes they do not. You have to look at the structure of the sentence to figure it out. The grammar card for Weeks 18 and 19 summarizes all the rules affecting commas before cc's.

Last week you learned to add a comma when a coordinating conjunction is joining two main clauses. However, if there is not a second subject after the coordinating conjunction, then it is not MC, cc MC. Instead, the pattern is **MC cc 2nd verb**.

The MC cc 2nd verb pattern has one subject performing two verb actions. This means you have only two items in a series (two verbs). Since there are only two verbs (two items in the series), there should not be a comma separating them.

The trick is to look for that second subject after the cc. If there is no subject, it probably should not have a comma.

MC cc 2nd verb examples:

- He bowed and walked away.
  - ➤ After *and* is the verb *walked*, not a second subject, so no comma.
- She fled to the lake and plunged in.
  - ➤ After *and* is the verb *plunged*, not a second subject, so no comma.

One of the reasons students have trouble with this is that sometimes coordinating conjunctions need a comma before them and sometimes they do not. Emphasize to your students that they need to look at the structure of the sentence to figure it out.

See Grammar Glossary: Parts of Speech: Coordinating Conjunctions, page G-12, for a quick list of all the rules affecting commas before cc's.

Now that your students have learned a few comma rules, ask them where they put commas and why. That will help them internalize the comma rules.

DAY 1

In your rewrite, combine his first two sentences with a *which* clause. Also note that Robin is not finished speaking.

#1 *MC* *S* *V* *prep* *MC* *V* *S* *DC S/w-w* *which* *V* *cc*

¶ [robin hood then ~~than~~ **proclaimed** to the stranger], "[here is my staff], (it is long and

MC V *cc* *V* *AC cl S* *V*

tough). now [wait my coming and meet me] (if you dare).

Combine sentences with a which

Check that students combined the sentences correctly and put a comma in front of the new *which* clause. See ✎ **1.**

Ask: What noun does *which* describe and where is it? Answer: *staff*, which is immediately before the *which* clause.

Fixes

Indent. Is this a new topic, speaker, place, or time? Answer: Yes, Robin is now addressing the stranger rather than talking to himself, so this counts as a new speaker.

Homophones and usage. *then*, meaning *next* or *immediately afterward*.

Quotations. Check that students placed a comma after *stranger* to separate the speaking verb (*proclaimed*) from the quotation it sets up. The comma goes immediately before the quotation, not after the verb.

Check for quotation marks around the words spoken but not at the end because Robin will continue to speak: *"Here ... .*

Commas with cc's.

Ask what the first *and* joins. Answer: two adjectives (*long and tough*), so no comma.

Ask what the second *and* joins. Answer: Two verbs with the same subject (an implied *you*). Ask: Should there be a comma? Answer: No, because *and* joins only two items in a series. Rule: **MC cc 2nd verb**, so no comma. See ✎ **2.**

Commas with adverb clauses. Ask: How should we punctuate mid-sentence adverb clauses? Answer: No comma. Rule: **MC AC**. Mid-sentence adverb clauses are not set off with commas.

End marks. This is a statement so add a period.

Grammar Notations

Subjects and verbs. *Robin Hood proclaimed, staff is, which is, wait, meet, you dare.* See ♡.

Prepositional phrases. *to the stranger.* Check underlines and ask students to show how this fits the pattern: **preposition + noun (no verb)**.

Clauses and sentence openers.

- #1 subject opener and MC: *Robin Hood then proclaimed to the stranger.*
- MC: *Here is my staff.*
- DC (w-w clause): *which is long and tough.*
- MC: *wait my coming and meet me.*
- AC (adverb clause): *if you dare.*

proclaimed: announced openly

✎ **1. Teacher's note.** This clause takes a comma because it is nonessential. It adds information but does not affect the meaning of the main clause (*Here is my staff*).

✎ **2. Teacher's note.** **MC cc 2nd verb** is just another way of explaining the pattern **a and b** but with compound verbs instead of other parts of speech. It is helpful to contrast **MC cc 2nd verb** with **MC, cc MC**. These patterns are nearly identical, except in the first there is not a second subject-verb pair after the cc, only a second verb, so no comma. It is only when the cc joins two main clauses (or three or more items) that it requires a comma before it.

♡ **Grammar lovers.** In clauses starting with *here is* or *there is*, the subject is the noun that comes after the verb, not *here* or *there*. It may help to recast this clause: *my staff is here.* **Also:** The subject of *wait* and *meet* is an implied *you*. This is in the imperative, or command, voice.

DAY 2

#1 MC S   V   V   AC cl   S   prep   V   prep   prep
[we will fight] (until the lesser of us **catapults** into the stream from ~~to / two /~~ too forceful a

blow)."

Fixes

Indent. Is this a new topic, speaker, place, or time? Answer: No, Robin is still speaking.

Homophones and usage. *too*, meaning *of an excessive amount*.

Quotations. Check that students continued writing where they left off with no quotation marks until the end of the speech after *blow*.

Commas with adverb clauses. Remind your students that *until* is not one of the basic www words but is another word in that category.

Ask: Should there be a comma before *until*? Answer: No. Ask: What is the rule? Answer: **MC AC**. Mid-sentence adverb clauses are not set off with commas.

End marks. This is a statement so add a period inside the closing quotation marks.

Grammar Notations

Subjects and verbs. *We will fight, lesser catapults.*

✧ **Advanced.** Students may try to mark *us* as the subject. If they do, ask if we say *us catapult* or *we catapult*. Since we say *we catapult*, *us* cannot be the subject. You might also ask them if "the lesser catapults into the stream" makes sense. It does, so *lesser* is the subject. *See ♡.*

Prepositional phrases. *of us, into the stream, from too forceful a blow.*

Check underlines and ask students to show how these fit the pattern: **preposition + noun (no verb)**. Note: In *from too forceful a blow, forceful* is an adjective and *too* an adverb, so there is no verb between *from* and *blow*.

Clauses and sentence openers.

- #1 subject opener and MC: *We will fight.*
- AC (adverb clause): *until the lesser of us catapults into the stream from too forceful a blow.*

Sidebar

catapults: thrusts quickly or suddenly.

This verb comes from *catapult*, a machine used to hurl large stones at a castle wall in a siege.

The **lesser** refers to the person who is not as capable as the other, the less capable of the two men.

♡ **Grammar lovers.** *us* is an objective pronoun since it functions as the object of the preposition *of*.

DAY 3

#1 MC S   V   MC V   S   #1 MC S V   DC
                                                                                              S/w-w V

¶ " [i̲ eagerly await the combat]!" [cried the stranger]. "[i̲t̲s̲/it's a fair test to prove] (who is

        prep   cc MC S   V   V
more **adept** with the staff), and [it will determine the better man]."

Fixes

adept: expert; very skilled

Indent. Is this a new topic, speaker, place, or time? Answer: Yes, a new speaker.

Quotations. Check that students placed quotation marks around the words spoken: *"I … combat!" cried the stranger. "It's … man."*

Exclamation mark + close quotes after *combat* because the stranger is excited. A comma is acceptable here, but an exclamation mark makes more sense.

✧ **Advanced.** Keep *cried* lowercase because it sets up the quotation before it and is therefore part of that same sentence, even though the quotation itself closes with an exclamation mark.

Homophones and usage. *It's a fair test.* Ask: What does *It's* mean? Answer: *It is.* The contraction is the one with the apostrophe: *it's.*

Commas with cc's. It will help to discuss the clauses first (see Grammar Notations).

Ask: Do we need a comma before the cc *and*, and why? Answer: Yes. Rule: **MC, cc MC**. When a coordinating conjunction joins two main clauses, it needs a comma before it.

End marks. Period after *man* inside closing quotation marks.

Grammar Notations

Subjects and verbs. *I await, cried stranger, it's* (S = *it*; verb = *is*), *who is, it will determine.*

✧ **Advanced.** If students marked *to prove,* you might explain that it is an infinitive, formed from a verb but not functioning as one.

Prepositional phrases. *with the staff.* Check underlines and ask students to show how this fits the pattern: **preposition + noun (no verb).**

Who-which **clauses.** Have students read the clause aloud: *who is more adept with the staff. See* ♡.

♡ **Grammar lovers.** This *who-which* clause is not like typical *who-which* clause dress-ups. It functions as the object of *prove* and is therefore essential to the sentence, so no commas.

Clauses and sentence openers.

- #1 subject opener and MC: *I eagerly await the combat!*
- MC: *cried the stranger.*
- #1 subject opener and MC: *It's a fair test to prove.*
- DC (w-w clause): *who is more adept with the staff.*
- MC: *it will determine the better man.*

DAY 4

#1 *MC S*   *V*   *prep*   *prep*   *cc*   *AC cl S*   *V*

¶ [he **nimbly** twirled his staff above his head between his fingers and thumb] (until it whistled

prep   *cc*   *MC S*   *V*   *prep*

through the air), and then ~~than~~ [he stepped onto the bridge].

Fixes

Indent. Is this a new topic, speaker, place, or time? Answer: Yes, a new topic, pulling out of his speech and focusing on his actions.

Homophones and usage. *then*, meaning *immediately afterward*.

Commas with adverb clauses. Ask: Should we put a comma before the adverb clause (*until it whistled through the air*)? Answer: No comma with mid-sentence adverb clauses. Rule: **MC AC**.

Commas with cc's. *See* ✏.

Ask: Should we put a comma before the first cc *and*? Answer: No, because it joins only two nouns, *fingers and thumb*.

Ask: Should we put a comma before the second cc *and*? Answer: Yes. Rule: **MC, cc MC**. When a coordinating conjunction joins two main clauses, it needs a comma before it.

End marks. This is a statement so add a period.

Grammar Notations

Subjects and verbs. *He twirled; it whistled; he stepped.*

Prepositional phrases. *above his head, between his fingers and thumb, through the air, onto the bridge.* Check underlines and ask students to show how these fit the pattern: **preposition + noun.**

Clauses and sentence openers.

- #1 subject opener and MC: *He nimbly twirled his staff above his head between his fingers and thumb.*
- AC (adverb clause): *until it whistled through the air.*
- MC: *he stepped onto the bridge.*

Style

If desired, have your students identify the best dress-ups from their sentences this week. Discuss their answers. Choose among these:

Strong verbs. *catapults, twirled, whistled.*

Quality adjectives. *adept.* See ♡.

-ly adverbs (not the first word of any sentence). *nimbly.*

nimbly: quickly and lightly in movement

✏ **Teacher's note.** Remember to discuss clauses before commas if needed.

♡ **Grammar lovers.** *adept* from Day 3 is a subject complement (a.k.a. predicate adjective) because it follows a linking verb and describes the subject, *who*.

STUDENT REWRITE

Robin Hood then proclaimed to the stranger, "Here is my staff, which is long and tough. Now wait my coming and meet me if you dare. We will fight until the lesser of us catapults into the stream from too forceful a blow."

"I eagerly await the combat!" cried the stranger. "It's a fair test to prove who is more adept with the staff, and it will determine the better man."

He nimbly twirled his staff above his head between his fingers and thumb until it whistled through the air, and then he stepped onto the bridge.

Week 20

No New Concepts

LEARN IT

There are no new concepts this week. See if you can answer the questions below. If not, check your grammar cards for the answers.

1. What does an adjective do?

2. What is the adjective test?

3. What is the difference between coordinate and cumulative adjectives?

4. What trick can help you tell the difference?

5. Why do you need to know? (Hint: it is a comma rule.)

Do you remember what these vocabulary words mean? If not, look them up in your vocabulary list in the back of your notebook.

- toppled
- hastened
- insatiable
- despoiled
- oppression
- yeomen
- vowed
- plundered
- succor

Teacher's answers

1. describes a noun or pronoun

2. the _____ pen

3. coordinate adjectives each describe the noun separately; the first cumulative adjective describes the second adjective plus noun together

4. coordinate if you can reverse their order or put *and* in between

5. coordinate adjectives take a comma, cumulative do not

Page 42, *Fix It! Grammar:* **Robin Hood, Student Book 2**

DAY 1

#3 ly   *MC*   *S*   *prep*   *V*   *prep*   *DC*   *V*

surely, [the knights of king arthur's round table never met in a **stouter** fight] (~~then~~/than did

S

these ~~to~~/two ~~/too~~).

Fixes

stouter: braver and more forceful

Indent. Is this a new topic, speaker, place, or time? Answer: No new topic. This is all about the actual fight.

Capitalization.

- *Surely*—first word of sentence.
- *King Arthur's, Round Table*—proper nouns.

Homophones and usage.

- *than* compares the fights of King Arthur's knights to this combat between Robin and the stranger. Use *than* for comparison. *Then is an adverb meaning soon afterward or at that time.*
- *two*, the number, referring to the two men.

End marks. This is a statement so add a period.

Grammar Notations

Subjects and verbs. *knights met, did two* (these two did).

- ✿ **Advanced.** If students overlook *two*, ask who or what is doing the action of *did*. Explain that the subject will be a word in the sentence.

Prepositional phrases. *of King Arthur's Round Table, in a stouter fight.*

Check underlines and ask students to show how these fit the pattern: **preposition + noun (no verb).**

Clauses and sentence openers.

- #3 -ly adverb opener: *Surely.*
- MC: *the knights of King Arthur's Round Table never met in a stouter fight.*
- DC: *than did these two. See* ✏.

✏ **Teacher's note.** If students ask, *than* is a subordinating conjunction here, so it starts a dependent clause, which cannot stand alone.

DAY 2

♡
#1 *MC S*   *V*   *prep*   *DC cl*   *S*   *V*   *MC S*   *V*

[robin quickly stepped upon the bridge], (where his **adversary** stood). first, [he dodged a blow

cc   *V*   *prep*

and then, ~~than~~ delivered its ~~it's~~ match to the stranger's head].

Fixes

Indent. Is this a new topic, speaker, place, or time? Answer: No.

Homophones and usage.

- *then*, meaning *next*.
- *its match*. Ask: What does *its* refer back to? Answer: *the blow* (the match of the blow, or its equal).

Commas with cc's.

Remind students that cc's must join the same part of speech, and then ask: What specific words does the cc *and* join? Answer: *dodged and delivered* (two verbs).

Then ask: Does this cc take a comma before it? Answer: No, because it joins only two verbs, not two main clauses. Rule: **MC cc 2nd verb** (no comma).

✏ **Teacher's note.** Why does it matter? Figuring out exactly what the cc's are connecting shows us whether commas are needed and where.

End marks. This is a statement so add a period.

Grammar Notations

Subjects and verbs. *Robin stepped, adversary stood, he dodged … delivered.*

Prepositional phrases. *upon the bridge, to the stranger's head.* Check underlines and ask students to show how these fit the pattern: **preposition + noun (no verb)**.

Clauses and sentence openers.

- #1 subject opener and MC: *Robin quickly stepped upon the bridge.*
- DC (www clause): *where his adversary stood. See* ♡.
- MC: *he dodged a blow and then delivered its match to the stranger's head.*

---

adversary: opponent; person who opposes or attacks

Check that students understand **match** to mean *something resembling something else*. Robin's blow is as powerful as the stranger's.

♡ **Grammar lovers.** This DC is a nonessential adjective clause instead of an adverb clause because it describes a noun (*bridge*), which explains why it needs a comma. However, this is too advanced for this level. See Adjective Clauses in the Grammar Glossary: Sentences, Clauses, and Phrases section (page G-17).

DAY 3

#5 *AC cl*   *S*   *V*   *V*   *MC*   *S*   *V*   *V*   *V*   *prep*

(if the strike had met its ~~it's~~ mark), [the man would have tumbled speedily into the water],

cc MC   *S*   *V*   *prep*

but [the stranger **parried** robin's blow to the right].

Fixes

Indent. Is this a new topic, speaker, place, or time? Answer: No.

Homophones and usage. *its mark*. Ask: What does *its* refer back to? Answer: *the strike* (the strike's mark).

Commas with adverb clauses. Ask: Is there a comma after *mark*, and why? Answer: Yes, because it is a #5 clausal opener, which always takes a comma. Rule: **AC, MC**. *See* 🖊.

Commas with cc's. Ask: Is there a comma before the coordinating conjunction *but*, and why? Answer: Yes, because it joins two main clauses. Rule: **MC, cc MC**. *See* 🖊.

End marks. This is a statement so add a period.

Grammar Notations

Subjects and verbs. *strike had met, man would have tumbled, stranger parried.*

Ask: Which of these are helping verbs? Answer: *had*, which helps out *met*; *would have*, which helps *tumbled*.

Prepositional phrases. *into the water, to the right.*

Check underlines and ask students to show how these fit the pattern: **preposition + noun (no verb)**.

Clauses and sentence openers.

- #5 opener and AC (adverb clause): *If the strike had met its mark.*
- MC: *the man would have tumbled speedily into the water.*
- MC: *the stranger parried Robin's blow to the right.*

parried: warded off; turned aside

🖊 **Teacher's note.** Discuss parts of speech or clauses before discussing commas, as needed.

DAY 4

In your rewrite, combine the two sentences with a *which* clause.

```
                                                                    DC  S/w-w
#2 prep          MC                    S                V        which   V     V
in response [the seven-foot man just as fiercely returned another blow], (it could have easily

          V
leveled a weaker opponent).
```

Connect sentence with which

Check that students combined the sentences correctly and put a comma in front of the new *which* clause. *See* ✎.

Ask: What noun does *which* describe and where is it? Answer: *blow*, which is immediately before the *which* clause.

Fixes

Indent. Is this a new topic, speaker, place, or time? Answer: No.

End marks. This is a statement so add a period.

Grammar Notations

Subjects and verbs. *man returned, which could have leveled.* Ask: Which of these are helping verbs? Answer: *could have*, which helps out *leveled.*

✎ **Teacher's note.** *As does not start an adverb clause, so students should not label it. If they are confused, remind them that clauses have a subject and a verb, and fiercely is only an adverb.*

Prepositional phrases. *In response.* Check for underlines.

Clauses and sentence openers.

- #2 prepositional phrase opener: *In response.*
- MC: *the seven-foot man just as fiercely returned another blow.*
- DC (w-w clause): *which could have easily leveled a weaker opponent.*

Style

If desired, have your students identify the best dress-ups from their sentences this week. Discuss their answers. Choose among:

Strong verbs. *dodged, tumbled, parried, leveled.*

Quality adjectives. *stouter.*

-ly adverbs (not the first word of any sentence). *speedily, fiercely.*

leveled: brought to the level of the ground; laid low

✎ **Teacher's note.** This *who-which* clause takes a comma because it is nonessential. It describes the blow more fully but does not change the meaning of the main clause, which says the stranger returned the blow.

STUDENT REWRITE

Since this passage continues without another indentation, be sure students continue writing where last week's passage left off.

Surely, the knights of King Arthur's Round Table never met in a stouter fight than did these two. Robin quickly stepped upon the bridge, where his adversary stood. First, he dodged a blow and then delivered its match to the stranger's head. If the strike had met its mark, the man would have tumbled speedily into the water, but the stranger parried Robin's blow to the right. In response the seven-foot man just as fiercely returned another blow, which could have easily leveled a weaker opponent.

Week 21

No New Concepts

LEARN IT

There are no new concepts this week. See if you can answer the questions below. If not, check your grammar cards for the answers.

1. What do -ly adverbs modify?

2. What are the comma rules for nouns of direct address (NDAs)?

Do you remember what these vocabulary words mean? If not, look them up in your vocabulary list in the back of your notebook.

- earnestly
- impoverished
- audacious
- escapades
- magnanimous
- vicariously
- melodiously
- gurgling

Have your students practice the concepts they have learned.

As you work through the sentences with your student, ask them where they put commas and why. That will help them internalize the comma rules.

DAY 1

#5 *AC cl*   *S*   *V*   *prep*   *AC cl*   *S* *V* *V* *MC S*

(when robin hood pushed the staff to the side) as **deftly** (as the stranger had done), [he

V   *DC* *S* *V*

showed his challenger] (that this was no easy fight).

✒ **Teacher's note.** Do not feel tied to the suggested questions. To a student who generally does well with the Fix Its, you might ask, "What commas did you add, and why?" Also, ask questions only at the point of need. If you check your student's work before discussing anything, you might narrow your questions and comments to just the problems your students had, reviewing rules only as needed.

deftly: nimbly; skillfully; cleverly

Fixes

Indent. Is this a new topic, speaker, place, or time? Answer: No.

Commas with adverb clauses. *See* ✒.

Ask: Is there a comma after *had done*, and why? Answer: Yes, because it is a #5 clausal opener, which always takes a comma.
Rule: **AC, MC.**

If students put the comma in the wrong place, guide them to see that the words that hang together in this #5 opener include another clause that continues the thought. The comma goes at the end of the entire thought.

End marks. This is a statement so add a period.

✒ **Teacher's note.** The construction "as … as" is an idiom, and idioms do not easily lend themselves to parts of speech breakdown. The first *as* does not start a prepositional phrase or an adverb clause so should not be marked.

Grammar Notations

Subjects and verbs. *Robin Hood pushed, stranger had done* (*had* = helping verb), *he showed, this was.*

If students are confused, point out that *was* is not a helping verb here because there is no other verb for it to help out. *See* ♡ **1.**

Prepositional phrases. *to the side.*

Check for underlines and ask students to show how this fits the pattern: **preposition + noun (no verb).**

Clauses and sentence openers.

- #5 opener and AC (adverb clause): *When Robin Hood pushed the staff to the side.*
- AC (adverb clause): *as the stranger had done.*
- MC: *he showed his challenger.*
- DC: *that this was no easy fight. See* ♡ **2.**

♡ **1. Grammar lovers.** *Was* is a linking verb, linking the subject, *this,* to its subject complement, *fight.*

♡ **2. Grammar lovers.** The last DC, *that this was no easy fight,* is not an adjective clause but a noun clause. Noun clauses come after a verb (*showed*) and answer "what."

DAY 2

MC S   V   prep   prep

¶ **thus** [they stood], each <u>in his place</u>, one hour later, neither budging an inch <u>from the spot</u>

♡
DC cl   S   V

(where they began**)**.

Fixes

thus: in this way

Indent. Is this a new topic, speaker, place, or time? Answer: Yes, a new time.

Commas with clauses. Ask: Is there a comma after *spot*, and why? Answer: No comma before mid-sentence www clause starters. *See* ♡.

End marks. This is a statement so add a period.

Grammar Notations

Subjects and verbs. *they stood, they began.*

  ✧ **Advanced.** If students mark *budging* as a verb, you could mention that it does not function as a verb here because it does not have a subject and helping verb with it. Contrast "they were not budging an inch."

Prepositional phrases. *in his place, from the spot.*

  Check for underlines and ask students to show how these fit the pattern: **preposition + noun (no verb).**

Clauses and sentence openers.

- MC: *they stood.* Note: Students may count this as a #1 opener since only a short transitional word comes before the main clause or not label it at all.
- DC (www clause): *where they began. See* ♡.

♡ **Grammar lovers.** This is another situation where the www clause is actually an adjective clause instead of adverb clause because it modifies the noun (*spot*) right before it. However, it does not affect punctuation in this case because the clause is essential.

Institute for Excellence in Writing

DAY 3

#2 *prep*   *MC*   *S*   *V*   *V* *cc*   *V*   *AC cl* *S*   *V*   *V* *prep*

<u>in that hour</u> [both men had given and received many blows] (until they were covered <u>with</u>

                         cc

chafed <u>skin</u>**,** aching muscles**,** and bruised bones)**,** ~~to, two,~~ too **.**

Fixes

chafed: sore from rubbing

Indent. Is this a new topic, speaker, place, or time? Answer: No.

Homophones and usage. *too*, meaning *also*.

Commas with cc's. Ask: Should there be a comma before the first *and* in *given and received*, and why? Answer: No, because it joins only two verbs to the same subject. Rule: **MC cc 2nd verb**, or no comma with a compound verb.

Commas with adverb clauses. Ask: Should there be a comma before *until*, and why? Answer: No, because mid-sentence adverb clauses are not set off with commas.

Commas with items in a series. Check that students punctuated the three items in a series with commas.

Ask: Which words does this cc join? Answer: *skin, muscles, bones*.

Ask: What part of speech are they all? Answer: nouns.

Ask: What pattern? Answer: **a, b, and c.**

End marks. This is a statement so add a period.

Grammar Notations

Subjects and verbs. *men had given … received, they were covered.*

Note: *Received* is often misspelled so check students' spelling and remind them of the "*i* before *e* except after *c*" rule.

Ask: Which are helping verbs? Answer: *had*, which helps *given … received*; and *were*, which helps *covered.*

Prepositional phrases. *In that hour; with chafed skin, aching muscles, and bruised bones.* Check for underlines and ask students to show how these fit the pattern: **preposition + noun (no verb).**

✧ **Advanced.** If students are puzzled, explain that in the second phrase one preposition has three objects (*skin, muscles, bones*).

Clauses and sentence openers.

- #2 prepositional phrase opener: *In that hour.*
- MC: *both men had given and received many blows.*
- AC (adverb clause): *until they were covered with chafed skin, aching muscles, and bruised bone.* Do students see that this cannot stand alone as a sentence? It needs a main clause to be legal.

DAY 4

| #2 *prep* | | *MC* | *S* | *prep* | *V* | *cc* | *V* |

despite ~~there~~/their ~~they're~~ **fatigue**, [neither of them considered crying "enough!" or seemed

prep

likely to tumble off the bridge].

Fixes

fatigue: weariness from physical exertion

Indent. Is this a new topic, speaker, place, or time? Answer: No.

Capitalization.

Despite—first word of sentence.

✦ **Advanced.** *Enough.* This is not critical to teach if students do not catch on easily. Although *Enough* does not begin a complete quoted sentence, it functions like one since we often speak in fragments, so capitalize it instead of treating it as part of a longer quoted sentence.

Homophones and usage. *their fatigue*, possessive, meaning *the fatigue of Robin and the stranger*.

Quotations. Check that students placed quotation marks around "Enough!"

End marks. This is a statement so add a period.

Grammar Notations

Subjects and verbs. *neither considered … seemed. See 🖊.*

Prepositional phrases. *Despite their fatigue, of them, off the bridge.*

Check for underlines and ask students to show how these fit the pattern: **preposition + noun (no verb).**

Coordinating conjunctions. Ask: What specific words does *or* join? Answer: two verbs (*considered or seemed*), so no comma.

✦ **Advanced.** Ask students if a comma would go before *or* if the quotation were not there. Answer: No, since it joins only two verbs to one subject (**MC cc 2nd verb**); the exclamation mark is there for the quotation. Point out that there is not a second subject after *or* so there are not two MCs.

Clauses and sentence openers.

- #2 prepositional phrase opener: *Despite their fatigue.*
- MC: *neither of them considered crying "Enough!" or seemed likely to tumble off the bridge.*

🖊 **Teacher's note.** Both *crying* (a gerund) and *to tumble* (an infinitive) are verbals that do not function as verbs. If students label them as verbs, you could simply mention that they do not function as verbs here.

Style

If desired, have your students identify the best dress-ups from this week's sentences. Discuss their answers. Choose among:

Strong verbs. No especially strong verbs this week. Students might mark *tumble*, which is fine at this level. It is a strong word but not technically a verb since infinitives (*to tumble*) do not function as verbs.

Quality adjectives. *chafed.*

-ly adverbs (not the first word of any sentence). *deftly.*

STUDENT REWRITE

Since this passage continues without another indentation, be sure students continue writing where last week's passage left off.

When Robin Hood pushed the staff to the side as deftly as the stranger had done, he showed his challenger that this was no easy fight.

Thus they stood, each in his place, one hour later, neither budging an inch from the spot where they began. In that hour both men had given and received many blows until they were covered with chafed skin, aching muscles, and bruised bones, too. Despite their fatigue, neither of them considered crying "Enough!" or seemed likely to tumble off the bridge.

Week 22

No New Concepts

LEARN IT

There are no new concepts this week. See if you can answer the questions below. If not, check your grammar cards for the answers.

1. Explain the difference between *then* and *than*.

2. What is the pattern for a prepositional phrase?

Do you remember what these vocabulary words mean? If not, look them up in your vocabulary list in the back of your notebook.

- cavorted
- captivated
- sport
- tarry
- heed
- ranged
- spanned
- resolutely

> **Teacher's answers**
>
> 1. *then* (adverb) = next; immediately afterward
>   *than* (conjunction) = used for comparison
>
> 2. preposition + noun (no verb)

Have your students practice the concepts they have learned.

✏ **Teacher's note.** Remember to keep the exercise light and fun like a game. If your student groans when you say, "Time for Fix It!" something is wrong.

Page 46, *Fix It! Grammar:* **Robin Hood, Student Book 2**

DAY 1

#5 AC cl   S   V   cc   MC   S   V   DC S V

(as the two stopped to rest now and then), [each **combatant** privately believed] (he had never

prep   V

in his life witnessed such a skillful quarterstaff duel).

Fixes

Indent. Is this a new topic, speaker, place, or time? Answer: No.

Spelling. Check that students spell *duel* correctly. Point out it has a homophone, *dual*, which denotes two of something. *Duel* is the combat that people fight.

Commas with adverb clauses. Ask: Do we need a comma after *now and then*, and why? Answer: Yes, because this is the end of the #5 opener (introductory adverb clause), which always takes a comma. Rule: **AC, MC**. *See* ✎.

Commas with adjectives.

Ask students to find two adjacent adjectives. Answer: *skillful quarterstaff*.

Now ask them to identify these as coordinate or cumulative. Answer: The two tricks to test both show up negative: 1) *quarterstaff, skillful duel* is strange; 2) *skillful and quarterstaff duel* is awkward. They are therefore cumulative and do not take a comma.

End marks. This is a statement so add a period.

Grammar Notations

Subjects and verbs. *two stopped, combatant believed, he had witnessed.*

Prepositional phrases. *in his life.* Ask: Why is this a phrase and not a clause? Answer: It does not have a subject and a verb, which all clauses must have.

Coordinating conjunctions. Ask: What specific words does the cc *and* join? Answer: two adverbs, *now and then*, so no comma.

Clauses and sentence openers.

- #5 opener and AC (adverb clause): *As the two stopped to rest now and then.*
- MC: *each combatant privately believed.*
- DC: *[that] he had never in his life witnessed such a skillful quarterstaff duel.* If your students do not catch this, just explain that it is a dependent clause because the word *that* is implied.

combatant: a person who fights

✎ **Teacher's note.** Remember to check clauses first if needed.

DAY 2

#2 *prep*   *MC S*   *V*   *prep*   *DC*   *S*   *V*   *prep*

¶ at last [robin delivered the stranger such a blow upon the ribs] (that his jacket smoked like

prep

damp straw **thatching** in the sun).

Fixes

Indent. Is this a new topic, speaker, place, or time? Answer: Yes, a new topic: the beginning of the last stage of the fight.

Simile. If desired, teach that a simile is a vivid or striking comparison between unlike things, usually using *like* or *as*.

Ask students to identify the simile in this sentence. Answer: *like damp straw thatching in the sun*. Ask them to explain what it means. Answer: Damp straw heated by the sun will let off steam, which looks like smoke and makes it appear as if it is burning. Robin's blow was so powerful it made the stranger's jacket smoke in a similar way.

End marks. This is a statement so add a period.

Grammar Notations

Subjects and verbs. *Robin delivered, jacket smoked.*

Prepositional phrases. *At last, upon his ribs, like damp straw thatching, in the sun.* Ask students to explain how these fit the pattern: **preposition + noun (no verb)**.

The third phrase might be hard: *damp* and *straw* are cumulative adjectives here describing the thatching. *See* ♡.

Clauses and sentence openers.

- #2 prepositional phrase opener: *At last.*
- MC: *Robin delivered the stranger such a blow upon the ribs.*
- DC: *that his jacket smoked like damp straw thatching in the sun.*

thatching: material like straw or rushes used to cover roofs, a common roofing material in the Middle Ages

♡ **Grammar lovers.** *Thatching* is an -ing word that functions as a noun; -ing words used as nouns are called gerunds, but you do not need to teach this.

DAY 3

#1 MC   V   S   DC   S   V   *prep*   *prep*   *prep*

[so **shrewd** was the stroke] (that the stranger came within a **hairsbreadth** of falling off the

bridge).

Fixes

Indent. Is this a new topic, speaker, place, or time? Answer: No.

End marks. This is a statement so add a period.

Grammar Notations

Prepositional phrases. *within a hairsbreadth, of falling, off the bridge.* Ask students to explain how these fit the pattern: **preposition + noun (no verb)**. *See* ♡.

Clauses and sentence openers.

- #1 subject opener: *So shrewd was the stroke.* Since the subject does not start this clause, students may have trouble identifying it as a subject opener. It may help them see it is a main clause if you recast the sentence: *The stroke was so shrewd.*

- DC: *that the stranger came within a hairsbreadth of falling off the bridge.*

shrewd: sharp, keen, or piercing

hairsbreadth: a very small space or distance

♡ **Grammar lovers.** Again, -ing words are sometimes gerunds, as here with *falling*. It is the object of the preposition so must be a noun.

DAY 4

In your rewrite, combine the two sentences with a *which* clause.

MC S   V   cc   prep   V   prep

however, [he regained himself quickly and by a **dexterous** blow gave robin a crack on the

DC   S/w-w

which   V

crown], (~~it~~ caused the blood to flow).

Combine sentences with which

Check that students combined the sentences correctly and put a comma in front of the new *which* clause.

dexterous: skillful or adroit in the use of his hands

Check that students understand the meaning of **crown** here: *the top of his head.*

Fixes

Indent. Is this a new topic, speaker, place, or time? Answer: No.

Commas with cc's. Ask: Should there be a comma before *and*, and why? Answer: No, because this cc joins only two verbs to the same subject: *he regained himself … and … gave.* Rule: **MC cc 2nd verb**, compound verbs are not separated from their subject with a comma.

End marks. This is a statement so add a period.

Grammar Notations

Subjects and verbs. *he regained … gave, which caused.* Reminder: The subject of a *who-which* clause is usually the *who* or *which*.

Prepositional phrases. *by a dexterous blow, on the crown.* Ask students to explain how these fit the pattern: **preposition + noun (no verb)**.

Coordinating conjunctions. *and.*

   ✣ **Advanced.** Ask students to identify the specific words this cc joins. Answer: *regained, gave.* Remind them that the cc must join the same part of speech. It may help to read the sentence without the prepositional phrase: *He regained himself quickly and gave Robin a crack on the crown.*

Clauses and sentence openers.

- MC: *he regained himself quickly and by a dexterous blow gave Robin a crack on the crown.* Point out that this is one clause, not two, because the subject does not repeat itself after the cc *and.* There are two verbs with one subject.

- DC (w-w clause): *which caused the blood to flow.*

Style

If desired, have your students identify the best dress-ups from this week's sentences. Discuss their answers. Best possibilities:

Strong verbs. *witnessed, smoked, regained.*

Quality adjectives. *damp, shrewd, dexterous.*

-ly adverbs (not the first word of any sentence). *privately.*

STUDENT REWRITE
Since this passage continues without another indentation, be sure students continue writing where last week's passage left off.

As the two stopped to rest now and then, each combatant privately believed he had never in his life witnessed such a skillful quarterstaff duel.

At last Robin delivered the stranger such a blow upon the ribs that his jacket smoked like damp straw thatching in the sun. So shrewd was the stroke that the stranger came within a hairsbreadth of falling off the bridge. However, he regained himself quickly and by a dexterous blow gave Robin a crack on the crown, which caused the blood to flow.

Week 23

No New Concepts

LEARN IT

There are no new concepts this week. See if you can answer the questions below. If not, check your grammar cards for the answers.

1. Explain when to use *lie* versus *lay*.

2. What is the meaning of *there*, *their*, and *they're*?

Do you remember what these vocabulary words mean? If not, look them up in your vocabulary list in the back of your notebook.

- quickened
- brusquely
- interloper
- bide
- tan your hide
- numskull
- faintheart
- lethal

> **Teacher's answers**
>
> 1. You *lie* yourself down but *lay* down an object. The past tense is confusing: The hen *lay* down (past tense of *to lie*) after she *laid* an egg (past tense of *to lay*).
>
> 2. *there* = in that place
>   *their* = possessive
>   *they're* = they are (contraction)

Page 48, *Fix It! Grammar:* **Robin Hood, Student Book 2**

Institute for Excellence in Writing

DAY 1

#6vss MC ___ S _____ V _____ #5 AC cl _____ S ____ V _____ prep _____ MC _____ S

[the blow **inflamed** robin]. (although he then **smote** the other <u>with all his might</u>), [the stranger

V

again warded off the blow].

Fixes

Indent. Is this a new topic, speaker, place, or time? Answer: No.

Commas with adverb clauses. Ask: Should there be a comma after *might*, and why? Answer: Yes, because #5 openers take commas. Rule: **AC, MC**.

End marks. This is a statement so add a period.

inflamed: angered to the point of growing red in the face

smote: struck hard (past tense of the verb *to smite*)

Grammar Notations

Subjects and verbs. *blow inflamed, he smote, stranger warded.*

Prepositional phrases. *with all his might.*

Ask students to explain how this fits the pattern: **preposition + noun (no verb)**.

✧ **Advanced.** If students mark *off the blow*, that is fine. *Off* is not the start of a prepositional phrase here (if it were, the phrase would make some sense by itself, which *off the blow* does not!) but an adverb that goes with verb: *warded off.* However, the distinction is not significant.

Clauses and sentence openers.

- #6 vss and MC: *The blow inflamed Robin.*
- #5 opener and AC (adverb clause): *Although he then smote the other with all his might.*
- MC: *the stranger again warded off the blow.*

DAY 2

#2 prep   *MC S*   *V*   *DC*   *S*   *V*   *cc*

at once [he **thwacked** robin], only this time so squarely (that our hero lost his footing and

       V   *prep*

tumbled into the chilly water).

Fixes

Indent. Is this a new topic, speaker, place, or time? Answer: No, it continues the topic of the fight.

Commas with cc's. Ask: Should there be a comma before the cc *and*, and why?
Answer: No, because it joins only two verbs (*lost, tumbled*), not two main clauses.
Rule: **MC cc 2nd verb.**

End marks. This is a statement so add a period.

thwacked: struck a sharp blow with something flat

Grammar Notations

Subjects and verbs. *he thwacked, hero lost … tumbled.*

Prepositional phrases. *At once, into the chilly water.*

Ask students to explain how this fits the pattern: **preposition + noun (no verb).**

Clauses and sentence openers.

- #2 prepositional phrase opener: *At once.*

   Ask: Why is this a phrase and not a clause? Short answer: No verb!

- MC: *he thwacked Robin.*
- DC: *that our hero lost his footing and tumbled into the chilly water.*

DAY 3

<pre>
#2 prep   MC S   V   MC S V   V   prep   cc
¶ to this unexpected happenstance, [robin called back], "hah! [i'm floating into the flood and
</pre>

<pre>
      prep
out with the tide]!"
</pre>

Fixes

Indent. Is this a new topic, speaker, place, or time? Answer: Yes, a new speaker and paragraph.

Quotations. Check that students placed quotation marks around the words spoken: *"Hah … tide!"*

Ask: What punctuation belongs after *Robin called back*, and why? Answer: Comma with speaking verb and quotation it sets up.

End marks. Robin is speaking excitedly, so put an exclamation mark inside the closing quotation marks.

happenstance: chance happening or event

Flood does not mean an overflow of water here but *the rise of the tide.*

Grammar Notations

Subjects and verbs. *Robin called, I'm floating.*

Ask: Which are helping verbs? Answer: *am* (part of contraction *I'm,* or *I am*), which helps out *floating*.

Prepositional phrases. *To this unexpected happenstance, into the flood, with the tide.* Ask students to explain how these fit the pattern: **preposition + noun (no verb)**.

✧ **Advanced.** The adverb *out* is not part of the prepositional phrase.

Coordinating conjunctions. Ask: What part of speech does the cc *and* join? Answer: two prepositional phrases (*into the flood, with the tide*).

✧ **Advanced.** Ask: What punctuation belongs after *into the flood,* and why? Answer: None, because the cc *and* joins two prepositional phrases, not three or more. Do not use commas between only two items in a series unless they are main clauses. Pattern: **a and b**.

Clauses and sentence openers.

- #2 prepositional phrase opener: *To this unexpected happenstance.*
- MC: *Robin called back.*
- MC: *I'm floating into the flood and out with the tide.*

DAY 4

#1 MC S   V   V   prep   prep   AC cl   S   V

¶ [he could not help laughing at himself at his **sorry** plight] (because he recognized the humor

prep

in his **predicament**).

Fixes

Indent. Is this a new topic, speaker, place, or time? Answer: Yes, a new topic, Robin's amusement at his own situation.

Commas with adverb clauses. Ask: What punctuation belongs after *plight*, and why? Answer: None because mid-sentence adverb clauses are not set off with commas: **MC AC**.

End marks. This is a statement so add a period.

Grammar Notations

Subjects and verbs. *He could help, he recognized.* Note: *not* is not part of the verb but an adverb modifying the verb.

✧ **Advanced.** If students mark *laughing* as a verb, you could either let it go or explain that it is not a verb here because it does not have a helping verb and subject. The sentence does not say "He was laughing."

Prepositional phrases. *at himself, at his sorry plight, in his predicament.*

Ask students to explain how these fit the pattern: **preposition + noun (no verb)**.

Clauses and sentence openers.

- #1 subject opener and MC: *He could not help laughing at himself at his sorry plight.*
- AC (adverb clause): *because he recognized the humor in his predicament.*

Style

If desired, have your students identify the best dress-ups from this week's sentences. Discuss their answers. Choose among:

Strong verbs. *inflamed, smote, warded off, thwacked, tumbled.*

Quality adjectives. *unexpected, sorry* (meaning *unfortunate*).

-ly adverbs (not the first word of any sentence). *squarely.*

sorry: unfortunate or deplorable. Point out that usually we mean feeling sympathy when we use *sorry*, but, like many words, it has more than one meaning.

predicament: an unpleasantly difficult or perplexing situation

STUDENT REWRITE

Since this passage continues without another indentation, be sure students continue writing where last week's passage left off.

The blow inflamed Robin. Although he smote the other with all his might, the stranger again warded off the blow. At once he thwacked Robin, only this time so squarely that our hero lost his footing and tumbled into the chilly water.

To this unexpected happenstance, Robin called back, "Hah! I'm floating into the flood and out with the tide!"

He could not help laughing at himself at his sorry plight because he recognized the humor in his predicament.

Week 24

Rules for Writing Numbers

LEARN IT

Numbers

There are just a few rules for writing numbers in papers. Here are the basics:

- Spell out numbers that can be written in one or two words. Use figures for other numbers. Examples:

  - The stranger stood a full *seven* feet tall.

  - For *fourteen* days we have enjoyed no sport, my friends.

- Spell out all ordinal numbers (first, second, third ...), which are numbers that show an order or progression. Example: He reached for a *second* arrow.

There are some exceptions, but these two principles cover most situations that you will need.

Use the grammar card to help you remember the rules.

For a fuller discussion of the rules for writing numbers, see the Grammar Glossary: Additional Rules and Concepts: Numbers Rules, G-31. This week will cover the basics. There are several exceptions, but these two principles cover most situations young students will need.

Page 50, *Fix It! Grammar:* Robin Hood, Student Book 2

DAY 1

MC   S   V   prep   DC cl   S

then ~~then~~ **gaining his feet**, [the outlaw robin waded to the bank], (where the little fish

V   cc   V   prep

scattered and fled), frightened at his splashing.

Fixes

Indent. Is this a new topic, speaker, place, or time? Answer: No.

Homophones and usage. *then*, meaning *immediately afterward*.

Commas with clauses.

  ⚜ **Advanced.** If students ask why there is a comma before the DC after *bank*, explain that occasionally some of the www words like *where* need a comma. See ♡ **1.**

Commas with cc's. Ask: Should there be a comma before the cc *and*, and why? Answer: No, because this cc joins only two verbs with the same subject: *fish scattered and fled*. Rule: **MC cc 2nd verb.** Compound verbs are not separated by commas.

End marks. This is a statement so add a period.

Grammar Notations

Subjects and verbs. *Robin waded, fish scattered … fled.*

  ⚜ **Advanced.** If students marked *gaining, frightened,* or *splashing*, just explain that -ing words do not always function as verbs. Contrast these words as verbs: *He was gaining his feet. The noise frightened the fish. He was splashing.* See ♡ **2.**

Prepositional phrases. *to the bank, at his splashing.*

  Ask students to explain how these fit the pattern: **preposition + noun (no verb).**

Clauses and sentence openers.

- MC: *the outlaw Robin waded to the bank.*
- DC (www clause): *where the little fish scattered and fled.* See ♡ **1.**

---

gaining his feet: an idiom (expression where the words do not make literal sense) meaning *he found his footing again* or *got back on his feet*

♡ **1. Grammar lovers.** The DC in this sentence is another adjective clause because it modifies the noun *bank*. It takes a comma because it is nonessential to the main clause. See Grammar Glossary: Punctuation: Commas: Rule 15: Essential-Nonessential Elements: Advanced, page G-25; and Stylistic Techniques: Dress-Ups: Advanced Adverb Clause, page G-38.

♡ **2. Grammar lovers.** The words *gaining* and *frightened* are present and past participles (types of verbals), functioning as adjectives. *Splashing* is a gerund, an -ing word functioning as a noun, in this case, the object of the preposition *at*.

DAY 2

#1 *MC   V   MC V   S   AC cl   S   V   V*

¶ " [give me your ~~you're~~ hand]," [cried the stranger] (when robin had reached the bank).

#1 *MC S   V   V   DC   S   V   prep*

" [i must admit] (that ~~your~~ you're a brave, sturdy soul), **wielding** a **hearty** stroke with

your ~~you're~~ staff !"

Fixes

Indent. Is this a new topic, speaker, place, or time? Answer: Yes, a new speaker and paragraph.

Commas with adverb clauses. Ask: Should there be punctuation before *when*, and why? Answer: No, mid-sentence adverb clauses do not need commas. Rule: **MC AC**.

Commas with adjectives.

Ask: Should there be a comma in *brave sturdy soul*? To determine, apply the tests: 1) Can we say *sturdy, brave soul*? Yes. 2) Can we say *brave and sturdy soul*? Yes. Both sound fine, so these are coordinate adjectives and need a comma between them.

Check that students do not put a comma between the last adjective and the noun it modifies, only between the adjectives: *brave, sturdy soul.*

Homophones and usage.

- *your hand* and *your staff*, possessives.
- *you're a brave soul*, the contraction meaning *you are*.

Quotations. Check that students placed quotation marks around the words spoken: *"Give … hand," cried the stranger … bank. "I must admit … your staff."*

Ask: Should there be any punctuation after *Give me your hand*, and why? Answer: Yes. Rule: **Quotation + comma + speaking verb** (*cried*). When a speaking verb sets up a quotation, it also needs a comma.

✧ **Advanced.** The period after *bank* is correct because the stranger speaks two complete sentences, which need something stronger than a comma to connect them.

End marks. End with either a period or an exclamation inside the closing quotation marks.

Grammar Notations

Subjects and verbs. *give* (with *you* understood), *cried … stranger, Robin had reached, I must admit, you're* (*you are*).

Ask: Which of these are helping verbs? *had*, which helps *reached*; *must*, which helps *admit*.

✧ **Advanced.** If students ask, *wielding* does not function as a verb here because it does not have a subject and helping verb (as in, *you were wielding*).

Continued on next page ▶

wielding: handling actively or using effectively

hearty: forceful; violent

Clauses and sentence openers.

- #1 subject opener and MC: *Give me your hand.* Remind students that imperative (command) voice still counts as a #1 opener even though the subject, *you*, is not stated.
- MC: *cried the stranger.*
- AC (adverb clause): *when Robin had reached the bank.*
- #1 opener and MC: *I must admit.*
- DC: *that you're a brave, sturdy soul. See ♡.*

♡ **Grammar lovers.** The last clause is a noun clause, answering the question *what* after the verb. *That* clauses do not take commas.

DAY 3

| #2 prep | MC | | S | V | prep | prep | prep |

¶ by this time, [~~there~~/their ~~they're~~ heads hummed like a hive of bumblebees on a **scorching**

june day].

Fixes

scorching: very hot; burning

Indent. Is this a new topic, speaker, place, or time? Answer: Yes, pulling out of his speech and turning to how they felt.

Capitalization.

- *By*—first word of sentence.
- *June*—capitalize names of months.

Homophones and usage. *their heads,* possessive.

Simile. If desired, ask students to identify the simile and discuss how effective it is. Answer: *like a hive of bumblebees on a scorching June day.* The humming sound bees make is from their wings beating rapidly, about 180 beats each second! We can imagine how their heads felt by thinking about how a hive full of bumblebees would sound. Similes are decorations in *Excellence in Writing*.

Commas with adjectives. Ask students to find two adjacent adjectives. Answer: *scorching June.* Now ask them to apply the tests to identify these as coordinate or cumulative: 1) *June scorching day* sounds awkward; 2) *scorching and June day* also sounds awkward. They are therefore cumulative and do not take a comma.

End marks. This is a statement so add a period.

Grammar Notations

Subjects and verbs. *heads hummed.*

✧ **Advanced.** If students mark *scorching* as a verb, ask them what it describes. Answer: the noun *day.* Only adjectives describe nouns, so it cannot be a verb.

Prepositional phrases. *By this time, like a hive, of bumblebees, on a scorching June day.*

Clauses and sentence openers.

- #2 prepositional phrase opener: *By this time.*
- MC: *their heads hummed like a hive of bumblebees on a scorching June day.*

DAY 4

In your rewrite, combine the two sentences with a *which* clause.

¶ then ~~, then~~ [robin hood **clapped** his horn to his lips and blew ~~3~~ blasts], (~~they~~ echoed sweetly down the forest paths).

(marked: MC S V prep cc V three which DC S/w-w V prep)

Combine sentences with a which

Check that students combined the sentences correctly and put a comma in front of the new *which* clause. See ✐.

Ask: What noun does *which* describe and where is it? Answer: *blasts*, which is immediately before the *which* clause.

Fixes

Indent. Is this a new topic, speaker, place, or time? Answer: Yes, a new topic, Robin's three horn blasts.

Homophones and usage. *then*, meaning *next* or *immediately afterward.*

Numbers. *three.* Spell out numbers that can be written in one or two words.

Commas with cc's. Ask: Should we put a comma before the cc *and*, and why? Answer: No, because this cc joins only two verbs to the same subject. *Robin Hood clapped … and blew.* Rule: **MC cc 2nd verb.**

End marks. This is a statement so add a period.

Grammar Notations

Subjects and verbs. *Robin Hood clapped … blew, which echoed.*

Clauses and sentence openers.

- MC: *Robin Hood clapped his horn to his lips and blew three blasts.*

  Since there is only a short transitional word before this MC, students may mark it as a #1 opener or not mark it at all. Technically, this is a "T" (transition) opener.

- DC (w-w clause): *which echoed sweetly down the forest paths.*

Style

If desired, have your students identify the best dress-ups from this week's sentences. Discuss their answers. Choose among:

Strong verbs. *scattered, fled, hummed, clapped* (an object against something), *echoed.*

Quality adjectives. *sturdy, hearty, scorching.*

-ly adverbs (not the first word of any sentence). *sweetly.*

clapped: struck an object (the horn) against something quickly and forcefully

✐ **Teacher's note.** This *who-which* clause takes a comma because it is nonessential, describing the blasts but not changing the meaning of the main clause, which tells us that Robin blew three blasts.

STUDENT REWRITE

Since this passage continues without another indentation, be sure students continue writing where last week's passage left off.

Then gaining his feet, the outlaw Robin waded to the bank, where the little fish scattered and fled, frightened at his splashing.

"Give me your hand," cried the stranger when Robin had reached the bank. " I must admit that you're a brave, sturdy soul, wielding a hearty stroke with your staff!"

By this time, their heads hummed like a hive of bumblebees on a scorching June day.

Then Robin Hood clapped his horn to his lips and blew three blasts, which echoed sweetly down the forest paths.

Week 25

No New Concepts

LEARN IT

There are no new concepts this week. See if you can answer the questions below. If not, check your grammar cards for the answers.

1. How does a dependent clause differ from a main clause?

2. Name the clause starters (subordinating conjunctions). Hint: the reminder acronym sounds like a website.

3. What is the comma rule for #5 clausal openers?

4. What is the comma rule for adverb clauses that do not begin a sentence?

Do you remember what these vocabulary words mean? If not, look them up in your vocabulary list in the back of your notebook.

- craven
- sparring
- countered
- sturdily
- hefty
- genially
- furtively
- deemed

> **Teacher's answers**
>
> 1. Both have a subject and verb, but a dependent clause cannot stand alone as a sentence, whereas a main clause can.
>
> 2. *when, while, where, as, since, if, although, because*
>
> 3. **AC, MC**. The comma comes after the whole clause, not after the www word.
>
> 4. **MC AC**. No comma.

For the rest of the year, have your students practice the concepts they have learned.

✎ **Teacher's note.** You have nine weeks of *Fix It!* lessons remaining with no new concepts being introduced. This affords your students plenty of practice to be able to master the concepts.

DAY 1

MC V　　S　prep　　　　　　　　　　MC　　　S　V

¶ "~~a~~ye," [replied ~~r~~obin to his worthy opponent], "[~~your~~/you're a tall, brave one], ~~to /two /~~too,

cc MC S　V　　　　　V　prep　　　prep　　　　　　　DC S/w-w　V　　　V　　prep

for [~~i~~ have never **faced** from here to ~~c~~anterbury a man] (who could topple me off a bridge)

AC cl　S　　V　　V

(as you have done)."

Fixes

Indent. Is this a new topic, speaker, place, or time? Answer: Yes, a new speaker and paragraph.

Capitalization.
- *Aye*—first word of sentence.
- Do not capitalize *you're*. See Quotations below.
- *Robin, I, Canterbury*—proper nouns. Canterbury is a famous city in England.

Homophones and usage.
- *you're a tall one*, the contraction meaning *you are*.
- *too*, meaning *also*.

Quotations. Check that students placed quotation marks around the words spoken: *"Aye,"* *replied Robin … opponent, "you're … done."*

Ask: What commas, if any, go with the quotations? Answer: commas around the interrupter: *"Aye," replied Robin to his worthy opponent, "you're … ."*

It may help students see that the second part continues his same sentence if you drop the narrative in between: *"Aye, you're a tall, brave one."*

Commas with adjectives. Ask: Should we put a comma between *tall* and *brave*? Answer: Yes, the two tests both show up positive: 1) *sturdy, brave soul* sounds right; 2) *brave and sturdy soul* also sounds right. They are therefore coordinate and need a comma.

Commas with cc's. Ask: Why do we need a comma before the cc *for*? Answer: **MC, cc MC**. Note: The comma also sets off the transition *too*, but without *too* we would still need the comma to help the cc join the two main clauses. *See* ✏.

End marks. This is a statement so add a period inside closing quotation marks.

Grammar Notations

Subjects and verbs. *replied Robin, you're (you are), I have faced, who could topple, you have done.*

Prepositional phrases. *to his worthy opponent, from here, to Canterbury, off a bridge.*

***Who-which* clauses.** Ask: What noun does this clause describe and where is it? Answer: *man*, which comes right before the *who* clause with prepositional phrases in between.

　✧ **Advanced.** This clause specifies which man is intended—the one who could topple Robin—so is essential and therefore not set off with a comma.

Continued on next page ▶

faced: confronted courageously or opposed. Note that while *faced* could mean facing in the direction of, "confronting bravely" better fits the context.

Aye is an old-fashioned word meaning *yes* and pronounced like the long *i* sound.

✏ **Teacher's note.** Discuss parts of speech or clauses before discussing commas, as needed.

Clauses and sentence openers.

- MC: *replied Robin to his worthy opponent.*
- MC: *you're a tall, brave one.*
- MC: *I have never faced from here to Canterbury a man.*
- DC (w-w clause): *who could topple me off a bridge.*
- AC (adverb clause): *as you have done.*

DAY 2

#3 ly   MC   S   cc   S   V   prep   prep   *two*   cc ⌄ prep

¶ suddenly, [the distant twigs and branches rustled <u>with the coming of men</u>], a **score** or ~~3~~ of

strong yeomen.

Fixes

Indent. Is this a new topic, speaker, place, or time? Answer: Yes, a new topic, leaving Robin's speech and turning attention to his band of men.

Numbers. *two.* Spell out numbers that can be written in one or two words.

Commas with items in a series. Ask: Do we need a comma before either of the cc's, and why? 1) Not before *and* because it joins two nouns, not three or more items in a series. 2) Not before *or* because it joins two numbers, not three or more.

End marks. This is a statement so add a period.

Grammar Notations

Subjects and verbs. *twigs … branches rustled.*

Clauses and sentence openers.

- #3 -ly adverb: *Suddenly.*
- MC: *the distant twigs and branches rustled with the coming of men.*

score: a group of twenty. This means that twenty to forty of Robin Hood's men came to the bugle call.

In the Middle Ages, this was a common meaning of *score*, fallen out of use by now but most famously employed by Abraham Lincoln in the Gettysburg Address: "Four score and seven years ago," or eighty-seven years before.

DAY 3

#1 *MC S   V   prep*   *prep*   *prep*

[they burst from ~~there~~/their ~~/they're~~ hiding places with robin's **steadfast** friend will stutely in

                                                                    MC V   S   MC   V   S   #1 MC   S   V   prep   prep

front]. ¶"good master," [cried will], "[how is this]? [~~your~~/you're drenched from head to foot]."

Fixes

steadfast: faithful and firm in purpose

Indent. Is this a new topic, speaker, place, or time? Answer: Not the first sentence, which continues the topic of the arrival of the Merry Men, but the second sentence starts a new paragraph because of a new speaker.

Capitalization.

- *They, Good, You're*—first word of sentences. Do not capitalize *how* because it continues a sentence within his speech.
- *Robin's, Will Stutely, Will*—proper nouns.

Homophones and usage.

- *their hiding places*, possessive.
- *You're drenched*, the contraction for *you are.*

Quotations. Check that students placed quotation marks around the words spoken: *"Good master," cried Will, "how … foot."*

Ask: What commas go with the quotations? Answer: commas around the interrupter: *"master," cried Will, "how … "*

✧ **Advanced.** The comma after *master* has a double purpose. It closes the quotation before a speaking verb and sets off the NDA *good master.*

End marks. This is a statement so add a period.

Grammar Notations

Subjects and verbs. *They burst, cried Will, is this* (not *how is* because *how* is an adverb), *You're.*

Like its synonym *wet, drenched* acts as an adjective here, but it is fine if students label it a verb. *See* ♡.

Clauses and sentence openers.

- #1 subject opener and MC: *They burst from their hiding places with Robin's steadfast friend Will Stutely in front.*
- MC: *cried Will.*
- MC: *how is this?*
- #1 subject opener and MC: *You're drenched from head to foot.*

♡ **Grammar lovers.** When past participles follow a *be* verb, is it a linking verb + subject complement (a.k.a. predicate adjective) or a helping verb + action verb? In this case, since no one physically drenched Robin Hood, *drenched* functions as an adjective describing his physical condition. You do not need to teach the concept, however, because it is too advanced for this level.

DAY 4

¶ "<u>well</u>, my friend," [answered <u>robin</u>], still amused, "[this **stout** fellow has tumbled me into the water and has given me a beating]!"

(with grammar notation marks above: MC, V, S, MC, S, V, V, prep, cc, V, V)

Fixes

Indent. Is this a new topic, speaker, place, or time? Answer: Yes, a new speaker and paragraph.

Capitalization. Do not capitalize *this* because it continues a sentence in his speech.

Quotations. Check that students placed quotation marks around the words spoken: *"Well, my friend," … "this … beating!"*

Put commas around the interrupter because it has a speaking verb setting up the quotation: *"friend," answered … amused, "this … "*

Notice that the comma after *friend* has a double duty: it sets off the NDA and separates the quotation from the speaking verb.

Commas with NDAs. Put commas around *my friend* because NDAs (nouns of direct address) take commas.

Commas with cc's.

Ask: Does the cc *and* need a comma before it, and why? Answer: No, because it joins only two verbs. Rule: **MC cc 2nd verb** (not **MC, cc MC**). *See* ✎.

The trick is to look for a subject after *and*. If you cannot find it but only a verb instead, as here, it is likely the **MC cc 2nd verb** pattern and therefore no comma.

End marks. This is exclamatory so could take either an exclamation mark or a period. Let students choose.

Grammar Notations

Subjects and verbs. *answered Robin, fellow has tumbled … has given.* Note that *fellow* is the subject of two verbs.

Ask: Which of these are helping verbs? Answer: *has* (helps *tumbled*); *has* (helps *given*).

Clauses and sentence openers.

- MC: *answered Robin.*
- MC: *this stout fellow has tumbled me (into the water) and has given me a beating.*

Style

If desired, have your students identify the best dress-ups from this week's sentences. Discuss their answers. Choose among:

Strong verbs. *topple, rustled, burst, drenched, tumbled.*

Quality adjectives. *worthy, distant, steadfast, stout.*

-ly adverbs. No -ly dress-ups this week. *Suddenly* is an opener.

---

stout: strong of body; hearty; sturdy.

Note: In Week 20 *stout* described the fight and meant forceful and brave. When the word describes a person or object, it suggests strength and usually heaviness or bulkiness.

✎ **Teacher's note.** With three or more verbs, commas would be needed for items in a series, but not for two.

STUDENT REWRITE

"Aye," replied Robin to his worthy opponent, "you're a tall, brave one, too, for I have never faced from here to Canterbury a man who could topple me off a bridge as you have done."

Suddenly, the distant twigs and branches rustled with the coming of men, a score or two of strong yeomen. They burst from their hiding places with Robin's steadfast friend Will Stutely in front.

"Good master," cried Will, "how is this? You're drenched from head to foot."

"Well, my friend," answered Robin, still amused, "this stout fellow has tumbled me into the water and has given me a beating!"

Week 26

No New Concepts

LEARN IT

There are no new concepts this week. See if you can answer the questions below. If not, check your grammar cards for the answers.

1. How many words can be in a #6 vss?

2. What is the main difference between a clause and a phrase?

3. A vss must be a sentence, and a sentence must have at least one main clause. What is the difference between a main clause and a dependent clause?

4. What words commonly start dependent clauses?

Do you remember what these vocabulary words mean? If not, look them up in your vocabulary list in the back of your notebook.

- towered
- husky
- muttered
- proclaimed
- catapults
- adept
- nimbly
- stouter

> **Teacher's answers**
>
> 1. 2–5
>
> 2. *clause:* has subject + verb
>   *phrase:* does not have verb
>
> 3. *main clause:* can stand alone as a sentence
>   *dependent clause:* cannot
>
> 4. www words: *when, while, where, as, since, if, although, because*
>   also: *that, who, which*

DAY 1

Choose the best end mark to follow *himself*, *Stutely*, *lads*, and *stranger*. Check for proper capitalization, too.

#1 MC   *S*   *V*   *V*   *prep*   *cc*   *MC V*   *S*

¶ " [then ~~than~~ he will not go without a **trouncing** and **ducking** himself]!" [cried will stutely].

#1 MC   V   *#2 prep*   *MC S*   *cc*   *twenty*   *S*   *V*   *prep*

" [have at him, lads]!" ¶ at that, [will and ~~20~~ other men sprang upon the stranger].

Fixes

Indent. Is this a new topic, speaker, place, or time? Answer: Two new paragraphs, one for Will's words (new speaker) and another for a new topic.

Homophones and usage. This time *then* means *in that case.*

Numbers. *twenty.* Spell out numbers that can be written in one or two words.

Quotations. Check that students placed quotation marks around the words spoken: *"Then … himself!" … "Have … lads!"*

Note: This time, the first narrative is not set off with a comma despite its speaking verb (*cried*) because there is an exclamation mark ending the quotation instead.

Commas. Ask students where to put commas and why.

- Insert a comma before *lads* because it is a noun of direct address (NDA) but not after it because it ends the sentence.
- Ask: Do the cc's need commas? Answer: No comma before either since both *and*'s join only two items that are not MCs (*trouncing and ducking, Will and men*).

End marks.

- Exclamation mark after *himself* and inside the closing quotation marks; keep *cried* lowercase.
- Period to close the first sentence after *Stutely.*
- Exclamation after *lads* since his invitation is highly exclamatory. Check that it is inside the closing quotation marks.
- Period at the end to close the last statement.

Grammar Notations

Subjects and verbs. *he will go, cried Will Stutely, have at* (*you* is the understood subject; *have at* is a verb phrase), *Will … men sprang.*

Prepositional phrases. *without a trouncing and ducking himself, At that, upon the stranger.*

- ✿ **Advanced.** The first one fits the pattern because *trouncing* and *ducking* are not verbs but nouns here, indicated by the article that comes before them (articles always precede nouns).

Clauses and sentence openers.

- #1 subject opener and MC (ignoring the opening adverb): *Then he will not go without a trouncing and ducking himself.*
- MC: *cried Will Stutely.*
- #1 subject opener (with you understood) and MC: *Have at him.*
- #2 prepositional phrase opener: *At that.*
- MC: *Will and twenty other men sprang upon the stranger.*

Sidebar (right margin):

trouncing: severe beating

ducking: plunging of the body under water

Check that students understand "Have at him" to mean an invitation to attack the stranger.

DAY 2

#5 AC   cl   S   V   MC   S   V   prep
(although they moved quickly), [the giant was ready], striking down men with his stout staff.

#3 ly   cc   MC S V   V   prep   prep
slowly and surely, however, [he was pressed down by the **considerable** number of men].

Fixes

Indent. Is this a new topic, speaker, place, or time? Answer: No, it continues the fight between the Merry Men and the stranger.

Commas. Ask students where they added commas, and why.

Insert a comma after *quickly* because it is the end of the #5 opener. Rule: **AC, MC.**

Ask: Should there be a comma before the cc *and*? Answer: No, it joins two -ly adverbs, so no comma.

End marks. This is a statement so add a period.

Grammar Notations

Subjects and verbs. *they moved, giant was* (*ready* is an adjective), *he was pressed down* (*down* is part of the verb phrase).

✧ **Advanced.** If students mark *striking* as a verb, simply explain that it is not one here because it is not coupled with a subject and helping verb. The sentence does not say, "The giant was striking."

Prepositional phrases. *with his stout staff, by the considerable number, of men.* Ask students to explain how these fit the pattern: **preposition + noun (no verb).**

Clauses and sentence openers.

- #5 opener and AC (adverb clause): *Although they moved quickly.*
- MC: *the giant was ready.*
- #3 -ly adverb opener: *Slowly and surely.*
- MC: *he was pressed down by the considerable number of men.*

DAY 3

Choose the best end mark to follow *wait*, *off*, *again*, and *him*. Check capitalization too.

MC   V #1 MC   V   MC V   S   prep   AC cl

¶ "[wait]**!** [everybody**,** back off]**!**" [called robin], **convulsing** <u>with laughter</u> (until his sore

S   V   #1 MC S V   cc MC V

sides ached again)**.** "[he is a blameless man]**,** so [harm him no more]**."**

Fixes

Indent. Is this a new topic, speaker, place, or time? Answer: Yes, a new speaker and paragraph.

Quotations. Check that students placed quotation marks around the words spoken: *"Wait ... off!" ... "He ... more."*

The interrupter is again not set off with a comma despite its speaking verb (*called*) because there is an exclamation mark before the verb instead of the usual comma.

Commas. *See* ✏ **1.**

Ask: Is a comma needed after *Everybody*, and why? Answer: Yes, to set off the NDA. If students do not catch this, it is not critical because it is not a typical noun of direct address. Just explain the principle and move on!

Ask: Is a comma needed before *until*, and why? Answer: No, because mid-sentence adverb clauses are not set off with commas. Rule: **MC AC.**

Ask: Is a comma needed before the cc *so*, and why? Answer: Yes, because it joins two main clauses. Rule: **MC, cc MC.**

End marks.

Exclamation marks after *Wait* and *off* inside the closing quotation marks; keep *cried* lowercase.

Period to close the first sentence after *again*.

Period at the end to close the last statement.

Grammar Notations

Subjects and verbs. *Wait* (subject, *you*, is understood), *back off* (adverb goes with verb; technically *you* is the subject, but it is fine if students mark the NDA *Everybody* as the subject), *called Robin, sides ached, He is, harm* (subject, *you*, is understood).

Adverb clause starter (subordinating conjunction). *until.* This is not one of the www words, but it starts an adverb clause. If students do not mark it, simply point it out, show the subject and verb, and help them bracket the clause.

Clauses and sentence openers.

- MC: *Wait!* Technically this does not count as a #6 vss because it is too short, only one word since the subject is understood but not stated.
- #1 subject opener and MC: *Everybody, back off!* See ✏ **2.**
- MC: *called Robin.*
- AC (adverb clause): *until his sore sides ached again.*
- #1 subject opener and MC: *He is a blameless man.*
- MC: *harm him no more.*

convulsing: shaking violently (with laughter)

✏ **1. Teacher's note.** Discuss parts of speech or clauses before discussing commas, as needed.

✏ **2. Teacher's note.** *Everybody, back off!* is a #1 and not a #6 vss because the sentence does not end until *ached again.* The quotation connects to the rest of the sentence because of the speaking verb. However, it is fine if students mark this as a vss.

DAY 4

Think of the rules you have learned to determine what punctuation should go after *proposal*.

#3 *ly*   MC S   V   MC V   S   MC V   S   V   *prep*

¶ openly [robin then set forth his proposal]. "[**hark** you, honest stranger]: [will you stay with

      cc   *V*   *prep*

me and be one of us]?"

Fixes

Indent. Is this a new topic, speaker, place, or time? Answer: New topic. In the last sentence, Robin was speaking to the Merry Men; now he is addressing the stranger.

Quotations. Check that students placed quotation marks around the words spoken: *"Hark … us."*

Commas.

Ask: Did you add any commas? Answer: Before *honest stranger*, an NDA.

Ask: Why should there not be a comma before the cc *and*? Answer: It joins only two verbs (*will stay* and *be*) to the same subject (*you*). Rule: **MC cc 2nd verb** (no comma).

End marks.

Ask: What punctuation did you place after *proposal*? Answer: A period. Commas set up quotations only when there is a speaking verb introducing them. *See* ♡ **2.**

In the second sentence Robin is asking a question, so close with a question mark inside the quotation marks.

Grammar Notations

Subjects and verbs. *Robin set forth* (verb phrase), *Hark you, will you stay … be.*

Ask: Which of these are helping verbs? Answer: *will*, which helps *stay* and *be*.

Clauses and sentence openers.

- #3 -ly adverb opener: *Openly.*
- MC: *Robin then set forth his proposal.*
- #1 subject opener and MC: *Hark you, honest stranger.*
- MC: *will you stay with me and be one of us?*

Style

If desired, have your students identify the best dress-ups from this week's sentences. Discuss their answers. Choose among:

Strong verbs. *sprang, pressed down, befall.*

Quality adjectives. *stout, blameless.*

-ly adverbs (not the first word of any sentence). *quickly, surely.*

hark: listen attentively

♡ **1. Grammar lovers.** The **colon** is correct after *Hark you, honest stranger.* Use a colon after a main clause to mean *an explanation follows*. It is the best way to indicate the relationship between these MCs.

♡ **2. Grammar lovers.** The verb phrase *set forth* sets up a direct object, *proposal*, not the quotation itself.

STUDENT REWRITE

"Then he will not go without a trouncing and ducking himself!" cried Will Stutely. "Have at him, lads!"

At that, Will and twenty other men sprang upon the stranger. Although they moved quickly, the giant was ready, striking down men with his stout staff. Slowly and surely, however, he was pressed down by the considerable number of men.

"Wait! Everybody, back off!" called Robin, convulsing with laughter until his sore sides ached again. "He is a blameless man, so harm him no more."

Openly Robin then set forth his proposal. "Hark you, honest stranger: will you stay with me and be one of us?"

Week 27

No New Concepts

LEARN IT

There are no new concepts this week. See if you can answer the questions below. If not, check your grammar cards for the answers.

1. Name the coordinating conjunctions. (Hint: the reminder acronym is FANBOYS.)

2. What is the comma rule when two main clauses are combined with a coordinating conjunction?

Do you remember what these vocabulary words mean? If not, look them up in your vocabulary list in the back of your notebook.

- adversary
- parried
- leveled
- deftly
- thus
- chafed
- fatigue
- combatant

Teacher's answers

1. *for, and, nor, but, or, yet, so*

2. **MC, cc MC**
   The comma goes before the cc, never after.

Teacher's note.
If you are continuing to do the grammar notations, it helps to go over those before addressing the fixes, especially when it comes to the commas.

Page 56, *Fix It! Grammar:* **Robin Hood, Student Book 2**

DAY 1

Robin will continue speaking in the next passage.

#1 MC S   V   MC S   V V   V *three* prep   cc   V   prep

[robin continued], "[you will be given 3̶ suits of lincoln green each year and partake of a

prep   DC S   V

share in the **lucrative** things] (that come our way).

Fixes

lucrative: profitable

Indent. Is this a new topic, speaker, place, or time? Answer: No new paragraph. Robin is still making an offer to the stranger.

Capitalization.

- *Robin, You*—first word of sentence and of quoted sentence.
- *Lincoln*—capitalize words derived from proper nouns.

Numbers. *Three.* Spell out numbers that can be written in one or two words.

Quotations. Check that students placed quotation marks at the start of his words but not at the end since he will continue speaking: *"You … way.*

Ask: Did you add commas with this quotation, and why? Answer: After *Robin continued.* Rule: **speaking verb + comma + quotation**.

Commas with cc's. Ask: Did you put a comma before the cc *and*, and why? Answer: No, because this cc joins only two verbs (*will be given* and *partake*), not two main clauses. Rule: **MC cc 2nd verb**, so no comma.

End marks. This is a statement so add a period.

Grammar Notations

Subjects and verbs. *Robin continued, you will be given … partake, that come.* See ✏.

Clauses and sentence openers.

- #1 subject opener and main clause: *Robin continued.*
- MC: *You will be given three suits of Lincoln green each year and partake of a share in the lucrative things.*
- DC: *that come our way.* See ♡.

✏ **Teacher's note.** If students think that *things* is the subject of *come*, either let it go or explain that the word *that*, like a *who* or *which*, is the true subject but it refers back to *lucrative things*.

♡ **Grammar lovers.** This DC is an adjective clause because it describes the noun, *things*, that comes right before the clause. Usually use *that* in place of *which* in essential adjective clauses.

DAY 2

#1 MC S   V   V   cc   #1 MC
                                                                                            S V   V
[you shall enjoy **succulent** venison and the stoutest tasting ale]. [i will appoint you my

            cc MC   V   S   V   #1 MC
                                                                                    V   MC V S
right-hand man], for [never have i watched such an able staff fighter]. [tell me]: [will you

V   prep
become one of my men]?"

Fixes

Indent. Is this a new topic, speaker, place, or time? Answer: No. Students should continue writing where they left off.

Commas with adjectives. *stoutest tasting* and *able staff.*

These are both cumulative adjectives, but it is unlikely students would want to put a comma between them anyway.

If it helps, put both through the two tests: *tasting stoutest ale* and *staff able fighter* sound awkward, as do *stoutest and tasting ale* and *able and staff fighter*, so these are cumulative adjectives and do not take commas.

Commas with cc's. Ask: Did you put a comma before the cc *and*, and why? Answer: No, because it joins only two nouns (*venison* and *ale*), which is two items in a series, not three or more, so no comma.

Ask: Is there another cc to evaluate and does it need a comma, and why? Answer: Yes: *for*. Yes, it needs a comma because it joins two main clauses. Rule: **MC, cc MC**.

End mark and closing quotation marks. Robin is asking a question, so end with a question mark inside the closing quotation marks.

Grammar Notations

Subjects and verbs. *You shall enjoy, I will appoint, have I watched, Tell* (with the subject, *you*, understood), *will you become.*

Ask: Which of these are helping verbs? Answer: *shall* (helps *enjoy*), *will* (helps *appoint*), *have* (helps *watched*), *will* (helps *become*).

Clauses and sentence openers.

- #1 subject opener and MC: *You shall enjoy succulent venison and the stoutest tasting ale.*
- #1 subject opener and MC: *I will appoint you my right-hand man.*
- MC: *never have I watched such an able staff fighter.*
- #1 subject opener and MC: *Tell me. See ✎.*
- MC: *will you become one of my men?*

succulent: juicy and tender

✎ **Teacher's note.** *Tell me* is not a vss because it connects to the MC after it with the colon. If students mark it as a #6 and the MC after it as a #1, let it go.

The **colon** is correct after *Tell me*. Use a colon after a main clause to mean *an example or explanation follows.* It is the best way to indicate that the question right after—*will you become one of my men?*—is what Robin wants the stranger to tell him. Colons can set up lists, sentences, quotations—any construction—but a main clause must come before the colon.

DAY 3

The stranger is not finished speaking.

#1 MC S V   MC V   S   AC cl S V   prep
¶ " [that i know not]," [replied the stranger sorely] (since he was still **nettled** about his

#5 AC cl S V   cc
thrashing). " (if you handle your ~~you're~~ bow and arrows worse ~~then~~ than your ~~you're~~

MC S V
hand-made staff), [i won't].

✎ **Teacher's note.** If students are puzzled by the stranger's apparent change of attitude, explain that although he praised Robin Hood's skill with the staff before, now he is angry and offended at being set upon by Robin's men and therefore more inclined to criticize him.

nettled: irritated; provoked

Fixes

Indent. Is this a new topic, speaker, place, or time? Answer: Yes, a new speaker and paragraph.

Quotations. Check that students placed quotation marks around the words spoken except at the end since he has more to say: *"That … not," … "if … won't.*

Commas. Ask students where they added commas. Also discuss where they should not have placed them but may have done so.

- After *know not.* Rule: **quotation + comma + speaking verb** (*replied*).
- Not before *since.* Rule: **MC AC** (mid-sentence adverb clauses are not set off with commas).
- No comma with *bows and arrows* (two nouns).
- After *staff.* Rule: **AC, MC** (#5 clausal openers are set off with commas).

Homophones and usage.

- *your* is possessive: the bow and arrows belonging to you.
- *than* compares Robin's handling of his bow and arrows to his handling of the staff.
- *your* is possessive: the staff belonging to you.

End marks. This is a statement so add a period.

Grammar Notations

Subjects and verbs. *I know, replied stranger, he was* (See ♡)*, you handle, I will* (from *won't,* the contraction for *will not*).

Prepositional phrases. *about his thrashing.*

✦ **Advanced.** -ing words sometimes function as nouns, as *thrashing* does as the object of the preposition.

Continued on next page ▶

♡ **Grammar lovers.** Regarding *he was nettled about his thrashing:* Grammarians sometimes disagree about whether a certain word after a *be* verb is a predicate adjective or part of the verb. One might argue that since someone has been nettling the stranger, *nettled* is part of the verb. In this construction, however, the stranger is not nettled by someone but about his thrashing, so *nettled* works like the adjective *angry* and functions as a subject compliment (a.k.a. predicate adjective). Since choosing verb or adjective does not affect punctuation, it really does not matter. See Passive versus Active Voice; Additional Rules and Concepts; Grammar Glossary, page G-33.

Clauses and sentence openers.

- #1 subject opener and MC: *That I know not.*
  - ✧ **Advanced.** Technically, this sentence begins with the direct object instead of the subject, but we still label it a #1 since it is one main clause with no other opener before it. If students have trouble seeing this, it is fine to let it go!
- MC: *replied the stranger sorely.*
- AC (adverb clause): *since he was still nettled about his thrashing.*
- #5 opener and AC (adverb clause): *If you handle your bow and arrows worse than your hand-made staff.*
- MC: *I won't.* If students have trouble with this, show that there is a subject and a verb and that no other word comes in front to make it a dependent clause. To hear that it can stand alone as a sentence, it helps to recast it without the contraction: *I will not!*

DAY 4

#1 MC   S   V   prep   #1 MC S   V

[~~your/~~you're not fit to be a yeoman in my own country]!" ¶ [he paused a moment].

                                        DC

#5 AC cl   V   S   S/w-w V   V   DC   S V   MC S

¶ "(if there ~~/their/they're~~ is any man here) (who can shoot better) (~~then/~~than i can)," [he

            V   MC   S V   V

finally **conceded**], "[then ~~/than~~ i will consider joining you]."

Fixes

Indent. Is this a new topic, speaker, place, or time? Answer: No new topic with his first words since the stranger is still speaking. Start a new paragraph with *He paused* because it pulls out of his speech and with *"If there …* because he is speaking again. If students want to keep all this in one paragraph, that is fine, but starting new paragraphs helps communicate that there is a pause in his thinking.

Homophones and usage.

- *You're* (you are) not fit.
- if *there* (pronoun setting up clause) is any man.
- better *than* I can (comparison).
- *then* (at that time) I will consider.

Quotations. Since this is a continuation of his speech, students should not put quotation marks at the beginning but should continue writing where they left off. Check that they placed quotation marks around the rest of the words spoken: *country!"* … *"If … can,"* … *"then … you."*

Commas. Ask students where they added commas and why.

- After *can* but before closing quations because it comes at the end of the #5 opener and because it separates the quotation from the interrupter. See ✎.
- After *conceded* because it is the end of the interrupter and because it is a speaking verb setting up the quotation. Pattern: **quotation + comma + narrative interrupting the speech + comma + quotation.**

End marks. This is a statement so add a period inside the closing quotation marks.

Continued on next page ▸

conceded: admitted or yielded

Check that students understand he is challenging Robin Hood and his men to an archery contest.

✎ **Teacher's note.** Notice that the #5 opener includes all three dependent clauses because they are all one thought.

Grammar Notations

Subjects and verbs. *You're, He paused, is man, who can shoot, I can, he conceded, I will consider.* Note: The helping verbs are *can* (shoot) and *will* (consider).

Address any of the following if questions arise: **1)** *You're* includes the subject and verb; **2)** *to be* is an infinitive, which is formed from a verb but does not function as one; **3)** *there* is a pronoun that sets up the clause; the true subject is *man*; **4)** *joining* looks like a verb but acts as the direct object of *consider* so is actually a noun here.

***Who-which* clauses.** Ask: What noun does this clause describe and where is it? Answer: *man*, which comes before the *who* clause. See ✎ **1.**

Clauses and sentence openers.

- #1 subject opener and MC: *You're not fit to be a yeoman in my own country.*
- #1 subject opener and MC: *He paused a moment.*
- #5 opener and AC (adverb clause): *If there is any man here.*
- DC (w-w clause): *who can shoot better.*
- DC: *than I can.* See ✎ **2.**
- MC: *he finally conceded.*
- MC: *then I will consider joining you.* Regarding *then* before this clause, see ✎ **2.**

Style

If desired, have your students identify the best dress-ups from this week's sentences. Discuss their answers. Choose among:

Strong verbs. *partake, conceded.*

Quality adjectives. *lucrative, succulent, able, nettled.* Allow students to count *nettled* as either a verb or an adjective. See ♡ on page 167.

-ly adverbs (not the first word of any sentence). *sorely.*

✎ **1. Teacher's note.** This clause specifies what man is meant—the one who can outshoot the stranger—so is essential and therefore not set off with a comma.

✎ **2. Teacher's note.** *Than* is a subordinating conjunction, which makes a clause dependent. By contrast, the adverb *then* does not affect the clause because it is not a subordinating conjunction. When you add *then* to a main clause, it is still a main clause.

STUDENT REWRITE

Since this passage continues without another indentation, be sure students continue writing where last week's passage left off.

Robin continued, "You will be given three suits of Lincoln green each year and partake of a share in the lucrative things that come our way. You shall enjoy succulent venison and the stoutest tasting ale. I will appoint you my right-hand man, for never have I watched such an able staff fighter. Tell me: will you become one of my men?"

"That I know not," replied the stranger sorely since he was still nettled about his thrashing. "If you handle your bow and arrows worse than your hand-made staff, I won't. You're not fit to be a yeoman in my own country!"

He paused a moment.

"If there is any man here who can shoot better than I can," he finally conceded, "then I will consider joining you."

Week 28

No New Concepts

LEARN IT

There are no new concepts this week. See if you can answer the questions below. If not, check your grammar cards for the answers.

1. Name the coordinating conjunctions. (Hint: the reminder acronym is FANBOYS.)

2. What is the comma rule for two verbs combined with a coordinating conjunction?

3. What words can be handy for combining sentences that share a common noun? (Hint: this is a dress-up.)

Do you remember what these vocabulary words mean? If not, look them up in your vocabulary list in the back of your notebook.

- thatching
- shrewd
- hairsbreadth
- dexterous
- inflamed
- smote
- thwacked
- happenstance

✏ **Teacher's note.** Remember to keep the discussion light and fun—make it a game.

Teacher's answers

1. *for, and, nor, but, or, yet, so*

2. a.k.a. compound verbs, no comma: **MC cc 2nd verb**

3. *who* and *which*

DAY 1

Think about whether to start a new paragraph when Robin addresses Will Stutely. Also, at the end of this passage, Robin is not finished speaking.

#1 MC S   V   #1 MC S   V   V prep   AC cl S   V   V   prep

¶ [robin accepted the challenge]. "[i will **stoop** to you] (as i have never stooped to man

MC V   prep   **four**   cc

before). ¶ "friend stutely, [cut down a white piece of bark 4 fingers tall and wide].

Fixes

Indent. Is this a new topic, speaker, place, or time? Answer: Yes, twice: **a)** The first sentence sets up the first part of the quotation (new speaker) and can go in the same paragraph. **b)** Start another paragraph when Robin turns away from addressing the stranger to give Will Stutely instructions—new topic.

Numbers. *four*. Spell out numbers that can be written in one or two words.

Quotations. *"I will … before. "Friend … wide.* Robin will have more to say Day 2, so do not close his speech with quotation marks.

✦ **Advanced.** When there is a new topic within one person's speech, close the first paragraph with no quotation marks (*man before.*) but open the next with opening quotation marks (*"Friend …).* When the first paragraph does not close with quotation marks, it indicates that he is not finished; when the second paragraph opens with quotation marks, it reminds us that someone is still speaking.

Ask: Why is there no comma before the first quotation? Answer: There is no speaking verb setting it up.

Commas. Ask students where they added commas. Also discuss where they should not have placed them but may have done so.

- There should not be a comma before the *as* adverb clause. Rule: **MC AC**.
- NDA: *Friend Stutely*, which should be set off with a comma.

End marks. This is a statement so add a period.

Grammar Notations

Subjects and verbs. *Robin accepted, I will stoop, I have stooped, cut.* See ♡.

✦ **Advanced.** In *cut down*, *down* is an adverb. Ask: Which makes more sense, *cut down* or *down a white piece*? Only the first, so *down* goes with the verb rather than starting a prepositional phrase.

Clauses and sentence openers.

- #1 subject opener and MC: *Robin accepted the challenge.*
- #1 subject opener and MC: *I will stoop to you.*
- AC (adverb clause): *as I have never stooped to man before.*
- MC: *cut down a white piece of bark four fingers tall and wide.*

stoop: lower oneself; descend from one's level of dignity.

Robin Hood considers it stooping because the stranger has insulted him.

♡ **Grammar lovers.** The subject of *cut* is not *Friend Stutely* but an understood *you*. NDAs do not do double duty as subjects. Although *Stutely* and *you* are one and the same in the story line, the words have different functions grammatically. Also, there would not be a comma between a subject and its verb, but there needs to be a comma after the NDA.

DAY 2

#1 MC V   *prep*   *#5 AC cl*   *S   V*

[nail it fourscore yards distant <u>on yonder white oak</u>]. ¶ "(if, stranger, you hit that target),

MC   *S   V   V*

[then ~~than~~ you can **dub** yourself an archer]."

Fixes

Indent. Is this a new topic, speaker, place, or time? Answer: Not with the first sentence because Robin is still talking to Will Stutely. In the second sentence, he addresses the stranger again, so start a new paragraph.

Quotations. This passage does not begin with quotation marks because Robin is still speaking here in the same paragraph as the Day 1 speech. There are no close quotation marks after "white oak" to indicate that Robin is not finished speaking. However, start the new paragraph with open quotation marks to remind the reader that someone is still speaking. End with quotations after *archer* because Robin is now finished. Fix: *"If, stranger … archer."*

Homophones and usage. *then,* meaning *at that time.*

Commas. Ask students where they added commas. Also discuss where they should not have placed them but may have done so.

- No comma in *yonder white oak* because it has cumulative adjectives. Both tests sound strange: *white yonder oak; yonder and white oak.*
- Commas around *stranger* to set off this NDA.
- Comma after *target* at the end of the #5 opener. Rule: **AC, MC.** Check clauses first if needed.

End marks. This is a statement so add a period inside the closing quotation marks.

Grammar Notations

Subjects and verbs. *nail* (*you* the implied subject), *you hit* (the NDA is not the subject), *you can dub.* Helping verbs: *can* (helps *dub*).

Clauses and sentence openers.

- #1 subject opener and MC: *Nail it fourscore yards distant on yonder white oak.*
- #5 opener and AC (adverb clause): *If, stranger, you hit that target.*
- MC: *then you can dub yourself an archer.* Note: The adverb *then* does not affect the clause.

dub: call or invest with a name or title of dignity

Ask if students know how far **fourscore** yards is. Answer: four times a score, which is twenty, so eighty in all.

DAY 3

> #1 MC S   V   V   MC   V   S #1 MC V   cc
> ¶ "aye, [i surely will strike the mark]," [answered he]. "[hand me a stout bow and a straight,
>
>   #5 AC cl S V   MC V   prep
> broad arrow]. (if i hit it not), [**thrash** me blue with bowstrings]!"

Fixes

thrash: beat soundly

Indent. Is this a new topic, speaker, place, or time? Answer: Yes, a new speaker and paragraph.

Quotations. Check that students placed quotation marks around the words spoken: *"Aye … mark"* and *"Hand … bowstrings."*

Commas. Ask students where they added commas or other punctuation and why. Also discuss where they should not have placed punctuation but may have done so.

- Comma after *mark*. Rule: **quotation + comma + speaking verb**. See End marks, below.
- No comma after *bow* because *and* joins only two nouns (*bow* and *arrow*), not three or more items in a series.
- Comma with coordinate adjectives: *straight, broad arrow*. Both tests sound right, so these are coordinate, not cumulative, and take a comma: 1) *broad, straight arrow*; 2) *straight and broad arrow*.
- Comma at the end of the #5 opener: *If I hit it not, … .*

End marks. Period after *answered he*. There is a complete quoted sentence before and after the interrupter, so close the interrupter with a period before starting the next sentence.

Exclamation mark after *bowstrings* to close his exclamatory speech. Check that the exclamation mark is inside the closing quotation marks.

Grammar Notations

Subjects and verbs. *I will strike, answered he, hand* (with the subject, *you*, understood), *I hit, thrash* (with the subject, *you*, understood).

Clauses and sentence openers.

- #1 subject opener and MC: *I surely will strike the mark.* Students may count this as a #1 opener or not since only a short transitional word comes before the MC.
- MC: *answered he.*
- #1 subject opener and MC: *Hand me a stout bow and a straight, broad arrow.*
- #5 opener and AC (adverb clause): *If I hit it not.*
- MC: *thrash me blue with bowstrings.*

DAY 4

In your rewrite, combine the first two sentences with a *which* clause.

DC S/w-w

#1 MC S   V   cc   **which** V   cc   #1 MC S   V

¶ [he chose a bow and a straight shaft], ̶i̶t̶ (ˇwas well feathered and smooth). [he stepped

prep   prep

up to the mark with **alacrity**].

Combine sentences with a *which*

Who-which clauses. Check that students combined the sentences correctly and put a comma in front of the new *which* clause.

Ask: What noun does *which* describe and where is it? Answer: *shaft,* which is immediately before the *which* clause. See ✎.

Fixes

Indent. Is this a new topic, speaker, place, or time? Answer: Yes, a new topic, pulling out of his speech and turning to his actions.

Commas. If students put a comma in front of either cc, explain that they both join only two items in a series (not MCs), so no comma in either case: *bow and shaft; well feathered and smooth.* Pattern: **a and b**.

End marks. This is a statement so add a period.

Grammar Notations

Subjects and verbs. *He chose, which was, He stepped* (*up* is an adverb modifying *stepped*).

Clauses and sentence openers.
- #1 subject opener and MC: *He chose a bow and a straight shaft.*
- DC (w-w clause): *which was well feathered and smooth.*
- #1 subject opener and MC: *He stepped up to the mark with alacrity.*

Style

If desired, have your students identify the best dress-ups from this week's sentences. Discuss their answers. Choose among:

Strong verbs. *stoop, dub.*

Quality adjectives. *yonder, feathered.*

-ly adverbs (not the first word of any sentence). *surely.*

alacrity: cheerful readiness or promptness

✎ **Teacher's note.** This *who-which* clause is nonessential because it simply describes the already identified shaft, so it is set off with a comma.

STUDENT REWRITE

Robin accepted the challenge. "I will stoop to you as I have never stooped to man before.

"Friend Stutely, cut down a white piece of bark four fingers tall and wide. Nail it fourscore yards distant on yonder white oak.

"If, stranger, you hit that target, then you can dub yourself an archer."

"Aye, I surely will strike the mark," answered he. "Hand me a stout bow and a straight, broad arrow. If I hit it not, thrash me blue with bowstrings!"

He chose a bow and a straight shaft, which was well feathered and smooth. He stepped up to the mark with alacrity.

Week 29

No New Concepts

LEARN IT

There are no new concepts this week. See if you can answer the questions below. If not, check your grammar cards for the answers.

1. Explain the comma rules for conversation.

2. Do commas and periods go before or after closing quotation marks?

3. Which of the following numbers should be spelled out?

   a) 150

   b) 100

   c) 68

   d) 10

   e) 7

   f) 3rd

Do you remember what these vocabulary words mean? If not, look them up in your vocabulary list in the back of your notebook.

- sorry
- predicament
- gaining his feet
- wielding
- hearty
- scorching
- clapped
- faced

Teacher's answers

1. Use commas when a speaking verb sets up a quotation.

2. "Before," like "these words."

3. Spell out all except **a)** since 150 would take three words to spell out (*one hundred fifty*).

a) 150	**d)** ten
b) one hundred	**e)** seven
c) sixty-eight	**f)** third

Page 60, *Fix It! Grammar:* **Robin Hood, Student Book 2**

DAY 1

In your rewrite, combine the sentences with a *who* clause set off with commas.

DC S/w-w
MC   S **who** V   prep   prep   V
¶ meanwhile, [robin's men, (~~lie~~/lay off to the side of the **prodigious** oak), ~~. they~~ watched]

AC cl   S   V   prep   prep
(as the stranger shot at the small white square fixed to its~~/it's~~ front).

Combine sentences with a who

Who-which clauses. Check that students combined the sentences correctly. Ask: What noun does *who* describe and where is it? Answer: *men*, which is immediately before the *who* clause.

prodigious: extraordinary in size

Fixes

Indent. Is this a new topic, speaker, place, or time? Answer: Yes, a new topic: the archery contest between the stranger and Robin.

Homophones and usage.

- *lay*, the past tense of *to lie*. The men are lying themselves on the ground, not laying an object.
- *its* front. Ask: What does *it* refer back to? Answer: *the oak* (the front of the oak).

Commas.

- Check that they put commas on both sides of the new *who* clause. See ✎.
- Check that they did not put a comma before the adverb clause (*as the stranger …*). Rule: **MC AC**, or mid-sentence adverb clauses are not set off with commas.
- If they put a comma in the phrase *small white square*, have them apply the adjective test: **1)** *white, small square* sounds awkward; **2)** *small and white square* also sounds awkward. These are therefore cumulative adjectives and should not have a comma.

End marks. This is a statement so add a period.

✎ **Teacher's note.** This *who* clause takes commas because it is nonessential; it simply adds information without affecting the meaning of the main clause.

Grammar Notations

Subjects and verbs. *men watched, who lay, stranger shot.*

Clauses and sentence openers.

- MC: *Robin's men … watched.*
- DC (w-w clause): *who lay off to the side of the prodigious oak.*
- AC (adverb clause): *as the stranger shot at the small white square fixed to its front.*

DAY 2

#3 ly   MC S   V   prep   cc   V   prep

deftly [he drew the arrow to his cheek and loosed the shaft], sending it so straight down the

       DC   S   V   prep

path (that it **cleft** the mark in the very center).

Fixes

Indent. Is this a new topic, speaker, place, or time? Answer: No.

Commas. Ask students if they added commas or other punctuation and why. Answer: No comma before cc and because it joins two verbs (*drew* and *loosed*). Rule: **MC cc 2nd verb.**

End marks. This is a statement so add a period.

Grammar Notations

Subjects and verbs. *he drew … loosed, it cleft.*

If students mark *sending* as a verb, simply mention that it is not a verb here because it is not coupled with a subject and helping verb. *See* ♡.

Coordinating conjunctions. *and.* Ask: What words does this cc join? Answer: two verbs, *drew* and *loosed.*

Clauses and sentence openers.

- #3 -ly adverb opener: *Deftly.*
- MC: *he drew the arrow to his cheek and loosed the shaft.*
- DC: *that it cleft the mark in the very center.*

cleft: split or divided as if by a cutting blow (past tense of *to cleave*)

Note: **To loose** as a verb means *to let loose.* In other words, *the stranger shot the arrow.* This verb is often confused with **to lose**, which means *to be deprived of.*

♡ **Grammar lovers.** *sending* is a participle that functions as an adjective here.

                                   Institute for Excellence in Writing

DAY 3

    #1 MC V   *AC cl S   V   MC V   S   #1 MC*   *S   V*

¶ "aha! [beat that] (if you can)!" [cried he]. ¶ [even the yeomen clapped ~~there~~/their /~~they're~~

prep

hands at such an unexpected, **keen** shot].

Fixes

keen: sharp; piercing

Indent. Is this a new topic, speaker, place, or time? Answer: Yes, twice: a) a new speaker and paragraph; b) a new topic by pulling out of his speech and turning to the yeomen's reaction.

Homophones and usage. *their* hands, possessive.

Quotations. Check that students placed quotation marks around the words spoken: *"Aha … can!"*

Since the stranger is speaking excitedly, it is appropriate to end his words with an exclamation, which preempts the normal comma between a quotation and its speaking verb. A comma here is also acceptable (*"Beat that if you can," cried he*), but do not use both.

Commas. Discuss the comma rules as follows. Be sure your students can explain why they added or omitted commas.

- No comma before the adverb clause (*if you can*) because mid-sentence adverb clauses do not take commas. Rule: **MC AC.**
- If students did not put the comma in *unexpected, keen shot*, ask them to apply the tests. 1) *keen, unexpected shot* sounds right; 2) *unexpected and keen shot* also sounds right. Both tests work, so these are coordinate adjectives and need a comma.

End marks. This is a statement so add a period.

Grammar Notations

Subjects and verbs. *Beat* (with the subject, *you*, understood), *you can, cried he, yeomen clapped.*

Prepositional phrases. *at such an unexpected, keen shot.*

Ask students to show how this fits the pattern: **preposition** (*at*) **+ noun** (*shot*) **and no verb in between** (middle words are not verbs: *such*=adverb, *an*=article, *unexpected*=adjective, *keen*=adjective).

Clauses and sentence openers.

- #1 subject opener and MC: *Beat that.*
- AC (adverb clause): *if you can.*
- MC: *cried he.*
- #1 subject opener and MC: *Even the yeomen clapped their hands at such an unexpected, keen shot.*
  - ✧ **Advanced.** *Even* is an adverb, which does not affect the main clause. Students may count this as either a #1 opener since *even* is so short or as a #T (transition) opener.

DAY 4

¶ taking up his bow and nocking an arrow with care, [robin hood shot with **unparalleled** skill]. [straight flew the arrow], piercing right through the stranger's shaft and splintering it.

(Grammar notation labels above the sentence: cc, prep, MC, S, V, prep, MC, V, S, prep, cc)

Fixes

Indent. Is this a new topic, speaker, place, or time? Answer: Yes, a new topic, Robin's turn.

Commas. Ask: Did you add commas or other punctuation, and why? Answer: None are needed. If students added a comma before either cc, point out that in both cases *and* joins only two -ing words, not main clauses or three items in a series. Notice that the words that cc's join have to be the same parts of speech, in this case, -ing words (present participles). *See* ♡ **1.**

End marks. This is a statement so add a period.

Grammar Notations

Subjects and verbs. *Robin Hood shot, flew arrow.*

✧ **Advanced.** If students mark any of the -ing words as verbs, just point out that they are not functioning as verbs here even though they express action. They need a subject (as in "The arrow was piercing" or "The arrow pierced") in order to function as a verb. *See* ♡ **1.**

Prepositional phrases. *with care, with unparalleled skill, through the stranger's shaft.* *See* ♡ **2.**

Clauses and sentence openers.

✧ **Advanced.** #4 -ing sentence opener, a participial phrase: *Taking up his bow and nocking an arrow with care.* You do not need to teach this, but if your students have learned about #4 openers, you could show this example.

▪ MC: *Robin Hood shot with unparalleled skill.*

▪ #1 subject opener (leads with MC though not with the subject): *Straight flew the arrow.*

Style

If desired, have your students identify the best dress-ups from this week's sentences. Discuss their answers. Choose among:

Strong verbs. *fixed, cleft.*

Quality adjectives. *prodigious, keen, unparalleled.*

-ly adverbs. No -ly dress-ups this week.

---

unparalleled: unequaled; unmatched

To **nock** an arrow is to cut a notch or groove at its end in order to hold it in place. Robin Hood shot his arrow straight down the middle of the shaft of the stranger's arrow, splitting it into separate pieces.

♡ **1. Grammar lovers.** These present participles all function as adjectives. *Taking* and *nocking* are #4 -ing sentence openers modifying *Robin Hood*, and *piercing* and *splintering* have the same function only come after the noun they modify (*arrow*) instead of before it.

♡ **2. Grammar lovers.** The word *up* does not start a prepositional phrase (*up his bow* does not make sense) but attaches to the verbal: *taking up.*

STUDENT REWRITE

Meanwhile, Robin's men, who lay off to the side of the prodigious oak, watched as the stranger shot at the small white square fixed to its front. Deftly he drew the arrow to his cheek and loosed the shaft, sending it so straight down the path that it cleft the mark in the very center.

"Aha! Beat that if you can!" cried he.

Even the yeomen clapped their hands at such an unexpected, keen shot.

Taking up his bow and nocking an arrow with care, Robin Hood shot with unparalleled skill. Straight flew the arrow, piercing right through the stranger's shaft and splintering it.

Week 30

No New Concepts

LEARN IT

There are no new concepts this week. See if you can answer the questions below. If not, check your grammar cards for the answers.

1. Explain when to use *to*, *too*, and *two*.

2. Explain when to use *its* and *it's*.

Do you remember what these vocabulary words mean? If not, look them up in your vocabulary list in the back of your notebook.

- score
- steadfast
- stout
- trouncing
- ducking
- considerable
- convulsing
- hark

> **Teacher's answers**
>
> **1.** *To* is the preposition: *to the right; to the store*. It is also the "to + verb" form of a verb: *to rush; to seize*. *Two* is the number, 2. *Too* means *also* or *too much*.
>
> **2.** *its* = possessive
> *it's* = it is (think it⁺s)

DAY 1

#1 MC   *S*   *V*   *prep*   *cc*   *V*   *prep*   *DC*

[then ~~than~~ all the yeomen leaped to ~~there~~/their ~~they're~~ feet and shouted for joy] (that

S   *V*   *V*

~~there~~/their ~~they're~~ master had shot so **flawlessly**).

Fixes

flawlessly: with no faults; perfectly

Indent. Is this a new topic, speaker, place, or time? Answer: No.

Homophones and usage.

- *then*, meaning *next* or *immediately afterward*.
- *their* feet, *their* master: possessives.

Commas. Ask: Did you add commas or other punctuation, and why? Answer: No needed commas.

If students added a comma before the cc *and*, ask them to tell you what it joins and the rule why no comma. Answer: two verbs (*leaped and shouted*). Rule: **MC cc 2nd verb**.

End marks. This is a statement so add a period.

Grammar Notations

Subjects and verbs. *yeomen leaped … shouted, master had shot* (*had* = helping verb).

Clauses and sentence openers.

- #1 subject opener and MC (ignoring the opening adverb): *Then all the yeomen leaped to their feet and shouted for joy.*
- DC: *that their master had shot so flawlessly.*

DAY 2

#2 prep · prep · MC V · S · MC S V · #1 MC
¶ "by the <u>great yew bow</u> of <u>saint</u> <u>withold</u>," [cried the stranger],"[that is a shot indeed]! [never

V S · V · prep · #3 ly MC · S V V · cc
have i <u>witnessed</u> its~~it's~~ <u>like</u> in all my <u>life</u>]! [truly i will be your~~you're~~ man **henceforth** and **ay**]."

Fixes

Indent. Is this a new topic, speaker, place, or time? Answer: Yes, a new speaker.

Capitalization. *By, Saint Withold, Never, I, Truly, I.* Do not capitalize *that* because it continues the sentence in his speech.

Homophones and usage.

- *its* like, the possessive, with *like* meaning match or equal.
- *your* man, the possessive.

Quotations. Check that students placed quotation marks around the words spoken: *"By ... Withold"* ... *"that ... ay."*

Commas. Ask: Did you add commas or other punctuation, and why?

- Ask if the adjectives in *great yew bow* are coordinate (comma) or cumulative (no comma). Tests: 1) *yew, great bow?* Yuck! 2) *great and yew bow?* Just as bad! Both sound awkward, so these adjectives are cumulative and do not take a comma.
- Commas with the interrupter: *"Withold," cried the stranger, "that ... ."*

    Ask: What is the pattern for using these commas? Answer: **quotation + comma + interrupter with speaking verb** (*cried*) **+ comma + rest of quoted sentence**.

- If students put a comma before the cc *and* (*henceforth and ay*), explain that it is joining two adverbs and ask them for the rule.

    The rule is to use no comma between only two items in a series unless they are main clauses. Pattern: **a and b.**

End marks. This is a statement so add a period inside the closing quotation marks.

Grammar Notations

Subjects and verbs. *cried stranger, that is, have I witnessed, I will be* (helping verbs: *have, will*).

- ✧ **Advanced.** *That* is a pronoun functioning as the subject of a main clause with *is* its verb.

Clauses and sentence openers.

- #2 prepositional phrase opener: *By the great yew bow of Saint Withold.*
- MC: *cried the stranger.*
- MC: *that is a shot indeed.*
- #1 subject opener (ignoring the adverb *Never*) and MC: *Never have I witnessed its like in all my life.*
- #3 -ly adverb opener: *Truly.*
- MC: *I will be your man henceforth and ay.*

henceforth: from this point forward; from now on

ay: ever or always. This word is pronounced like the long *a* sound; it is now archaic, or no longer used. Contrast the word *aye*, which is pronounced like a long *i* sound and means *yes*.

Yew, pronounced like *you*, is a kind of evergreen tree.

DAY 3

#1 MC   S   V   V   MC   V

¶ "[then i have gained a superior man this day]," [affirmed ~~there~~/their ~~they're~~ **sportive**

S   (Q)   V   S V

leader]. "[what name do you go by], good fellow?"

Fixes

sportive: playful and merry

Indent. Is this a new topic, speaker, place, or time? Answer: Yes, a new speaker and paragraph.

Homophones and usage. *their leader*, possessive.

Quotations. Check that students placed quotation marks around the words spoken: *"Then … day," … "What … fellow?"*

  ✧ **Advanced.** The period after *leader* is correct because he is speaking two separate sentences, which need a period to connect them.

Commas. Ask: Did you add commas or other punctuation, and why?

  Comma before *affirmed*. Rule: **quotation + comma + speaking verb** (*affirmed*).

  Comma before *good fellow*, a NDA.

End marks. Robin is asking a question, so close with a question mark inside the quotation marks.

Grammar Notations

Subjects and verbs. *I have gained, affirmed leader, do you go by* (*by* is part of the verb phrase *go by*, meaning *be known by*).

  Ask: Which are helping verbs? Answer: *have*, which helps *gained*; *do*, which helps *go by*.

Clauses and sentence openers.

- #1 subject opener (ignoring the adverb *Then*, which does not affect the clause) and MC: *Then I have gained a superior man this day.*
- MC: *affirmed their sportive leader.*
- Q: *What name do you go by.*

    This is a new opener that has not been discussed before: Explain that questions can be labeled "Q." If desired, add it to the Sentence Opener grammar card.

DAY 4

#5 *AC*   *cl*   *S*   *V*   *MC S*   *V*   *MC*   *V*   *S*

¶ "(where i come from), [men call me john little]," [responded the stranger **proudly**].

Fixes

Indent. Is this a new topic, speaker, place, or time? Answer: Yes, a new speaker and paragraph.

Quotations. Check that students placed quotation marks around the words spoken: *"Where … Little."*

Commas. Ask: Did you add commas? If so, explain why.

Comma after #5 opener: *Where I come from, men* … . Rule: **AC, MC**.

Comma before *responded*. Rule: **quotation + comma + speaking verb** (*responded*).

End marks. This is a statement so add a period.

Grammar Notations

Subjects and verbs. *I come from* (adverb goes with verb), *men call, responded stranger*.

Clauses and sentence openers.

- #5 opener and AC (adverb clause): *Where I come from*.
- MC: *men call me John Little*.
- MC: *responded the stranger proudly*.

Style

If desired, have your students identify the best dress-ups from this week's sentences. Discuss their answers. Choose among:

Strong verbs. *leaped, witnessed, affirmed*.

Quality adjectives. *superior, sportive*.

-ly adverbs (not the first word of any sentence). *flawlessly, proudly*.

proudly: with pleasure over something regarded as honorable to the speaker. This word sometimes has a negative connotation, implying too much pride or arrogance, but Little John takes appropriate pride in his given name.

STUDENT REWRITE

Since this passage continues without another indentation, be sure students continue writing where last week's passage left off.

Then all the yeomen leaped to their feet and shouted for joy that their master had shot so flawlessly.

"By the great yew bow of Saint Withold," cried the stranger, "that is a shot indeed! Never have I witnessed its like in all my life! Truly I will be your man henceforth and ay."

"Then I have gained a superior man this day," affirmed their sportive leader. "What name do you go by, good fellow?"

"Where I come from, men call me John Little," responded the stranger proudly.

Week 31

No New Concepts

LEARN IT

There are no new concepts this week. See if you can answer the questions below. If not, check your grammar cards for the answers.

1. What are the comma rules for items in a series?

2. What is the comma rule for a #5 clausal opener?

Do you remember what these vocabulary words mean? If not, look them up in your vocabulary list in the back of your notebook.

- lucrative
- succulent
- nettled
- conceded
- stoop
- dub
- thrash
- alacrity

Teacher's answers

1. Three or more items in a series take commas, but not two or more (except for two MCs). Put the comma before the cc, never after.

   Patterns: **a, b, and c**
   a and b

2. Always use commas after #5 clausal openers, even if they are short.

Page 64, *Fix It! Grammar:* **Robin Hood, Student Book 2**

Institute for Excellence in Writing

DAY 1

In your rewrite, combine the first two sentences with a *who* clause and commas around it. Also, Will is not finished speaking.

#1 MC   S   *who* V   *spoke up*   MC S V

¶ [then will stutely, ~~spoke up. he~~ (enjoyed a humorous **quip**), .] "no, little stranger, [i do not

V   cc   V   V

like your ~~you're~~ name but would not have it any other way].

Combine sentences with a who

Who-which clauses. Check that students combined the sentences correctly with commas around the new *who* clause.

Ask: What noun does *who* describe and where is it? Answer: *Will Stutely*, which is immediately before the *who* clause. *See ✎.*

Fixes

Indent. Is this a new topic, speaker, place, or time? Answer: Yes, a new speaker.

Homophones and usage. *your name*, the possessive.

Quotations. Check that students placed quotation marks at the beginning of Will's speech but not at the end because he is not finished: *"No … way.*

Commas. Ask: Did you add other commas, and why?

- Commas around *little stranger*, NDA.
- No comma before *but* because it joins only two verbs (*do like* and *would have*), not two main clauses. Rule: **MC cc 2nd verb**.

End marks. This is a statement so add a period. If students prefer an exclamation, that works, too.

Grammar Notations

Subjects and verbs. *Will Stutely spoke up* (the adverb *up* is part of the verb phrase), *who enjoyed, I do like … would have.*

Ask: Which of these are helping verbs? Answer: *do*, which helps *like*; *would*, which helps *have.*

Clauses and sentence openers.

- #1 subject opener (ignoring the adverb *Then*) and MC: *Then Will Stutely … spoke up.*
  - ✦ **Advanced.** Students may confuse this with a speaking verb that needs a comma before the quotation it sets up, but this is a complete thought—*he spoke up*—rather than a verb like *said* setting up the quotation. Contrast this: *He remarked, "No, I do not like … ."*
- DC (w-w clause): *who enjoyed a humorous quip.*
- MC: *I do not like your name but would not have it any other way.*

quip: witty remark

✎ **Teacher's note.** This *who* clause is nonessential and needs commas because it simply adds information but does not identify the noun it describes more specifically. If you remove it from the sentence, Will Stutely still spoke up; the main clause information does not change.

DAY 2

#5 AC cl   S   V   cc   MC   S   V   prep
(since 'little' is indeed your /you're true name)—and clearly [your /you're small of bone and

                MC S   V   V   V   cc MC S   V   V
tendons]—[you shall fittingly be named little john], and [i will be your godfather]."

Since the story has made the point that Little John is not little but a tall, husky man, Will Stutely is being humorous by saying his size matches his name.

He is also playing with the idea that Little John is the new infant in the family whom they have humorously christened by renaming him Little John instead of John Little. Will becomes, then, the godfather (guardian or sponsor) of this new member of the family.

tendons: the tissue that connects muscles and bones

Fixes

Indent. Is this a new topic, speaker, place, or time? Answer: No new topic because Will is still speaking and on the same subject.

Homophones and usage.

- *your true name*, the possessive.
- *you're small of bone*, the contraction meaning *you are* small of bone.

Quotations. Check that students put quotation marks only at the end since this speech is a continuation: *Since … godfather."*

Commas. Ask: Did you add commas? If so, explain why.

- ✧ **Advanced.** The first cc *and* does not connect two items but is a digression in his thoughts (an aside). The dashes help communicate that this is a side thought. *See* ✐.
- ✧ **Advanced.** Usually there would be a comma at the end of the #5 opener after *name* (Rule: **AC, MC**), but the dashes to set off the aside preempt the normal comma. *See* ✐.
- No comma before the second cc *and* because this cc joins two nouns (*bones* and *tendons*).
- Comma before the third cc *and* because it joins two main clauses: *you shall be named Little John, and I will be your godfather.* Rule: **MC, cc MC**.

End marks. This is a statement so add a period inside the closing quotation marks.

✐ **Teacher's note.** The em dashes (longest dash marks) correctly set off a thought that interrupts the main flow of the sentence. Em dashes can also be used to draw attention to something.

Grammar Notations

Subjects and verbs. *'Little' is, you're (you are), you shall be named, I will be.*

Ask: Which of these are helping verbs? Answer: *shall be* (helps *named*); *will* (helps *be*).

- ✧ **Advanced.** Words referred to as words are italicized or put in quotation marks. In quotes or italics, "Little" means "the word Little" or "the name Little." In this case, single quotes (' ') are used for a quotation within another quotation.

Clauses and sentence openers.

- #5 opener and AC (adverb clause): *Since 'Little' is indeed your true name.*
- MC: *you're small of bone and tendons.*
- MC: *you shall fittingly be named Little John.*
- MC: *I will be your godfather.*

DAY 3

#1 MC   S   cc   S   V   AC cl   S   V

¶ [then robin hood and his entire band **guffawed** out loud] (until the stranger began to grow

enraged).

Fixes

Indent. Is this a new topic, speaker, place, or time? Answer: Yes, a new topic. Will is no longer speaking and the focus is on the men's response.

Commas. Ask: Did you add commas? Explain why.

No comma before *and* since it joins only two nouns (*Robin Hood* and *band*).

No comma before *until*. Rule: **MC AC**, or mid-sentence adverb clauses do not take commas.

End marks. This is a statement so add a period.

> **guffawed:** laughed loudly and boisterously

Grammar Notations

Subjects and verbs. *Robin Hood ... band guffawed, stranger began.*

Point out that *guffawed* has a compound subject: *Robin Hood and his band.*

Adverb clause starter (subordinating conjunction). *until.* This is not one of the www words but it starts an adverb clause. If students do not mark it, simply point it out, show the subject and verb, and help them bracket the clause.

Clauses and sentence openers.

- #1 subject opener (not counting the adverb *Then*) and MC: *Then Robin Hood and his entire band guffawed out loud.*

- AC (adverb clause): *until the stranger began to grow enraged.*

DAY 4

Choose the best punctuation after *staff*.

#1 MC   S   V   prep   prep   prep   MC   V

¶ " [you dare to make a fool of me after witnessing my skill with the staff]!" [snapped

S   #1 MC S   V   V   cc MC   S   V   V

john little]. " [you will have sore bones], and [such misfortune will come **posthaste**]."

Fixes

Indent. Is this a new topic, speaker, place, or time? Answer: Yes, a new speaker.

Quotations. Check that students placed quotation marks around the words spoken but not the intervening narrative: *"You dare … staff!" … "You will have … posthaste."*

Since he snaps an angry response, which is exclamatory, use an exclamation mark instead of the usual comma after *staff*. Also, do not capitalize *snapped*. Since it sets up the quotation before, it is part of the same sentence.

Commas with cc's. Comma before the cc *and* because it joins two main clauses. Rule: **MC, cc MC**.

End marks. He ends with a statement so add a period + closing quotation marks.

Grammar Notations

Subjects and verbs. *You dare, snapped John Little, You will have, misfortune will come.* Ask: Which of these are helping verbs? Answer: *will* (helps *have*), *will* (helps *come*).

Prepositional phrases. *of me, after witnessing, with the staff.*

   ✦ **Advanced.** If students are confused, explain that *witnessing* is formed from a verb but functions as a noun here (the object of the preposition).

Clauses and sentence openers.
- #1 subject opener and MC: *You dare make a fool of me after witnessing my skill with the staff.*
- MC: *snapped John Little.*
- #1 subject opener and MC: *You will have sore bones.*
- MC: *such misfortune will come upon you posthaste.*

Style

If desired, have your students identify the best dress-ups from their sentences this week. Discuss their answers. Choose among:

Strong verbs. *guffawed, snapped.*

Quality adjectives. *humorous, enraged.*

   ✦ **Advanced.** If students do not recognize that *enraged* from Day 3 functions as an adjective, there is no need to teach it now. *See* ♡.

-ly adverbs (not the first word of any sentence). *fittingly.*

---

posthaste: with the greatest possible speed or promptness

✎ **Teacher's note.** Discuss parts of speech or clauses before discussing commas, as needed.

♡ **Grammar lovers.** Even though *enraged* follows an infinitive, it acts like any subject complement after a linking verb (*grow enraged*).

STUDENT REWRITE

Then Will Stutely, who enjoyed a humorous quip, spoke up. "No, little stranger, I do not like your name but would not have it any other way. Since 'Little' is indeed your true name—and clearly you're small of bone and tendons—you shall fittingly be named Little John, and I will be your godfather."

Then Robin Hood and his entire band guffawed out loud until the stranger began to grow enraged.

"You dare to make a fool of me after witnessing my skill with the staff!" snapped John Little. "You will have sore bones, and such misfortune will come posthaste."

Week 32

No New Concepts

LEARN IT

There are no new concepts this week. See if you can answer the questions below. If not, check your grammar cards for the answers.

1. What is the pattern for a prepositional phrase?

2. What part of speech must the prepositional phrase not have?

Do you remember what these vocabulary words mean? If not, look them up in your vocabulary list in the back of your notebook.

- prodigious
- cleft
- keen
- unparalleled
- flawlessly
- henceforth
- sportive
- proudly

> **Teacher's answers**
>
> 1. preposition + noun
>
>   It begins with a preposition and ends with a noun.
>
> 2. no verb

Page 66, *Fix It! Grammar:* Robin Hood, Student Book 2

Institute for Excellence in Writing

DAY 1

Robin is not finished speaking.

¶ "no, my **capital** fellow," [urged robin hood], "[calm your, ~~you're~~ rage], for [the name

actually fits you well]. from this day [we will address you as little john].

Fixes

Indent. Is this a new topic, speaker, place, or time? Answer: Yes, a new speaker and paragraph.

Capitalization. Do not capitalize *calm* because it continues a sentence in his speech.

Homophones and usage. *your rage,* the possessive.

Quotations. Check that students placed quotation marks around the words spoken but not at the end since Robin has not finished his speech: *"No ... fellow" ... "calm ... Little John.*

Commas. Ask: Did you add commas, and why?

- Set off with commas *my capital fellow* because it is a noun of direct address (NDA).
- Add commas to set off the interrupter because it has a speaking verb setting up the quotation and because Robin has not finished his sentence: *"fellow," urged Robin Hood, "calm ... .*
- Check that the comma after *fellow* is inside the closing quotation marks.

    The comma after *fellow* is there for two reasons: the NDA and the quotation.

- Comma before the cc *for* to join two main clauses with a comma plus coordinating conjunction: **MC, cc MC**. Remind students that a cc is not strong enough by itself to hold two MCs together. It also needs a comma.

End marks. This is a statement so add a period.

Grammar Notations

Subjects and verbs. *urged Robin Hood, calm* (with the subject *you* understood), *name fits, we will address* (*will* is a helping verb).

Prepositional phrases. *From this day, as Little John.*

If students labeled *as* a subordinating conjunction, show them the preposition list and ask them to find *as* on it. Then ask them which pattern fits: an adverb clause, which must have a subject and verb; or a prepositional phrase, which does not have a verb. Since there is no verb in *as Little John,* this *as* is a preposition. *See ✎.*

Clauses and sentence openers.

- MC: *urged Robin Hood.*
- MC: *calm your rage.*
- MC: *the name actually fits you well.*
- #2 prepositional phrase opener: *From this day.*
- MC: *we will address you as Little John.*

capital: excellent or first-rate.

Note that this is the same spelling for the capital city of a state or an important city in a country. See also Week 5 Day 4 (page 36), where **capital** meant *punishable by death: a capital offense.*

✎ **Teacher's note.** Remind students that words can function as more than one part of speech. We have to look at how they are used in the sentence to determine their function.

DAY 2

#6 vss
MC   V   *#1 MC S   V   V*   *prep*

[come, my merry men]! [we will prepare a **christening** feast for our new, fair infant]."

Fixes

Indent. Is this a new topic, speaker, place, or time? Answer: No, Robin is still speaking and on the same topic.

Quotations. No open quotation marks since it is part of the same speech but close quotation marks to signal the end of Robin's speech: *infant.*"

Commas. Ask: Did you add commas, and why?

- Set *my Merry Men* off with a comma because it is a noun of direct address (NDA).
- If students did not add a comma between *new* and *fair*, have them try the two tests: 1) *our fair, new infant* sounds right; 2) *our new and fair infant* sounds right. Therefore, these are coordinate adjectives and need a comma.

End marks. This is a statement so add a period inside the closing quotation marks.

christening: a baptism ceremony that includes giving a name to the child

---

Grammar Notations

Subjects and verbs. *Come* (subject, *you*, is understood), *we will prepare* (*will* is a helping verb).

Prepositional phrases. *for our new, fair infant.*

Ask students to explain why this *for* is a preposition instead of a coordinating conjunction. Answer: It fits the preposition pattern: *for* = preposition; *infant* = noun; none of the middle words is a verb. Also, if it were a coordinating conjunction, it would be joining two or more items, which it is not.

Clauses and sentence openers.

- #6 vss and MC: *Come, my Merry Men.*
- #1 subject opener and MC: *We will prepare a christening feast for our new, fair infant.*

DAY 3

¶ turning ~~there~~/their ~~they're~~ backs upon the stream, [the men plunged into the forest and

retraced ~~there~~/their ~~they're~~ steps] (until they reached ~~there~~/their ~~they're~~ dwelling deep in

the ancient woodland), (which had never yet been **surveyed**).

(Grammar markings above the text: prep, MC, S, V, prep, cc, V, AC cl, S, V, prep, DC, S/w-w, V, V, V)

Fixes

Indent. Is this a new topic, speaker, place, or time? Answer: Yes, a new place.

Homophones and usage. *their backs, their steps, their dwelling*: all possessives.

Commas. Ask: Did you add commas, and why?

Ask: Why should there not be a comma before *and*? Answer: It joins a compound verb (*plunged* and *retraced*) with one subject. Rule: **MC cc 2nd verb.**

Ask: Why should there not be a comma before *until*? Answer: Mid-sentence adverb clauses do not take commas. Rule: **MC AC.** *See* ✏ **1.**

End marks. This is a statement so add a period.

Grammar Notations

Subjects and verbs. *men plunged … retraced, they reached, which had been surveyed.* Ask: Which are helping verbs? Answer: *had been*, which helps *surveyed.*

***Who-which* clauses.** Ask: What noun does this *which* clause describe and where is it? Answer: *woodland*, which comes immediately before *which*. *See* ✏ **2.**

Clauses and sentence openers.

- ✧ **Advanced.** #4 -ing participial phrase opener: *Turning their backs upon the stream.* Students do not need to mark these.
- MC: *the men plunged into the forest and retraced their steps.*
- AC (adverb clause): *until they reached their dwelling deep in the ancient woodland.* *See* ✏ **3.**
- DC (w-w clause): *which had never yet been surveyed.*

surveyed: the extent, boundaries, and physical details of an area determined by using precise measurements

✏ **1. Teacher's note.** Although *until* is not one of the standard www words, it can serve as a clause starter (subordinating conjunction).

✏ **2. Teacher's note.** This is a nonessential *which* clause so takes a comma.

✏ **3. Teacher's note.** Did your students remember that *until* can start an adverb clause? If not, simply point it out, show the subject and verb, and help them place parentheses around the clause.

DAY 4

#2 *prep*   *MC S   V   V*   *prep*   *cc*   *prep*   *cc*   *V*

in a clearing [they had built huts from bark and branches of trees and **fashioned** couches

prep   *prep*   *#1 MC S prep*   *V*

of soft brush covered with deerskin]. [an oak with branches spreading broadly around stood

there ~~their / they're~~].

Fixes

Indent. Is this a new topic, speaker, place, or time? Answer: No.

Homophones and usage. *There* means *in that place.*

Commas. Ask: Did you add commas, and why? See ✎.

  Ask: Why should there not be a comma before the first *and*? Answer: It joins only two nouns (*bark* and *branches*), not three items in a series.

  Ask: Why should there not be a comma before the second *and*? Answer: It joins two verbs (*built* and *fashioned*) to the same subject (*they*). Rule: **MC cc 2nd verb**.

End marks. This is a statement so add a period.

Grammar Notations

Subjects and verbs. *they had built … fashioned, stood … oak (an oak stood).*

  ✧ **Advanced.** If students mark *covered* or *spreading* as verbs, you might explain that they derive from verbs but function as adjectives here. Contrast the same words used as verbs: *soft brush was covered with deerskin; the branches were spreading around.*

Prepositional phrases. *In a clearing, from bark and branches, of trees, of soft brush, with deerskin, with branches.*

  ✧ **Advanced.** *around* is an adverb at the end of this sentence, not a preposition. You can tell this because it is not in a prepositional phrase.

Clauses and sentence openers.

- #2 prepositional phrase opener: *In a clearing.*
- MC: *they had built huts from bark and branches of trees and fashioned couches of soft brush covered with deerskin.*
- #1 subject opener and MC: *An oak with branches spreading broadly around stood there.*

Style

Have your students identify the best dress-ups from this week's sentences. Discuss their answers. Choose among:

Strong verb: *urged, plunged, retraced, fashioned.*

Quality adjective: *capital, ancient.*

-ly adverb: *broadly.*

---

fashioned: made; gave a particular form to

✎ **Teacher's note.** Because the cc's are in close succession, students may misread this as a series of three or more items in a row. Guide them to see what the cc's actually join, reminding them that cc's must join the same parts of speech.

STUDENT REWRITE

"No, my capital fellow," urged Robin Hood, "calm your rage, for the name actually fits you well. From this day we will address you as Little John. Come, my Merry Men! We will prepare a christening feast for our new, fair infant."

Turning their backs upon the stream, the men plunged into the forest and retraced their steps until they reached their dwelling deep in the ancient woodland, which had never yet been surveyed. In a clearing they had built huts from bark and branches of trees and fashioned couches of soft brush covered with deerskin. An oak with branches spreading broadly around stood there.

Week 33

No New Concepts

LEARN IT

There are no new concepts this week. See if you can answer the questions below. If not, check your grammar cards for the answers.

1. What is a main clause?

2. What do MCs usually start with?

3. What is a dependent clause?

4. What words do DCs usually start with?

Do you remember what these vocabulary words mean? If not, look them up in your vocabulary list in the back of your notebook.

- quip
- tendons
- guffawed
- posthaste
- capital
- christening
- surveyed
- fashioned

Teacher's answers

1. MC = a group of words with a subject and verb that *can* stand alone as a sentence

2. The subject or an article (*a, an, the*) and/or adjectives + subject

3. DC = a group of words with a subject and verb that *cannot* stand alone as a sentence

4. www.asia.b words, *who, which, that*

DAY 1

♡1

#2 *prep*   #1 *MC V*   *S prep*   *DC cl*   *S*   *V*   *V*

beneath the oak [was a seat of **downy** green moss], (where robin hood was positioned to sit),

cc   *prep*

feasting and enjoying merrymaking with his fearless men.

Fixes

Indent. Is this a new topic, speaker, place, or time? Answer: No, the passage continues to describe the Merry Men in their home deep in the woods.

Commas.

Ask: Should there be a comma between the two adjectives in *downy green moss*? Short answer: No. Apply the test: 1) *green, downy moss* sounds awkward; 2) *downy and green moss* also sounds awkward. Therefore, these are cumulative adjectives and should not have a comma.

Ask: Should there be a comma before *and*? Answer: No, because this cc joins only two items (*feasting* and *enjoying*), not three or more. Pattern: **a and b.**

End marks. This is a statement so add a period.

Grammar Notations

Subjects and verbs. *was … seat, Robin Hood was positioned.*

✧ **Advanced.** If students mark the -ing words, point out that they are not verbs here because none of them has a subject or helping verb. *See* ♡ **1.**

Prepositional phrases. *Beneath the oak, of downy green moss, with his fearless men.*

Clauses and sentence openers.

- #2 prepositional phrase opener: *Beneath the oak.*
- MC: *was a seat of downy green moss.*
- DC: *where Robin Hood was positioned to sit. See* ♡ **2.**

downy: fluffy and soft like down, the soft under-feathers of birds

♡ **1. Grammar lovers.** *Feasting* and *enjoying* function as adjectives; *merrymaking* functions as a noun.

♡ **2. Grammar lovers.** This DC is again an adjective instead of adverb clause because it modifies the noun (*moss*) right before it. The comma before *where* is correct because its clause is nonessential. If we remove it from the sentence, it does not change the meaning of the rest of the sentence. See Adjective Clauses; Sentences, Clauses, and Phrases; Grammar Glossary, page G-17.

DAY 2

#1 MC   S   V   prep   *DC* S/w-w   V   V   prep   prep

¶ [here they found the rest of the band], (who had recently returned with a **brace** of well-fed

        #1 MC   S   V   cc prep   V

deer). [then they built great fires and after a time roasted the does].

brace: a pair; two of certain game

Fixes

Indent. Is this a new topic, speaker, place, or time? Answer: Arguably, yes. The last several sentences are wrapping up the story and ending it with a feast. It is also fine not to start a new paragraph here. Let students choose.

Spelling. Check that students spell the plural of *doe* correctly: *does*. Even though it is spelled like the verb *does* (e.g., *he does*), it is pronounced with a long *o* sound.

Commas with cc's. Ask: Should there be a comma before the cc *and*? Answer: No, because it joins only two verbs (*built* and *roasted*), not two main clauses or three items in a series. Rule: **MC cc 2nd verb.** See ✐.

End marks. This is a statement so add a period.

✐ **Teacher's note.** Remind students that cc's must join the same parts of speech. (E.g., two verbs, two nouns, etc.)

Grammar Notations

Subjects and verbs. *they found, who had returned, they built … roasted.*

Prepositional phrases. *of the band, with a brace, of well-fed deer, after a time.*

Who-which clauses. Ask: What noun comes immediately before the *who* clause? Answer: *band*, which *who* refers back to.

Clauses and sentence openers.

- #1 subject opener and MC (ignoring the adverb *Here* at the beginning): *Here they found the rest of the band.*
- DC (w-w clause): *who had recently returned with a brace of well-fed deer.*
- #1 subject opener and MC (ignoring the adverb *Then* at the beginning): *Then they built great fires and after a time roasted the does.*

Institute for Excellence in Writing

DAY 3

#1 MC S   V   prep   AC cl   S   V   V   MC S   V   prep

[they brought forth a large barrel of ale]. (when the feast was prepared), [they settled down on

prep

the **verdant** green in the clearing].

Fixes

Indent. Is this a new topic, speaker, place, or time? Answer: No.

Commas. Ask: Did you add commas, and why? Answer: Comma needed after *prepared*.
Rule: **AC, MC**, or commas follow #5 clausal openers.

End marks. This is a statement so add a period.

verdant: covered with growing plants or grass

Grammar Notations

Subjects and verbs. *they brought* (the adverb *forth* goes with this verb), *feast was prepared* (*was* is a helping verb), *they settled* (the adverb *down* goes with this verb).

Clauses and sentence openers.

- #1 subject opener and MC: *They brought forth a large barrel of ale.*
- #5 opener and AC (adverb clause): *When the feast was prepared.*
- MC: *they settled down on the verdant green in the clearing.*

DAY 4

#1 MC   *S*   *V*   *prep*   *#2 prep*   *MC S*   *V*   *second*

[robin hood placed little john at his right hand]. from that time forward [he was to be ~~2nd~~

prep   *AC cl*   *S*   *V*   *V*   *prep*

in command] (as robin had promised after ~~there~~/their ~~they're~~ **valorous interchange**

prep

in the forest).

Fixes

Indent. Is this a new topic, speaker, place, or time? Answer: No.

Numbers. *second.* Spell out ordinal numbers, which indicate an order.

Homophones and usage. *their interchange,* possessive.

Commas. Ask: Should there be a comma before *as*? Answer: No comma is needed with mid-sentence adverb clauses. Rule: **MC AC**.

End marks. This is a statement so add a period.

Grammar Notations

Subjects and verbs. *Robin Hood placed, he was, Robin had promised* (had is a helping verb).

Prepositional phrases. *at his right hand, From that time, in command, after their valorous interchange, in the forest.*

Clauses and sentence openers.
- #1 subject opener and MC: *Robin Hood placed Little John at his right hand.*
- #2 prepositional phrase opener: *From that time forward.*
- MC: *he was to be second in command.*
- AC (adverb clause): *as Robin had promised after their valorous interchange in the forest.*

Style

If desired, have your students identify the best dress-ups from this week's sentences. Discuss their answers. Choose among:

Strong verbs. *positioned.*

Quality adjectives. *downy, fearless, verdant, valorous.*

-ly adverbs (not the first word of any sentence). *recently.*

valorous: courageous; having boldness in facing danger

interchange: a back and forth exchange

STUDENT REWRITE

Since this passage continues without another indentation, be sure students continue writing where last week's passage left off.

Beneath the oak was a seat of downy green moss, where Robin Hood was positioned to sit, feasting and enjoying merrymaking with his fearless men.

Here they found the rest of the band, who had recently returned with a brace of well-fed deer. Then they built great fires and after a time roasted the does. They brought forth a large barrel of ale. When the feast was prepared, they settled down on the verdant green in the clearing. Robin Hood placed Little John at his right hand. From that time forward he was to be second in command as Robin had promised after their valorous interchange in the forest.

Week	Parts of Speech Sentence Elements	Punctuation	Dress-Ups	Sentence Openers	Other Concepts	Vocabulary
1	articles nouns *who-which* clauses	end marks	*who-which* clause		capitals indentation	reigned glades expertise rambled
2	pronouns verbs coordinating conjunctions	commas with items in a series			its/it's	wrath dauntless readily carefree
3		quotations	strong verb		to/two/too there/their/they're	blithely fancifully convivially accosted shoddy
4	adjectives	commas with nouns of direct address (NDAs)			then/than	taunted champion top-notch retorted
5	-ly adverbs prepositions				your/you're	affronted composedly buck wager seethed capital
6			-ly adverb quality adjectives			impulsively hot-blooded opponent toppled hastened
7	subjects clauses and phrases					accounts reserved lavishly vendetta
8	main and dependent clauses		clause starters (www.asia.b words)		lie/lay	adroitly displaced famished narrowly
9						insatiable despoiled oppression yeomen
10				#1 subject #2 prepositional phrase		vowed plundered succor earnestly
11			combining sentences with a who-which	#3 -ly adverb		impoverished audacious escapades magnanimous vicariously

Week	Parts of Speech Sentence Elements	Punctuation	Dress-Ups	Sentence Openers	Other Concepts	Vocabulary
12	coordinate and cumulative adjectives	commas with quotations commas with adjectives before a noun		#5 clausal opener		melodiously gurgling cavorted captivated sport
13				#6 vss		tarry heed ranged spanned
14		commas with adverb clauses				resolutely quickened brusquely interloper
15			additional clause starters		whose/who's Review questions: indents and capitalization	bide tan your hide numskull faintheart
16					Review questions: articles and nouns	lethal craven sparring countered
17					Review questions: FANBOYS and MCs	sturdily hefty genially furtively
18	coordinating conjunctions	comma rule mc, cc mc				deemed towered husky muttered
19		comma rule mc cc 2nd verb				proclaimed catapults adept nimbly
20					Review questions: adjectives	stouter adversary parried leveled
21					Review questions: -ly adverbs and NDAs	deftly thus chafed fatigue
22					Review questions: prepositional phrases and *then/than*	combatant thatching shrewd hairsbreadth dexterous

Week	Parts of Speech Sentence Elements	Punctuation	Dress-Ups	Sentence Openers	Other Concepts	Vocabulary
23					Review questions: more usage	inflamed smote thwacked happenstance sorry predicament
24					rules for writing numbers	gaining his feet wielding hearty scorching clapped
25					Review questions: DCs	faced score steadfast stout
26					Review questions: #6 vss's and DCs	trouncing ducking considerable convulsing hark
27					Review questions: commas	lucrative succulent nettled conceded
28					Review questions: dress-up and more commas	stoop dub thrash alacrity
29					Review questions: numbers and quotations	prodigious cleft keen unparalleled
30					Review questions: more usage	flawlessly henceforth sportive proudly
31					Review questions: more commas	quip tendons guffawed posthaste
32					Review questions: prepositional phrases	capital christening surveyed fashioned
33					Review questions: more clauses	downy brace verdant valorous interchange

Fix It!
Grammar
Glossary

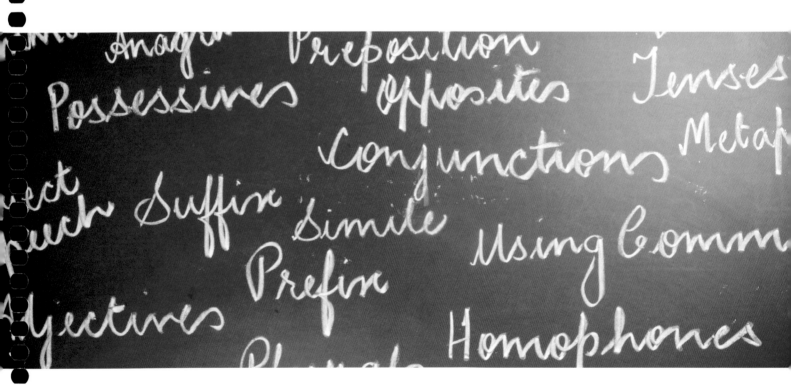

Pamela White

Institute for
Excellence in
Writing

Listen. Speak. Read. Write. Think!

Fix It!
Grammar

Glossary

Pamela White

THIRD EDITION

Contents

Making grammar friendly

This glossary is available for reference if you wish to refresh your memory or would like more information about a specific rule.

One goal of the Institute for Excellence in Writing is to make grammar friendly for younger students and beginning writers. Thus, the terms used in the early *Fix It! Grammar* books are layman's terms, such as *-ing opener* instead of participle and *who-which* instead of adjective clause.

However, grammar terms are useful to the teacher and the student over time, so they are gradually incorporated into the books as well as defined in the glossary.

With the repetition provided in the Fix Its, your students will learn the elements and rules of grammar in manageable increments.

Editing Marks

indent	¶
capitalize	≡
lowercase	/
delete	℮
insert	∨
space	#
close up	⌒

Parts of Speech

Many words can be used as different parts of speech. You have to look at how they are used in the sentence to determine their parts of speech. To see how these parts of speech are used as IEW dress-ups and sentence openers, see the Stylistic Techniques section beginning on page G-35.

Articles (ar)

Articles are the words *a, an, the*.

Articles always set up a noun, so when students see an article, they should know that a noun will follow soon after. Sometimes adjectives come between the article and its noun: *a tall stranger; the reluctant, timid soldier.*

Nouns (n)

Nouns are objects (things), people, animals, places, and ideas.

To determine if a word is a noun, apply these two tests, which work best for objects and animals:

> **1.** Is it countable? *two* _____
>
> **2.** Can an article come in front of it? *the* _____ *; a/an* _____ .

Common and Proper Nouns

Common nouns name general things and are not capitalized.

Proper nouns are capitalized and name specific people, places, animals, and sometimes objects with a name unique to that specific person, place, or animal. *The king* is a common noun, but *King James* is proper. A *beagle* is a common noun, but the name of my pet beagle *Benji* is proper.

Compound Nouns

These are two or more words combined to form a single noun. They can be written as separate words (*apple tree; shooting match*), as hyphenated words (*lady-in-waiting*), or as one word (*marksman; wintertime*). To spell compound words correctly, consult a dictionary.

Students may be confused how to use something like *apple tree* in key word outlines or in marking nouns. A compound noun is not an adjective + noun or two nouns but just a single noun. These are nouns that could have been written as a single word because they express a single thing.

Noun Functions

The two functions of nouns and pronouns that are most useful to understand are the subject and the object of a preposition.

Subjects are nouns or pronouns that perform a verb action. Identify subjects by finding the verb first and then asking, "Who or what is doing this action?" That is the subject.

Saying that a noun is a subject identifies how it functions or behaves in that sentence; it is different from the part of speech (noun or pronoun).

Subject-verb agreement means that the subject and its verb should agree in number. If the subject is singular, the verb should be singular; if the subject is plural, the verb should be plural. Students occasionally find it confusing that a singular verb often ends in *s* and a plural verb does not: *she walks* but *they walk*.

The **object of a preposition** is the noun or pronoun that is the last word in a prepositional phrase. See under Parts of Speech: Prepositions, page G-11; and Stylistic Techniques: Sentence Openers: #2 Prepositional Opener, page G-39.

Other Noun Functions (Advanced)

Direct and **indirect objects** are important mainly as they relate to pronoun usage (*The soldier treated him graciously*, not *The soldier treated he graciously*). Since these are objects, they must use objective pronouns (see under Pronouns on the next page).

Direct objects follow a verb and answer the question *what* or *who*. Example: *The third soldier built a fire.* Built what? *a fire* (direct object).

Indirect objects are rarer and appear only when there is a direct object. They usually come between the verb and direct object and tell who or what received the direct object. Example: *The little man gave the second soldier a purse.* Gave what? *the purse* (direct object). Who received it? *the soldier* (indirect object).

The difficulty is that indirect objects also seem to answer the question *who* or *what* (gave who? *the soldier*). Tip: To tell the difference, you should be able to insert *to* in front of the indirect object: *gave a purse to the second soldier.* He is not giving the soldier to someone else.

Subject complements, a.k.a. predicate nouns, are important for the same pronoun usage problem (*It was she*, not *It was her*). These are nouns that follow a linking verb and point back to the subject, so they *complement* the subject.

Subject complements use subjective, not objective, pronouns (see under Pronouns on the next page), which is the only reason to teach these to older students. Note: Adjectives can also be subject complements.

Appositives are nouns that rename the noun that comes before them. They are important because they are punctuated with commas if nonessential (*Robin Hood, the archer*) and without commas if essential (*the archer Robin Hood*).

Imperative mood is used to issue commands. The subject, *you*, is implied.

Example: *Tarry for me here.* Robin Hood is addressing his men, asking them to wait for him. *You* is the implied subject.

Pronouns (pr)

Personal pronouns refer back to a person or thing recently mentioned and substitute for that person or thing. They should agree in case, person, and number with the noun they refer to. Begin with having students identify basic pronouns and later work on pronoun agreement.

There are three cases:

Subjective case pronouns are used as the subject (or, infrequently, subject complements).

Objective case pronouns are used as objects of verbs or prepositions.

Possessive case pronouns show ownership. These do not have an apostrophe.

	Subjective pronouns	Objective pronouns	Possessive pronouns
1st person singular	I	me	my/mine
2nd person singular	you	you	your/yours
3rd person singular	he, she, it	him, her, it	his, her/hers, its
1st person plural	we	us	our/ours
2nd person plural	you	you	your/yours
3rd person plural	they	them	their/theirs
	who	whom	whose

Pronoun agreement: To agree in person means that first person pronouns should not shift suddenly to second or third. To agree in number means that a singular pronoun should refer back to a singular noun and a plural pronoun should refer to a plural noun.

There are several different categories of pronouns in addition to personal pronouns (relative, demonstrative, interrogative, indefinite, reflexive), but in practice, teach them only as they become relevant in writing.

Reflexive pronouns end in *self* or *selves* and refer back to a noun or pronoun in the same sentence.

Examples:

Princess Dorinda fancied *herself* quite chic.

The fish allowed *themselves* to be stroked.

Verbs (vb)

Verbs are words that express either action or a state of being. There are three types: action, linking, and helping verbs.

Action Verbs

Action verbs express action (as in *chop, budge, confide*) or ownership (as in *have, possess, own*).

Verb + Adverb (Advanced)

In identifying parts of speech, some students are confused by what look like prepositions after a verb but without the usual noun afterward. In this case, these words do not function as prepositions but as adverbs that must be coupled with that verb.

Examples: *Robin Hood set off; the Merry Men rose up; they cavorted about; stand back.*

Helping Verbs

Helping verbs appear with action verbs to help them along. Picture the helping verb as a Boy Scout who helps an elderly lady cross the street. One helps the other along!

Examples: *The magical purse would always refill with gold.* Would helps *refill.* *She had played him a trick.* Had helps out *played.*

Helping verbs:

> *am, is, are, was, were, be, being, been* (*be* verbs, which can also be linking verbs)
>
> *have, has, had*
>
> *do, does, did*
>
> *may, might, must, ought to*
>
> *would, will, could, can, should, shall*

Tip: Helping verbs communicate possibility (*can, could, might*, etc.) or time (*was, did, has*, etc.).

Linking Verbs

Linking verbs connect the subject to a noun or adjective that renames or describes it and is called the **subject complement** (a.k.a. predicate noun and predicate adjective).

Examples: *Robin Hood was* (linking verb) *an outlaw* (subject complement). *The combatants seemed* (linking verb) *weary* (subject complement). *The princess was* (linking verb) *artful and cunning* (subject complements).

Common linking verbs:

> *am, is, are, was, were, be, being, been* (*be* verbs, which can also be helping verbs)
>
> *seem, become* (always linking verbs)
>
> *appear, grow, remain, continue*
>
> *taste, sound, smell, feel, look* (verbs dealing with the senses)

Some of these verbs can also be action verbs. Tip: If you can substitute *seem* for the verb, it is probably a linking verb.

Be Verbs

Be verbs often stump students when identifying parts of speech because they do not show action. Since they dominate our language and perform important functions as helping and linking verbs, it is important students can recognize that they are verbs.

Ask students to memorize the *be* verbs: *am, is, are, was, were, be, being, been.*

Verbals: Infinitives, Participles, Gerunds (Advanced)

Verbals are words formed from a verb, but they usually do not function as a verb.

You do not have to teach students to identify whether a particular verbal is functioning as a noun or adjective or adverb. There is little point to drilling this harder concept except to mention that verbals are not verbs. Learning what function they take will not affect punctuation or help most students understand grammar, nor will it show up on the SAT or ACT.

As a strong verb dress-up? If students want to label a verbal as a strong verb, decide whether it is too advanced to direct them toward basic action verbs instead.

It helps older students to have a basic understanding of these verbals:

1. Infinitives are verbals formed by placing *to* in front of the simple present form of a verb (like *to sneeze*). Infinitives function as adjectives, adverbs, and nouns but never as verbs.

2. Participles often function as adjectives and come in two forms: present (-ing words) and past participles (-ed words). However, when participles are coupled with a subject and a helping verb, they function as verbs, as in *He **was splashing**, which frightened the fish. For years, she **had longed** to visit the world above the sea.*

a. Sometimes these participle-adjectives appear directly before the noun: *hunting skills; a botched case.*

b. Sometimes they are an -ing or -ed phrase coming before or after a main clause and modifying the subject of the main clause: *Springing to his feet, Robin Hood confronted the challenger.* (*Springing* describes *Robin Hood*, the subject after the comma.) See under Stylistic Techniques: Sentence Openers: #4 -ing Participial Phrase Opener, page G-41.

3. Gerunds are -ing words that function as nouns. Examples: *His splashing frightened the fish.* (*Splashing* is the subject of the sentence and therefore a noun.) *The fish were frightened by his splashing.* (*Splashing* is the object of the preposition *by* and therefore a noun.)

Split infinitives

A concern more of the past than the present, *split infinitives* are worth teaching advanced writers. To split one's infinitive is to insert one or more adverbs between "to" and the verb, as in "to foolishly insert."

Generally, split infinitives are acceptable but formerly frowned on, so avoid them when it is just as smooth to place the intervening adverb somewhere else.

Adjectives (adj)

Adjectives are words that describe or modify nouns and pronouns. Usually they come before the noun they modify, as in *the crowded room* or *covetous princess*.

Sometimes adjectives come after a linking verb, as in *the princess was **thrilled**; the soldiers were **penniless** and **forlorn***.

Comparative and Superlative Adjectives

Comparative adjectives (ending in *-er*) and superlative adjectives (ending in *-est*) are forms of adjectives comparing two or more nouns. Students sometimes have trouble recognizing that words ending in *-er* or *-est* can be adjectives. Have them drop the ending and ask if the word remaining is an adjective.

Example: *The noblest buck is the most noble buck.* Drop the ending and ask if *noble* can describe a noun. It can, so *noble* and *noblest* are both adjectives.

Some words form irregular comparatives and superlatives. The most common of these are *good* and *bad*:

> *good, better, best*
>
> *bad, worse, worst*

Caution students against using *more* or *most* with a comparative or superlative adjective. Not *more prouder* but *prouder*. Most one-syllable adjectives form the comparative and superlative by adding the suffix. Adjectives of three or more syllables form the comparative with *more* and the superlative with *most* in front of the regular adjective. Two-syllable adjectives have more complex rules, but usually whichever sounds better is correct.

Adverbs (adv)

Adverbs usually modify verbs or adjectives and answer the questions *how, when,* or *where*. Encourage students to identify what part of speech the adverbs modify.

Example: *The princess stoutly denied that she possessed stolen goods. Stoutly* tells us how she denied, so it is the adverb, and it comes right before the verb it describes.

Many adverbs end in *-ly*. See Stylistic Techniques: Dress-Ups: -ly Adverb, page G-35; and Sentence Openers: #3 -ly Adverb Opener, page G-40.

Imposter -ly's: Some *-ly* words are adjectives like *chilly, ghastly, ugly,* and *friendly*. If the word describes an object or person (*the ugly duckling*), it is an adjective and not an adverb.

Advanced: Adverbs can also modify other adverbs, but this is rare and usually awkward in the hands of young writers, giving such unhelpful constructions as *she spoke extremely quickly*.

Advanced: Comparative adverbs are usually formed by adding *more* or *most* in front of the adverb. If the adverb is short, sometimes the suffix is used, as in *deadliest*. If in doubt, students should check a dictionary.

Tip: When adjectives come after a linking verb, they are known as **subject complements** or **predicate adjectives**. See Parts of Speech: Verbs: Linking Verbs, page G-8.

Prepositions (prep)

Prepositions start phrases that usually show some relationship dealing with space (*on the branch*) or time (*in the morning*). If it is something a frog can do with a log or a squirrel with a tree, it is probably a prepositional phrase: *climbs on the log, sits in the branches, runs around the tree.*

A prepositional phrase always follows this pattern:

preposition + noun (no verb)

It begins with a preposition, ends with a noun, and does not have a verb in it. Since there is not a subject + verb, it is a phrase, not a clause. There may be other words in between the preposition and noun, but there will never be a verb: *in the act; by a great baron; of strong and goodhearted yeomen.*

First learning parts of speech helps students accurately identify prepositional phrases. Until the concept is mastered, guide them to see that the phrase begins with a preposition, ends with a noun, and has no verb in it.

The most common prepositions:

aboard	at	despite	near	throughout
about	because of	down	of	to
above	before	during	off	toward
according to	behind	except	on, onto	under
across	below	for	opposite	underneath
after	beneath	from	out	unlike
against	beside	in	outside	until
along	besides	inside	over	unto
amid	between	instead of	past	up, upon
among	beyond	into	regarding	with
around	by	like	since	within
as	concerning	minus	through	without

In the first stories of *Fix It!* students are asked to identify prepositional phrases. Removing prepositional phrases helps students see the underlying structure of their sentences better, which is the basis for being able to punctuate correctly.

Doubling as other parts of speech: A few words in the preposition list are sometimes another part of speech, so guide students to determine this based on the pattern. The two most important examples:

> **1.** Adverbs that follow a verb but do not start a prepositional phrase (*warded **off**; cried **out***).

> **2.** Subordinating conjunctions that start dependent clauses: *since, as, until, after, before.* See under Stylistic Techniques: Sentence Openers: #5 Clausal Opener, page G-42.

Younger students do not need to count the preposition *to* in an infinitive, as in *to float,* since infinitives work a little differently from prepositional phrases.

On not ending sentences with prepositions: This is a carryover from Latin and not a true rule in English. Andrew Pudewa quips that Winston Churchill gave the definitive answer to this problem when he remarked, "That is a rule up with which I will not put!"

If the sentence is more awkward to revise with the preposition placed earlier, it is better to have it at the end. Example: *I have only a plain blackthorn staff to meet you with.* The alternative is this stilted construction: *I have only a plain blackthorn staff with which to meet you.*

Misplaced prepositional phrases: The later stories deal with the problem of dangling prepositional phrases where misplaced prepositional phrases distort the meaning, often humorously.

Example: ***King Arthur declared on special days*** *he would not feast until someone narrated a bizarre tale that he could trust.* The king did not make this declaration on special days; instead, he declared he would not feast on them.

Revise by moving the prepositional phrase: *King Arthur declared* ***he would not feast on special days*** *until someone narrated a bizarre tale that he could trust.*

Coordinating Conjunctions (cc)

Coordinating conjunctions connect parts of speech, phrases, and clauses. Whatever they connect needs to be the same thing grammatically: two or more nouns, two or more present participles, two or more dependent clauses, two or more main clauses, and so forth.

Have students memorize the seven basic coordinating conjunctions using the mnemonic device FANBOYS, an acronym for the cc's: *for, and, nor, but, or, yet, so.*

Punctuation: The main problem with cc's is that sometimes they have a comma in front of them and sometimes they do not. See Punctuation: Commas, page G-21.

The principles to keep in mind:

    1. Use commas before cc's when they join

        a. two main clauses. Pattern: **MC, cc MC**. Example: *Usually Robin towered over others,* **but** *the stranger was taller by a head and a neck.*

        b. three or more items in a series. Pattern: **a, b, and c**. Example: *He ran to the window, opened it,* **and** *vaulted out.*

    2. Do not use commas before cc's when they join two items in a series unless those are MCs. Example: *fine gardens* **and** *wide lawns.*

    This applies to two verbs (a compound verb) with one subject. Pattern: **MC cc 2nd verb** (notice there is no comma). Example: *He bowed* **and** *walked away.*

Train students to locate cc's and then determine what same parts of speech or constructions they are joining. This matters because it shows whether or not the commas will be necessary: comma if three or more; no comma if only two unless MCs. It also matters because it helps students identify faulty parallelism. See sidebar.

Starting sentences with cc's: Strict grammarians forbid this on the basis that the job of cc's is to connect things of equal grammatical rank. Generally, encourage this avoidance, especially in academic papers, but it is not a hard and fast rule.

One clear exception is in dialogue, which can mimic real speech patterns. We often start our thoughts with *and* or *but.*

Faulty parallelism

Coordinating conjunctions should join parts of speech, phrases, or clauses of equal grammatical rank. When they do not, it is known as faulty parallelism, a concept middle and high school students should learn. It means that the items in a series are not parallel, that is, not the same part of speech, type of phrase, or type of clause.

Example: Once she **stole** into the throne room, **swinging** on the chandeliers, and **landed** at the feet of the scandalized courtiers.

Problem: The sentence sets up a parallel construction but is not consistent with its items in a series (bolded).

Corrected: Once she **stole** into the throne room, **swung** on the chandeliers, and **landed** at the feet of the scandalized courtiers.

Subordinating Conjunctions

In IEW's stylistic techniques, we begin by teaching students the because clause, then seven more common clause starters using the acronym **www.asia.b** for the words that can start dependent clauses:

> *when, while, where, as, since, if, although, because*

Later we add three more:

> *until, whereas, unless*

These are all subordinating conjunctions, so named because they start subordinate clauses, an older term for dependent clauses. There is no special need to teach the terminology (subordinating conjunction) except that it is important to distinguish these types of words from coordinating conjunctions (cc). For simplicity's sake, students can mark these clause starters with a *cl*.

The main difference is that when coordinating conjunctions (*for, and, nor, but, or, yet,* and *so*) are added to a main clause, we still have a main clause. When subordinating conjunctions (*when, while, where,* etc.) are added to a main clause, they turn it into a dependent clause. The punctuation changes too. See under Stylistic Techniques: Dress-ups: Clause Starters, page G-38; and Sentence Openers: #5 Clausal Opener, page G-42.

Advanced: Confusingly, *since, until,* and *as* sometimes function as prepositions, and *because of* is also a preposition. See tips for distinguishing them under Stylistic Techniques: Sentence Openers: #5 Clausal Opener, page G-42.

Advanced: Also confusingly, *as, where, when, while* and *whereas* sometimes start adjective clauses or function as coordinating conjunctions. See Sentences, Clauses, and Phrases: Clauses: Dependent Clauses (Advanced), page G-17; and Stylistic Techniques: Sentence Openers: #5 Clausal Opener, page G-42.

Conjunctive Adverbs (Advanced)

These words are a writer's plague—albeit an important group of words!—because they are often confused with subordinating conjunctions but need different punctuation.

Some common conjunctive adverbs: *however, therefore, then, moreover, consequently, otherwise, nevertheless, thus, furthermore, instead, otherwise.*

Learn this principle: When you add a conjunctive adverb to a main clause, it is still a main clause, which is not the case with subordinating conjunctions.

How this matters:

1. If conjunctive adverbs start a sentence, usually follow them with a comma as you would any transitional word or expression. The exception is short conjunctive adverbs like *then*, which do not require a pause.

> Examples: **Then** *they dropped it when we were older.* **Moreover***, didn't they realize cell phones were for emergencies only?*

2. If a conjunctive adverb falls between two main clauses that belong together in one sentence, put a semicolon before it and comma after: **MC; ca, MC.**

> Example: *Years of indulgence had spoiled her beyond recognition;* **however***, Lady Constance recalled a time in Dorinda's childhood when she had been a lovable child.*

> If the main clauses express two different ideas, separate them with a period.

The lady bent down and awarded Gawain a kiss. **Then** *she appealed to him to rhapsodize about the tribulations and treasures of true love.*

3. If conjunctive adverbs fall in the middle of a sentence, however, use two commas or none, depending on whether you need a clear pause around them.

Examples: *Chanticleer ignored her advice,* **however.** *Pertelote* **therefore** *argued more vehemently for laxatives from the garden. Chanticleer* **then** *countered with another round of dire dreams, which* **nevertheless** *failed to convince Pertelote.*

Interjections

Interjections are words that express a strong emotion, such as *ow, oh, ugh, whew*. They usually are set off with commas, but if they have a strong exclamatory message, you may put an exclamation mark after them. Alone, they do not count as a sentence.

"Oops! I do believe I've broken your leg."

"Oh, yes, benevolent frog!"

"Yuck! I won't touch another bite!"

Sentences, Clauses, and Phrases

Sentences

A sentence expresses one complete thought. To do so, it must have at least one main clause.

Sentence sense. Writers often string together more than one main clause in a sentence, often with the coordinating conjunction *and,* when those main clauses would be more powerful as separate sentences. When students are ready to understand the concept, discourage this practice.

Sentence fragments. A fragment is an error in which a sentence has phrases and/or dependent clauses but no main clause.

Servants came forth, attending to his horse. Welcoming the warrior. The second part is an unacceptable fragment.

In fiction and even in academic writing for some teachers, fragments that do not leave the reader hanging and that fit the flow of the paragraph are dramatic and effective. *Fix It!* stories permit such fragments, especially in dialogue when complete sentences would sound unnatural. The key is whether or not the fragment leaves the reader feeling as if something more is needed.

"Would you like me to rescue your ball?"

"Oh, yes!" (acceptable fragment)

Because students often use fragments ineffectively in formal writing, many teachers forbid the use of any fragment. Discuss which fragments in the *Fix It!* stories work well and which ones do not in order to arm students with the practice of recognizing sentence fragments. This will also help them distinguish phrases and dependent clauses from main, or independent, clauses.

Clauses and Phrases

Failure to recognize the basic clauses and phrases that form the underlying structure of sentences is at the heart of most students' inability to punctuate their sentences properly.

When older students struggle with knowing where to place their commas, this, along with knowing basic parts of speech, is most likely the root problem. They cannot recognize a main clause if they do not know what a subject-verb pair is, and they cannot know this if they do not distinguish nouns, pronouns, and verbs from other parts of speech.

The different levels of *Fix It!* teach grammar progressively in this way: beginning with basic parts of speech, then identifying phrases and clauses, and gradually adding in punctuation. Once students understand the basic structure of their sentences, they will know how to apply the punctuation rules.

Phrases

A phrase is a group of related words that does not have both a subject and a verb.

Prepositional phrases. Practically speaking, these are the only phrases worth teaching. Finding prepositional phrases helps get the "noise" out of the sentence and makes it easier for students to see their clauses. It also helps them properly identify #2 sentence openers. See Parts of Speech: Prepositions, page G-11; and Stylistic Techniques: Sentence Openers: #2 Prepositional Opener, page G-39.

Appositive. A convenient word for a simple concept, an appositive is a noun that renames the noun that comes right before it. Example: *Robin Hood,* **the archer.** The only reason appositives are worth flagging is that they usually are set off with commas but sometimes not. See under Punctuation: Commas: Rule 15: Essential-Nonessential Elements, page G-24.

Clauses

A clause is a group of related words that must have both a subject and a verb.

Main Clauses (MC)

These are clauses that can stand alone as a sentence.

a. *Main clause* is abbreviated *MC* in *Fix It!* The MC is also known as an independent clause or strong clause.

b. MCs usually start with a subject or with an article (*a, an, the*) and/or adjectives plus subject. Example: *The poor soldiers returned* follows the pattern of "Article (*The*) adjective (*poor*) subject (*soldiers*) verb (*returned*)."

Sometimes the subject-verb will be inverted, with the verb coming before the subject. Examples: *There gathered around him displaced countrymen.* subject-verb = countrymen gathered. *Up rose his Merry Men.* subject-verb = Merry Men are. These are still MCs.

c. When identifying MCs, include prepositional phrases in the middle or at the end of the clause but not ones that come before MCs. Follow common sense in determining which words must group with the basic subject and verb of the main clause.

d. Sometimes dependent clauses (like *who-which*'s) are included in a MC and needed for it to make sense. Example: *I have never met a man who could topple me off a bridge.* The MC includes the dependent who clause and does not makes sense as just *I have never met a man.*

Dependent Clauses (DC)

These are clauses that cannot stand alone as a sentence.

a. *Dependent clause* is abbreviated *DC* in *Fix It!* It is also known as a subordinate clause or weak clause.

b. DCs are basically main clauses with another word or words in front that turn the main clause into something that leaves us hanging, that cannot stand alone as a sentence.

For practical purposes, it is enough for younger students to recognize the dependent clause starters *who, which, that,* and the subordinating conjunctions, the www.asia.buwu words *when, while, where, as, since, if, although, because, until, whereas, unless.*

As an example, start with a main clause: *The foresters discovered them in the act.* Now add a www word: *Although the foresters discovered them in the act.* There is still a subject and verb, so this is a clause and not a phrase. However, the second version leaves us hanging. Although this is true, something else must also be true.

DCs (Dependent Clauses) must be attached to a MC (Main Clause) to be a legal sentence.

c. To simplify grammar, focus on teaching just two types of DCs: 1. *who-which* clauses, and 2. www.asia.b clauses. In *Fix It!* adverb clauses that begin with one of the www words are abbreviated as *AC*.

See Stylistic Techniques: Dress-Ups: *Who-Which* Clause, page G-36, and Clause Starters (www.asia.b), page G-38; and Stylistic Techniques: Sentence Openers: #5 Clausal Opener, page G-42.

Tip: Conjunctive adverbs like *however, therefore, then* and coordinating conjunctions like *and, or, but* do not turn a MC into a DC.

Dependent Clauses (Advanced)

Understanding DCs well and punctuating them perfectly every time can get complex. The amount of time it would take to teach most students these finer points of grammar is not always worth it, but it may help teachers to understand the following.

Dependent clauses function in different ways, which can affect their punctuation.

1. Adverb clauses, a.k.a. adverbial clauses (AC)

Most of the time, a clause starter from the www word list will start an adverb clause. It should not be set off with a comma if it falls in the middle or at the end of a sentence (**MC AC**), but it takes a comma after the clause if it is an opener (**AC, MC**).

2. Adjective clauses

This usually starts with a relative pronoun, mainly *who, which,* or *that.* Adjective clauses usually follow nouns or pronouns and describe the nouns they follow: *the **arrow that** Robin shot…; the **princess, who** was artful and cunning….*

Adjective clauses are set off with commas if they are nonessential to the rest of the sentence but not set off with commas if they are essential. See under Punctuation: Commas: Rule 15: Essential-Nonessential Elements, page G-24.

Unfortunately—and this is one of the areas where grammar gets messy—three of the subordinating conjunctions that are in the clause starter list, *as, where,* and *when,* sometimes start adjective clauses and thus act as relative pronouns. This matters because adverb clauses in the middle or end of sentences never take commas, but adjective clauses take commas when they are nonessential.

Contrast these examples:

*The roof is formed of shells, which open and close **as** the water flows over them. As* is a subordinating conjunction meaning *while;* it starts an adverb clause, so no comma.

*The outcome of joy is invariably woe, **as** all creatures know. As* is a relative pronoun meaning *a fact that;* it starts a nonessential clause and needs a comma.

Other messy exceptions are *while* and *whereas*, which can be subordinating conjunctions (no comma before them) or coordinating conjunctions (comma before them when they join main clauses).

Contrast these sentences:

> *The second soldier took the road to the right **while** he thought about his next plan of action.* No comma because *while* is a subordinating conjunction starting an adverb clause, and adverb clause dress-ups are not set off with commas. *While* means "at the same time that" here.

> *The second soldier took the path to the right, **while** the other two determined to travel down the road to the left.* Comma because *while* is a coordinating conjunction joining two main clauses (**MC, cc MC**). As a cc, *while* and *whereas* convey a contrast.

3. Noun clauses

These function as nouns. Most often, they follow a verb and begin with *that*, one of the words that confusingly can also begin an adjective clause. You can tell the difference because *that* adjective clauses follow a noun while *that* noun clauses follow a verb. Example: *People felt that Robin Hood was like them. That* follows the verb *felt* so starts a noun clause.

Tip: A clause is a noun clause if you can substitute a pronoun for it. Example: *People felt **that** Robin Hood was like them. People felt **it**.* Makes sense! But: *Robin returned to the town **that** he had left. Robin returned to the town **it**?* This does not make sense, so this *that* starts an adjective, not a noun, clause.

Where grammar gets even muddier is that *when, where, who* and other words sometimes start noun clauses. However, students will not run into these situations enough in marking dress-ups and openers to make it worth spending the time to teach noun clauses. Fortunately, students rarely have trouble punctuating noun clauses, so learning about them becomes a moot issue.

Punctuation

End Marks . ? !

A sentence may end with a **period**, **question mark**, or **exclamation mark**.

Do not double punctuate. Not *"You're sure?!"* or *"Hah!," he said.* But *"You're sure?"* and *"Hah!" he said.*

Rule 1. Use periods at the end of statements and in abbreviations.

> He bowed and walked away.

> **Advanced: Comma splices** and **fused sentences** occur when students join main clauses with only commas or with no punctuation. MCs need something stronger to hold them together, often a period. See under Semicolons, page G-26.

Rule 2. Periods (and commas) go inside closing quotation marks.

> "The better man should cross first."

Rule 3. Use question marks after direct questions.

> Did you ever hear the story of the three poor soldiers?

Rule 4. Use exclamation marks when the statement expresses strong emotion, but do not overuse them. When a character is said to exclaim something, the context begs for an exclamation mark.

> "No one calls me a coward!"

> "Hah!" the other exclaimed.

Quotations " "

Rule 1. Use quotation marks to enclose direct quotations but not indirect speech, which usually begins with *that*. Quotation marks should "hug" the words they enclose—that is, there should not be a space between the quotation mark and the word or punctuation it encloses.

> "It's no wonder that child has turned out so blemished," clucked Lady Constance. (direct)

> Secretly he thought that in beauty she surpassed Queen Guinevere herself. (indirect)

Rule 2. The attribution is the narrative that sets up a quotation with a speaking verb (*he said*). Set attributions off from quotations with commas. The attribution can come before, after, or in the middle of the quotation.

When using your computer, be sure you are creating *curly quotes* (" ") and not *straight quotes* (" ").

Straight quotes should be reserved for measurements, and only when the format is very tight, such as 6" 2' for six feet, two inches.

Patterns: **speaking verb, "quote"** or **"quote," speaking verb**

> He *answered,* "Hand me a stout bow and straight arrow."

> "I will join your band," *announced* the stranger.

> "You stand back," *responded* his adversary, "since I am the better man."

Rule 3. Commas and periods always go inside closing quotations (unless they are followed by parentheses, in which case they go after the parentheses).

> "It's gold, you know."

Rule 4. Exclamation marks and question marks go inside closing quotations when they are part of the material quoted; otherwise, they go outside. Also, use only one ending mark of punctuation—the stronger—with quotation marks, em dashes excepted.

> "If only I could have my ball back, I would bestow a handsome reward on my benefactor!"

> "Dorinda, who was at the door?" King Morton inquired.

Rule 5. If a quotation ends in an exclamation mark or question but is followed by an attribution, use a lowercase letter at the beginning of the attribution (unless it starts with a proper noun) because the attribution is part of the same sentence as the quotation.

> "Have at him!" cried Will Stutely.

Rule 6. When a spoken sentence is interrupted, close the first part and begin the second with quotation marks. Do not capitalize the first letter of the continuation.

> "By the great yew bow of Saint Withold," cried the stranger, "that is a shot indeed!"

Rule 7. When typing, place thoughts in italics instead of in quotation marks.

> *It's time she was humbled a little,* thought the wise soldier.

When handwriting, use quotation marks.

Rule 8. Use italics or place quotation marks around words referred to as words. Trick: Insert "the word(s)" or "the name" before the word in question to tell if this rule applies.

> Since "Little" is indeed your true name.... (Since the name "Little"...)

> He would have none of this recent drivel of dropping "sir" and "madam" when addressing one's elders. (dropping the words "sir" and "madam")

Rule 9. Use single quotation marks for quotations within quotations. This is the only time to use single quotations.

> "She also insisted on stripping the top coverlets from all the mattresses because, as she put it, 'They might be unclean.'"

Rule 10. In conversation, if someone is speaking and changes topic, start a new paragraph. However, close his first paragraph without a quotation mark and open his new paragraph with a quotation mark.

The missing quotation mark at the end of the first paragraph signals that he has not finished speaking. The opening quotation mark in the next paragraph reminds us that someone is still speaking.

> Robin accepted the challenge. "I will stoop to you as I never stooped to man before.

> ¶ "Friend Stutely, cut down a white piece of bark four fingers tall and wide."

Apostrophes '

Rule 1. Use an apostrophe with contractions, placing it where the letter(s) have been removed. Note that in formal writing contractions should be avoided, but they are acceptable in fiction, especially in dialogue.

"I'll figure out how to trick them."

"It's too bad, but we'd better go our separate ways."

Rule 2. Use an apostrophe to show possession. To form plural possessives, make the noun plural first; then add an apostrophe. An exception is irregular plural possessives like *children's* and *women's*.

the second soldier's turn

the soldiers' last night at the palace (the last night of all three soldiers)

Rule 3. Never use an apostrophe with possessive pronouns (*his, hers, its, theirs, ours, yours*) since they already show possession. Teach students the differences in these tricky pairs:

Possessive Pronoun	Contraction
its	it's (it is; remember by it's)
whose	who's (who is)
theirs	there's (there is)

Just like with quotation marks, when using your computer, be sure you are using curly apostrophes (') and not straight apostrophes (').

Commas ,

Rule 1. Adjectives before a noun

Use commas to separate two or more coordinate adjectives before a noun. **Coordinate adjectives** each independently describe the noun, as in *dewy, silent leaves*.

Do not use commas to separate **cumulative adjectives**, in which the first adjective modifies both the second adjective and the noun, as in *one fair morning*. The adjectives are cumulative if the last one deals with time, age, or color *or* if it forms a compound noun with the noun (*apple tree*).

Two tricks help distinguish coordinate from cumulative, but these are just tricks that depend on a quick response, not rules. If you think about it too long, it is harder to tell.

Adjectives are coordinate and need a comma if you can

    1. reverse their order.

    2. add *and* between them.

Examples: With *pointed, protruding nose*, it sounds right to say both *protruding, pointed nose* and *pointed and protruding nose*, so the adjectives are coordinate and the comma is necessary.

With *stout oak staff*, it sounds awkward to say either *oak stout staff* or *stout and oak staff*, so the adjectives are cumulative and should not have a comma.

Occasionally students will put a comma between an adjective and the noun it modifies, as in *the pointed, protruding, nose*. Be on the lookout for this and squash this habit if it forms!

Rule 2. Quotations

Use a comma with a verb of speaking that introduces a direct quotation, whether the verb comes before or after the quotation.

Older students who do not correctly punctuate their sentences rarely learn by memorizing punctuation rules. The problem goes back to understanding the underlying sentence structure. See under Sentences, Clauses, and Phrases: Clauses and Phrases, page G-15.

Students with weak understanding of when to punctuate should start with the first story of Fix It!

"King Mel loathes courtly balls," Lord Ashton *protested*.

Lord Ashton *protested*, "King Mel loathes courtly balls."

Rule 3. Nouns of Direct Address (NDAs)

Set off nouns of direct address (NDAs) with commas.

"*Fool*, you have killed the king's deer."

"For fourteen days we have enjoyed no sport, *my friends*."

Rule 4. Items in a series

Pattern: a, b, and c. Use commas to separate three or more items in a series. These items must be the same part of speech or same grammatical construction, such as phrases or clauses. The last two items are usually connected by a coordinating conjunction.

Robin was *mature, strong*, and *dauntless*. (three adjectives)

He *accepted* the match, *grabbed* his bow and arrow, and *started* off from Locksley. (three verbs)

The Oxford comma. Current trend is to keep the Oxford comma, which is the comma before the coordinating conjunction in three or more items in a series. Although the Oxford comma is optional if there is no danger of misreading, writers do not always recognize potential confusion. It is never wrong to include the Oxford comma, so it is easier to include it always.

Example: *To his hens, Chanticleer gave fine gifts, the pleasure of his singing and corn.* Ambiguity: Are "the pleasure of his singing and corn" the actual gifts, or are these three separate items? The Oxford comma clarifies that these are three separate items: *Chanticleer gave fine gifts, the pleasure of his singing, and corn.*

Pattern: a and b. Do not use commas with only two items in a series unless those items are main clauses.

You shall enjoy succulent *venison* and the stoutest tasting *ale*. (two nouns)

He will receive a *trouncing* and a *ducking* himself. (two -ing words)

Rule 5. Compound verb. Pattern: MC cc 2nd verb.

Do not use a comma before a coordinating conjunction that joins two verbs (a compound verb) with the same subject. It helps to think of this as joining only two items (two verbs) in a series. You will not see a second subject after the coordinating conjunction.

They *built* great fires and *roasted* the does. (two verbs)

He also *had* the little man in the red jacket for his guest and *treated* him graciously.

Rule 6. Main clauses with a coordinating conjunction. Pattern: MC, cc MC

Use a comma before a coordinating conjunction that joins two main clauses. You will see a subject and verb after the coordinating conjunction.

"*He is* of diminished princely stature, *and he doesn't care* for polo."

They had fought well in the wars, *but* now *they were* out of work and destitute.

Rule 7. Introductory prepositional phrases (#2 sentence openers)

Use commas after introductory prepositional phrases of five or more words. The comma is optional with fewer than five words. With short prepositional openers, let the pause test be your guide: If it sounds better with a pause, include a comma; if it does not need a pause, leave it out.

For advanced writers, emphasize that this is the only situation when quotations are set up with a comma. In research, quotations are often worked into the text with no punctuation or with a colon when they follow a main clause that they also illustrate.

Technically, the comma in the MC, cc MC pattern is optional when the clauses are short and there is no danger of misreading.

However, since it can cause confusion to omit it, it is easier to include it always.

On his journey north Gawain encountered few obstacles. (comma optional)

From stone *to* stone they cavorted about. (comma optional)

"*By* the faith *of* my heart, never have I been called a craven in all my life!"

With a string of opening introductory prepositional phrases, save the comma for the end of all of them, even if one of them is long.

> Not: During the long and arduous weeks, of preparation, for the ball, Mel was shuffled off to the hunting lodge.

> But: During the long and arduous weeks of preparation for the ball, Mel was shuffled off to the hunting lodge.

Advanced: When the introductory prepositional phrase is followed by a verb instead of noun or pronoun, do not add the comma.

> Behind them close on their heels *bounded* the cow and the calf.

Rule 8. Mid-sentence prepositional phrases

Prepositional phrases in the middle of sentences are not set off with commas.

> The stranger shot *at the small white square* fixed to its front.

Rule 9. Transitional expressions and interjections

Use a comma after introductory transitional expressions and interjections. Usually include commas on both sides of interrupting words or phrases that appear elsewhere in a sentence.

> *Meanwhile,* Robin's men lay off to the side of the prodigious oak.

> *Moreover,* didn't they realize cell phones were intended for emergencies only?

> The palace accountant ordered them a new HDTV, complete with a surround system, *too.*

> As grown-up girls, *however,* they could go when they pleased.

When an interjection expresses a strong emotion, use an exclamation mark instead.

> *Alas!* In an ox's stall this night I shall be murdered where I lie.

Rule 10. Introductory adverb clauses (#5 sentence openers). Pattern: AC, MC

Use commas after introductory #5 adverb clause sentence openers, even if they are short. An adverb clause is a type of dependent clause. See Stylistic Techniques: Sentence Openers: #5 Clausal Opener, page G-42.

> *Although* the foresters discovered them in the act, they narrowly escaped.

> *Since* the problem was obvious, he continued after a pause.

> *When* he finished, they thanked their old friend heartily for his kindness.

> *Because* the Sheriff of Nottingham was related to the slain forester, he had a vendetta to catch Robin Hood.

Rule 11. Adverb clause dress-up. Pattern: MC AC

Do not use a comma with mid-sentence adverb clauses. See Stylistic Techniques: Dress-Ups: www.asia.b words, page G-38. See exceptions in Rules 13 and 15 below.

> Robin observed him *as* he trimmed his staff.

> "Remain on the other side *while* I quickly make a staff."

"I will tan your hide *until* it's as many colors as a beggar's cloak *if* you touch your bow."

Rule 12. Comparisons.

Do not use a comma to separate parts of a comparison.

O disconsolate hens, louder was your keening *than* that of senators' wives in Rome.

Rule 13. Contrasting elements.

Use commas to separate contrasting parts of a sentence.

The ideas in this story are the cock's thoughts, not mine.

This is especially confusing with the www words *although, while,* and *whereas.* When they contrast the main clause before them, set them off with a comma, despite the more common rule **MC AC**.

"Now you flinch for fear, *although* you have felt no harm."

"Whatever I win in the woods I will award you in the evening, *while* all that you have gained you must bestow on me."

This sometimes applies to the cc *but* when it presents a strong contrast, even when it is joining only two items in a series that are not main clauses and therefore normally do not take a comma.

"Dreams are often a portent not just of joy, *but* of tribulations to come."

Rule 14. Participial Phrases (#4 sentence openers)

Use commas after introductory -ing participial phrases, even if they are short.

Excusing herself from the table, Dorinda hastened away.

Participial phrases in the middle or at the end of sentences are usually nonessential and therefore set off with commas.

Her sisters rose from the depths, *singing plaintively.*

Rule 15. Essential-Nonessential elements (a.k.a. restrictive-nonrestrictive)

Set off *who-which* clauses, appositives, participial phrases, and adjective clauses with commas if they are nonessential. Do not put commas around them if they are essential.

If the clause or phrase is necessary to the meaning of the rest of the sentence or if it specifies which one of something is being discussed, it is essential and should not be enclosed in commas.

If it does not alter the meaning of the rest of the sentence or if the person or thing is adequately identified, it is nonessential and needs commas, even though it may be adding important information. *Nonessential* should not be taken to mean unimportant.

Tricks to test:

1. Mentally remove the clause or phrase from the sentence to see if it alters the information in the rest of the sentence or specifies who or what is meant. If it does not, the element is nonessential and should be set off with commas.

2. Put parentheses around the clause or phrase. If the sentence still seems to work, the clause or phrase is probably nonessential.

Importantly, often whether or not you use commas changes the meaning. For example, it is correct to punctuate the following who clause as essential or nonessential: *Even the footmen, who once toadied to her, snubbed her.* With commas, it is saying that all footmen

Tip: Sometimes it is not crystal clear whether a clause or phrase is essential or nonessential. Ask these questions:

Does it affect the meaning of the rest of the sentence?

Does it specify which particular noun is intended?

Then use your best guess. Grammarians will not always agree on particular examples!

Tip: The concept of essential and nonessential elements does not apply to sentence openers, which have separate rules of punctuation. Test this out only on phrases and clauses in the middle or at the end of sentences.

snubbed her, and, incidentally, all once toadied to her. Without commas it is saying that only those footmen who used to toady to her now snubbed her: *Even the footmen who once toadied to her snubbed her.*

Examples:

"Be ready to heed my call, *which will sound as three short blasts upon the bugle horn.*" (nonessential which clause)

> If we remove the which clause from the sentence, the main clause meaning does not change: the speaker still wants them to be ready to heed his call. The which clause is therefore nonessential, even though it adds important information, and should be set off with commas.

He had shot a deer *that the king reserved for his own table.* (essential that clause, so no comma)

> This clause is essential because it specifies which particular deer. He did not shoot just any deer but one reserved for the king.

"It was agreed that the poor soldier *who had already suffered from the power of the apple* should undertake the task." (essential who clause)

> The who clause specifies which soldier—the one who had already suffered from the apple's power—so is needed in the sentence and therefore not set off with commas. It restricts the information to that particular soldier, which is why these are sometimes called restrictive clauses.

She had confessed the truth to Lady Constance, *who now played her trump card.* (nonessential who clause)

> Lady Constance is already sufficiently identified. The who clause adds an important detail but does not alter the meaning of the rest of the sentence so is nonessential and needs a comma.

the archer *Robin Hood* (essential appositive)

> Without his name, we would not know which archer is intended, so this is an essential appositive and should not be set off with a comma.

Robin Hood, *the archer* (nonessential appositive)

> It adds information but does not restrict the information to a particular Robin Hood or change the meaning of the rest of the sentence.

Robin Hood rose, *needing a change.* (nonessential participial phrase)

> He still rose, regardless of whether or not he needed a change. The participial phrase adds information but does not alter the meaning of the main clause.

Advanced: Sometimes *when, as,* and *where* start adjective clauses instead of adverb clauses. When they do, they can be essential or nonessential. This next example illustrates a nonessential adjective clause (*where*) and a nonessential participial phrase (*frightened*).

> Robin waded to the bank, *where* the little fish scattered and fled, *frightened* at his splashing.

Tip: The word *that* can replace *which* in essential clauses.

Tip: Most participial phrases are nonessential.

Semicolons ;

Rule 1. Use semicolons to join main clauses when they are so intricately linked they belong in the same sentence. Otherwise, use a period. Pattern: **MC; MC**

"He sounds like just my type; he sounds just like me!"

Advanced: Conjunctive adverbs (words like *therefore, however, nevertheless, moreover, furthermore*) do not turn a main clause into a dependent one; therefore, use a semicolon before the conjunctive adverb if it joins two main clauses that belong in one sentence. Use a period if the main clauses should be two sentences.

Run-ons. A **comma splice** is the error caused by joining two main clauses with only a comma when they need to be joined with something stronger, such as a semicolon, a period, or a comma plus a coordinating conjunction. A **fused sentence** is the error of joining two main clauses with no punctuation or coordinating conjunction.

Comma splice: *Gawain glanced up, the great ax descended.* Something stronger than a comma is needed to join these two main clauses.

There are four common solutions to run-ons, which work better or worse depending on the sentence:

1. Period: Gawain glanced up. The great ax descended.

2. Semicolon: Gawain glanced up; the great ax descended.

   a. Use a semicolon only when the two clauses are so inextricably linked (and often parallel in construction) that they are expressing one idea and need to go together in one sentence.

   b. A semicolon is more effective than a period here because it shows there is a link between these two ideas, but solutions 3 and 4 are better still.

3. Comma + cc: Gawain glanced up, *and* the great ax descended.

4. Adverb clause: Subordinate one of the clauses by starting it with one of the www.asia.b words:

   a. As Gawain glanced up, the great ax descended. (Comma needed after the introductory adverb clause: **AC, MC.**)

   b. Gawain glanced up as the great ax descended. (No comma needed with adverb clause dress-up: **MC AC.**)

   This is the best solution to this comma splice because the subordinating conjunction *as* explains how the two clauses are related: Gawain happened to glance up at the same time that the Green Knight lowered his ax.

A period is usually the easiest and often the best solution for run-ons, especially for younger students.

Advanced: Rule 2. Use semicolons to separate items in a series when the items contain internal commas. (Rare)

Highborn women lamented when Troy, that noble city celebrated by Homer, fell through trickery; when Pyrrhus, ancient Greek ruler, seized King Priam by the beard; and when the Romans, ruthless and crazed, torched Carthage to the ground.

Colons :

Rule 1. Use a colon after a main clause to introduce an explanation or a list when a phrase like *for example* or *that is* is not included. Lists take no punctuation if there is not a main clause setting them up.

"Yet one other boon I ask: please accept this simple souvenir from me."

Advanced: High school students will benefit from this pattern when they make a point and want to use a quotation to support that point. The colon is the perfect mark of punctuation to join the main clause to the quotation that illustrates it. Think of colons as meaning *see what follows* or *an example follows*.

Rule 2. In business or technical writing, use colons after subheads or words like *example* to set up what follows. Rarely use this in academic papers.

To: Example:
Fix: Dear Sir or Madam:

Rule 3. Use a colon to separate the hour and minutes when specifying time of day.

"We have a manicure scheduled for 10:15."

Hyphens -

Rule 1. Use hyphens in some compound nouns, such as *lady-in-waiting*. Consult a dictionary to check whether the compound noun should be written as one word (*marksman*), two words (*apple tree*), or hyphenated words.

Rule 2. Use hyphens with compound adjectives in front of a noun but usually not after a noun: jewel-encrusted crown, nineteenth-century author, well-attired people. Her crown was jewel encrusted. He lived in the nineteenth century. The people were well attired.

Rule 3. Use hyphens with compound numbers from *twenty-one* to *ninety-nine* and with spelled out fractions like *one-fourth*.

Rule 4. Use hyphens in phone numbers: 555-1212.

Em Dashes and Parentheses — ( )

Although em dashes and parentheses should be used sparingly, especially in academic writing, they can be effective tools when used properly. Distinguish between the **hyphen** (-), which joins things like compound words, and the **em dash**, which is longer (—).

Rule 1. Use em dashes in place of commas when you want to emphasize or draw attention to something. Use **parentheses** in place of commas to minimize the importance of something or to offer an aside. Em dashes are loud, parentheses quiet.

Chanticleer would raise his beak high on a fine summer evening and sing—to the jealousy of neighboring roosters for miles around—such ecstasy had he in his crowing.

(Notice that in fairy tales, characters don't have great curiosity about such oddities as talking frogs.)

Rule 2. Use em dashes to indicate an interruption in speech or a sudden break in thought.

His younger daughter—now there was another topic that brought red to his face.

Rule 3. Use em dashes to set off nonessential elements that have commas inside them.

The poor widow owned a few farm animals—three hefty sows, three cows, and a sheep dubbed Molly—with which she attempted to eke out a living.

Rule 4. Use parentheses for area codes in phone numbers: (260) 555-1212.

Pattern: **MC: illustrating list, example, or quotation**.

Remember, a main clause must come before a colon.

Advanced: When a main clause follows the colon, use a capital letter under two circumstances:

1) The colon introduces more than one sentence (rare).

2) It introduces a formal statement or quotation.

Example: *Charlemagne stated the dual boon of herbs: "An herb is the friend of physicians and the praise of cooks."*

Em dashes get their name from the fact that they are roughly the width of the upper-case M in the alphabet.

There is no key for a em dash on your keyboard, but there are shortcuts:

On a PC, type **ctrl-alt-minus sign**: specifically, the minus sign on the numeric keypad on the far right of the keyboard.

On a Mac, type **option-shift-hyphen**.

Ellipsis Points ...

Rule 1. Use ellipsis points to signal hesitation or a reflective pause, especially in dialogue in fiction. Rarely use them in formal papers for this reason.

"Ahem..." Lord Ashton cleared his throat conspicuously.

"Um... certainly... the mattress test."

Rule 2. In composition or academic writing, use three spaced periods (the ellipsis mark) to indicate an omission in a quotation. It is not necessary to use the ellipsis mark at the beginning or end of an excerpted passage.

Rule 3. In quoting another source, if the part you leave out spans more than one sentence, use four ellipsis points. The fourth one is actually a period.

Additional Rules and Concepts

Indentation Rules

Indent at the beginning of appropriate sentences to start new paragraphs. On the student pages, mark sentences that need indenting with the editing notation for a paragraph, which looks like a backwards P: ¶.

In copy work, indent by doing two things: 1. start on the next line, and 2. start writing ½ inch from the left margin.

Begin a new paragraph with the following:

1. A new speaker.

a. Start the paragraph at the beginning of the sentence in which someone is speaking, even if the quotation appears later in the sentence. Example: *She cried out with great force, "Thieves!"*

b. If a narrative sentence sets up the quotation, it can go in the same paragraph as the quoted sentence. Example: *The stranger came right to the point. "It is cowardly to stand there with a lethal arrow aimed at my heart."*

c. If narrative follows a quotation in a separate sentence but points directly back to the quotation, it can also go in the same paragraph. Example: *"It is cowardly to stand there with a lethal arrow aimed at my heart." The stranger did not mince words.*

2. A new topic.

a. This is the fuzziest to determine. Generally, if the narrator or a character switches topic or the focus, start a new paragraph.

b. The problem is that topics are a bit like a camera lens: they can sweep a broad scene or zoom in on details. If not much time is devoted to any of the details, you can safely combine different but related points in one paragraph, just as a photograph of the ocean—which takes in the water, sky, beach, swimmers, and even distant ships—can be as harmonious as one of a single shell on shore.

3. A new place.

a. Start a new paragraph when the story switches to a new scene.

b. If several switches are made in quick succession, such as a character's journey to find something, it may be less choppy to keep in one paragraph. Encourage older students to be flexible in making these choices, but if students are more comfortable with a stricter interpretation (hence more paragraphs), that is fine.

You may have noticed that this book does not follow this indentation format. These rules are perfect for students, though, because they typically do not have the typographic tools that book designers have, such as being able to control the space between paragraphs.

4. A new time.

    a. Same principles as with place: start a new paragraph with a new time unless there are several time shifts in close succession that make sense together in a single paragraph.

The rules for new paragraphs in fiction are less rigid than they are in academic writing. Do not get hung up on the details, but try to follow the main principles and aim for some consistency. If students make a reasonable case based on these principles for something other than what the book suggests, let them choose. In practice, paragraph divisions are clearer and more critical in academic writing, so we can be more flexible with fiction.

Capitalization Rules

Rule 1. Capitalize the first word of a sentence and of a quoted sentence, even when it does not begin the full sentence.

    The stranger responded, "You joke like a numbskull!"

Rule 2. Use lowercase to continue interrupted quotations.

    "Princess," he began, "you have a visitor at the door."

Rule 3. Capitalize proper nouns and words derived from proper nouns.

    Sherwood Forest; Robin Hood; Arthurian; Spartan

Rule 4. Capitalize people's titles when used with a name or as a substitute for a name in a noun of direct address. Do not capitalize titles when used without a name. Do not capitalize family members unless used as a substitute for a name or with a name.

    The Sheriff of Nottingham was related to the forester whom Robin Hood killed.

    The sheriff was related to the forester whom Robin Hood killed.

    "Can you clean the bullet from his wound, Doctor?"

    He succeeded his father as king.

An exception to Rule 4 is sir or madam as a noun of direct address: "Stand back, sir," demanded Robin.

Rule 5. Capitalize calendar names (days of the week and months) but not seasons.

    the month of June; in the spring; on Wednesday

Rule 6. Capitalize compass directions only when they refer to specific geographic regions, such as the South, or are part of a proper noun, such as North Carolina or New South Wales.

    On his journey north Gawain encountered few obstacles. (He is heading in a northward direction but not traveling to a region known as the North.)

Rule 7. Capitalize the first and last words of titles and subtitles and all other words except articles, coordinating conjunctions, and prepositions.

    A shy, small girl recited "Mary Had a Little Lamb."

    Your Knights of the Round Table are reputed superior in courtesy and arms.

    Note: Titles of long works like books, magazines, and movies should be italicized. Titles of short works like poems, short stories, and articles in magazines should be in quotation marks.

When writing longhand, it is customary to underline words that you will want to italicize.

Numbers Rules

Different style guides give different rules about how to write numbers. These simplified rules follow the principles of the Chicago Manual of Style.

Rule 1. Spell out numbers that can be expressed in one or two words; use figures for other numbers.

> The younger of his two daughters had racked up one thousand text messages on her cell phone in a single month!

Rule 2. Spell out ordinal numbers.

> In another year the second sister was permitted to rise to the surface.

Rule 3. Use numerals with dates.

> Exiting the hall, the stranger called back, "Meet me at the Green Chapel in one year and one day on January 1, 1400."

Rule 4. When numbers are mixed with symbols, use figures.

> "We can expect at least 40% of those invited to attend, or 238 guests."

Homophones and Usage

Homophones are words that sound alike but are spelled differently and have different meanings. Usage errors occur when students use one word when another is meant, often with words that are spelled similarly.

Encourage students to start a list of troublesome words to consult whenever they write.

Some common errors:

1. *there, their, they're; your, you're*

   a. *There* is the adverb pointing to a place or point: *over there; there is the spot.*

   b. *Their* and *your* are possessive pronouns: *their journey; your weapon.*

   c. *They're* and *you're* are contractions meanings *they are* and *you are*: *they're finished; you're spying.*

2. *to, two, too*

   a. *To* is the preposition: *to the soldiers' aid; to the right. To* is also used in infinitives, the "to + verb" form of a verb: *to rush; to seize.*

   b. *Two* is the number.

   c. *Too* means either *also* or *to an excessive degree* or *too much.* It is easy to remember because it has one too many o's!

3. *its, it's*

   a. *Its* is the possessive: *its bark* (the bark of the tree).

   b. *It's* is the contraction *it is*: *It's too bad.* Teach the difference by explaining that the apostrophe in *it's* is like a little *i*: *it^{i}s.*

   c. *Its'* is always incorrect.

4. *then, than*

   Use *then* to mean *next* or *immediately afterward.* Use *than* for a comparison. *After Alice drank the potion, she was then shorter than she was a moment before.*

5. *lie, lay*

> **a.** Simplify this problem pair by explaining that someone lies himself down but lays down an object.
>
> **b.** The three main verb forms:
>
> > i. to lie: *lie, lay, lain* (present, past, past participle)
> >
> > ii. to lay: *lay, laid, laid*
>
> One reason students have trouble with these words is that the past tense of *to lie* is the same as the present tense of *to lay*.
>
> **c.** For some students, memorizing a simple sentence can help with the confusing past tense forms: *Henny Hen lay down* (something she did to herself) *after she laid an egg* (something she did to an object).

6. *like, as*

> **a.** Simple explanation: Use *like* when comparing two nouns; use *as* or *as if* when comparing a noun to an idea (subject + verb).
>
> Not *She arranged her flowerbed as a whale* but *like a whale.*
>
> Not *It looks like it will be a lengthy convalescence* but *It looks as if it will be a lengthy convalescence.*
>
> **b.** When *as* means in the role, status or function of, it is a preposition.
>
> *Treat everything here as your own.*
>
> *"Come to the Green Chapel or be known as a coward."*

The word *like* is a preposition, not a conjunction, so it starts a prepositional phrase, which ends in a noun and does not have a verb. It should not start a clause.

To compare a noun to a clause, use *as, as if,* or *as though* instead of *like.*

7. *farther/farthest, further/furthest*

> Use *farther* and *farthest* as the comparative and superlative forms of *far*, referring to physical distance, no matter how short or long. Use *further* and *furthest* for everything else. *Further* means *to a greater extent* or *additional/in addition.*
>
> It is easy to remember the difference because *farther* and *farthest* derive from *far*, relating to distance. We do not say, "I am going fur down the road"!
>
> *She had earned a reputation for beauty reaching into the farthest kingdoms.* (physical distance)
>
> *She swam out farther from the shore.* (physical distance)
>
> *"I will no further descant on such matters."* (to a greater extent)
>
> Some dictionaries no longer distinguish these two, but most careful writers will.

8. *use to, used to*

> *Use to* is substandard English. The correct form is *used to.*
>
> *She used to bring pictures she had drawn to Lady Constance.*

9. *try and, try to*

> Use *try to* when trying to do something. *She tried to sprint across the hill* means she attempted to accomplish this feat. *She tried and sprinted across the hill* does not make sense because *tried* needs an object, as in *she tried climbing.*

10. *affect, effect*

    a. *Affect* as a verb means *to influence, act on,* or *produce a change in. Effect* as a noun is the result of that change. Most of the times this is how we use these words.

    Years of indulgence had the obvious effect (noun meaning the result) *of spoiling Dorinda.*

    Maybe Dorinda was too self-centered for anyone else to affect (verb form meaning to influence) *her deeply.*

    b. *Affect* and *effect* both have a noun and verb meaning, which is one reason they are so confusing. As a noun, a person's *affect* is his emotional appearance, feeling or emotion. As a verb, *to effect* is to bring about or accomplish something.

11. *between, among*

    Use *between* when dealing with two items, *among* with three or more.

    She wandered among the exotic botanical species. (more than two different species of plants)

    Dorinda held the napkin between her thumb and first finger. (two fingers)

Idioms

An idiom is an expression that cannot be understood literally, word for word. Example: *We had better go our separate ways. Had better* is an idiom meaning *ought to.* No one *has,* or *possesses,* something called *better*!

Do not expect students to determine parts of speech of words in idioms because often this will not make sense. When sentences begin with idioms, they do not always have to be labeled as certain openers.

Passive versus Active Voice (Advanced)

In active voice, the subject of the sentence is doing the verb action. Most sentences are written in active voice. Example: *The soldier invited the dwarf to warm himself by the fire.*

In passive voice, we start with the person or thing being acted upon, in the example above, the dwarf, and make it the new subject of the sentence: ***The dwarf was invited by the soldier*** *to warm himself by the fire.*

Passive voice follows this pattern: **Person/thing being acted on + be verb + past participle + by someone or something** (either in the sentence or understood). *The dwarf* (person being acted on) *was* (be verb) *invited* (past participle) *by the soldier* (by someone) *to warm himself by the fire.* If the sentence does not have all four elements, it is not in passive voice. That is, not every *be* verb is passive.

In writing, discourage older students from misusing passive voice because it is usually wordy and dull. Do not teach the concept to younger students.

Understanding passive voice helps instructors and older students even at this level with one tricky part of speech identification. When -ed past participles (see Parts of Speech: Verbals, page G-9) follow a *be* verb, it is unclear whether they are subject complements after a linking verb or part of the verb phrase.

One way to tell is that they are verbs if the sentence is in passive voice.

    Example: *The castle would be **demolished** by the soldiers.* Test for passive voice: *The castle* (subject being acted upon) *would be* (be verb) *demolished* (past participle) *by the* *soldiers* (*by* someone). Since this sentence is in passive voice, *demolished* is a verb, not an adjective.

The men were famished. Test: *The men* (subject) *were* (*be* verb) *famished. Famished* ends in -ed, so can it be a past participle? No: there is no one *famishing* the men so no *by* someone phrase. This makes *famished* an adjective, not a verb.

Two hundred pounds would be rewarded to the man who delivered Robin Hood to the king. Test: *Two hundred pounds* (subject being acted upon) *would be* (*be* verb) *rewarded* (past participle) *to the man who delivered Robin Hood to the king.* There is also a "*by* someone" phrase that is understood: *by the king.* Since this is in passive voice, the past participle is part of the verb and not an adjective.

Past Perfect Tense (Advanced)

Use the past perfect when relating the earlier of two events that occurred in the past. The more recent event is couched in past tense, the earlier event in past perfect. Form past perfect with *had* + the past participle of the verb.

One such frightful deluge swept away (past tense) *worthy King William, who had reigned* (past perfect) *in Flovenia for fourteen peaceful years.*

Subjunctive Mood (Advanced)

Used infrequently, the subjunctive mood expresses contrary-to-fact conditions with wish or if statements in the third person followed by a *be* verb. For present tense, all subjects take *be*; for past, *were.* To test: Ask if the statement is literally true. If not, use subjunctive.

*Kissing his hand, the little mermaid felt as if her heart **were** already broken.* Her heart is *not* already broken, so the subjunctive is correct: "as if her heart were" rather than "as if her heart was."

*Fearing lest his name **be** tarnished, Gawain began to despair of ever finding his implacable enemy.* His name will not be tarnished, so the subjunctive is correct: not "Fearing lest his name *is* tarnished," but "Fearing lest it *be* tarnished."

Stylistic Techniques

Fix It! stories teach the stylistic techniques of the Institute for Excellence in Writing. The list below reviews these techniques and offers pointers about how dress-ups and sentence openers reinforce grammar.

Dress-Ups

Dress-ups are ways of dressing up writing style, either by using stronger vocabulary (-ly adverb; strong verb; quality adjective) or by making the sentence structure more complex (*who-which* clause; www.asia.b clause).

Generally, hold older students to a more rigorous standard than younger students, encouraging all students to use word lists like a thesaurus to build their vocabulary when they work on dress-ups in their own writing.

The words marked as vocabulary dress-ups in the book have varying levels of strength. It is up to teachers to decide whether to count some of these words as "dress-up quality" or to allow words the book does not mark. The goal is to encourage interesting and specific vocabulary.

Two of the dress-ups, -ly adverbs and www.asia.b clauses, can also be sentence openers if they start a sentence. Count them as dress-ups if they come later in the sentence but as sentence openers if they are the first word in the sentence.

-ly Adverbs

Found anywhere except the first word in a sentence, this dress-up enriches by adding color and detail. Like other adverbs, the -ly adverb describes or modifies adjectives or verbs. See Parts of Speech: Adverbs, page G-10.

> The palace accountant *vehemently* complained about the princess's excessive texting.

Count only -ly words that are adverbs, not imposter -ly's, which are adjectives, like *princely, lonely, ugly,* and *ghastly*.

When they are ready, direct students to distinguish true -ly adverbs from adjectives by understanding how these parts of speech work. Even younger students can be asked what part of speech follows the -ly word.

The easiest way to check if an -ly word is an adverb or adjective is to place it in front of a noun. If that makes sense, it must be an imposter -ly (an adjective) since only adjectives can describe nouns. Then check it by placing it in front of a verb. If it works, it is a legitimate -ly adverb.

Examples: *She **cleverly** masqueraded herself as a poor girl.* *Cleverly* comes before and describes a verb (*masqueraded*), so it must be an -ly adverb. It also answers the adverb question *how*: *She masqueraded. How did she masquerade? She cleverly masqueraded.*

*"What nonsense this **silly** frog is talking!"* *Silly* comes before and describes a noun (*frog*), so it must be an imposter -ly, an adjective and not an adverb. It also does not answer the adverb question *how*.

Who-Which Clauses

A *who-which* clause is a dependent clause that begins with *who* or *which*. These clauses deepen content by adding new information to the sentence or minimize choppiness by combining two short sentences. See also Sentences, Clauses, and Phrases: Clauses, page G-16.

> Example: *Robin Hood cut straight a hefty staff, **which** measured six feet in length.*

To keep the *who* or *which* from stealing the main verb, remove the *who-which* clause from the sentence and confirm that a complete thought (a sentence) remains. If not, the *who* or *which* may have stolen the main verb.

> Example: *A bedraggled young woman, **who** stood at the door.* If I remove my who clause, I am left with only *A bedraggled young woman,* which is not a complete thought. I need something more: *A bedraggled young woman, who stood at the door, dripped water into her shoes.*

Use *who* for people, *which* for things or institutions. Animals are a special category. If they are just animals, use *which*. If they are beloved pets or if they take on human characteristics like the frog in "The Frog Prince," use *who*.

Younger students should form *who-which* clauses by placing the *who* or *which* immediately after the noun it describes. Many *who-which* clauses take commas. For younger students, you could simply require that they put commas around them all and only later teach essential and nonessential *who-which* clauses.

Advanced *Who-Which* Clauses

Punctuation. *Who-which* clauses are set off with commas if they are **nonessential** but take no commas if they are **essential**.

Essential which clauses usually start with *that* instead of *which*, but do not count these as dress-ups because the dress-up is for practicing who and which clauses.

That starts an adjective clause when it follows a noun. If it follows a verb, it is a noun clause instead. See under Punctuation: Commas: Rule 15: Essential-Nonessential Elements, page G-24, for further information about this important concept. See also Stylistic Techniques: Advanced Style: Noun Clauses, page G-44.

Question. When *who* or *which* asks a question, it begins a full sentence (a main clause), so *who* or *which* starting a question is not a *who-which* adjective clause, which is a dependent clause. Example: "Who was at the door?" does not count as a dress-up.

Whose. *Whose* is the possessive pronoun, used with people or things.

> Examples: There lived within the glades of Sherwood Forest a famous outlaw *whose* name was Robin Hood. The table *whose* legs were wobbly threatened to crash to the ground.

Who versus whom. Use *whom* instead of *who* when *whom* is the object of something (objective case), such as the object of a preposition or a direct object. Use *who* when it is

---

***Who-which* clauses** are adjective clauses, which usually modify the noun they follow. Older students may write which clauses to modify the entire idea that comes before.

Example: You have killed the king's deer, which is a capital offense. It is not the deer that is the offense but killing it—the full idea expressed in the main clause.

Advanced: The pronouns *who, that,* and *which* become singular or plural according to the noun they modify. Since the clause modifies the noun right before it, the verb must agree in number with that noun.

Example: Gawain was one of the knights who honor courtesy. The verb honor agrees with knights, not with one.

Also, if you teach *who-which* clauses as a dependent clause, it may help to understand that who or which is usually the subject of the clause.

in the subjective case, functioning as the subject of the sentence or, rarely, as a subject complement. See Parts of Speech: Pronouns, page G-7.

Trick: *he/him* substitution. If you can revise the sentence and substitute *he* or *they*, use *who*; if *him* or *them*, use *whom*.

> *He bellowed his challenge, as if doubting* **who/whom** *in the hall held rule.* He held rule, so *who* is correct.

> *I am not he of* **who/whom** *you speak.* You speak of *him*, so *whom*. (object of preposition)

Invisible *who-which*. *Who-which*'s followed by a *be* verb can be invisible for a more stylish sentence.

> Example: *Robin Hood started off from Locksley,* ~~which was~~ *the town where he lived. All had come to Sherwood Forest,* ~~which was~~ *a vast, uncharted wood.* In both cases, we could drop *which was* for a more elegant construction.

Strong Verbs

Teach younger students to recognize verbs by filling in these blanks with a form of the word in question: *yesterday he _____; today he _____; tomorrow he will _____.* (Yesterday he pitched; today he pitches; tomorrow he will pitch.)

As the most powerful part of speech, the verb can make or break a sentence. Challenge students to distinguish truly strong verbs from ordinary ones.

> Example: Compare ordinary: "It'll be the first thing I'll throw away when I make changes."

> versus strong: "It'll be the first thing I'll pitch when I redecorate."

Strong verb dress-ups should be action verbs, not helping or linking verbs. See Parts of Speech: Verbs, page G-8.

Quality Adjectives

Gradually teach students the difference between ordinary and quality adjectives. Quality adjectives are strong because they are more colorful, provide a stronger image or feeling, or add more detail and are more specific than ordinary adjectives. See also Parts of Speech: Adjectives, page G-10.

> Example: His advisers realized they had a *daunting* task.

Adjectives describe nouns. Teach how to locate adjectives with this simple test: The _____ person or object (thing).

> Examples: *the gurgling brook.* Is *brook* a person or thing? Yes, so *gurgling* is an adjective. Or *the confident stranger.* Is *stranger* a person or object? Yes, so *confident*, which describes the noun, must be an adjective.

www.asia.b Clauses

Initially, teach that dependent clauses may begin with one of these eight subordinating conjunctions: *when, while, where, as, since, if, although, because,* easy to learn by memorizing **www.asia.b**. IEW materials sometimes call these **the www words**. They usually start an adverb clause.

Eventually, students will learn that other words can start dependent clauses too, such as *until, whereas, wherever, whenever, as if, unless,* and sometimes *before* or *after*. See Sentences, Clauses, and Phrases: Clauses, page G-16, and Stylistic Techniques: Sentence Openers: #5 Clausal, page G-42.

A dependent clause cannot stand on its own as a sentence. It needs to be attached to a main clause to be a legal sentence.

Examples:

"Meet me *if* you dare."

"Your name, Little John, fits you ill *because* you are far from little!"

Robin Hood and his band guffawed loudly *until* the stranger began to grow enraged.

Remain on the other side *while* I quickly make a staff.

Most of the time, a www.asia.b word will begin an adverb clause. When an adverb clause occurs mid-sentence (the dress-up), it should not be set off with commas; when an adverb clause starts a sentence (the opener), it takes a comma after the clause. Teach simple patterns to help students remember these rules:

MC AC: no comma when an adverb clause falls in the middle or at the end of a sentence

AC, MC: comma at the end of a clause when the adverb clause comes before the main clause

Advanced: www.asia.b Words

The www words **since, as**, and **until** sometimes are prepositions instead of conjunctions. You can tell they do not start clauses if there is no subject and verb after them, as in *since childhood* or *as an archer* or *until the next day*. See under Sentence Openers: #5 Clausal Opener, page G-42, for tricks to tell the difference.

The www words **as, where**, and **when** can start adjective clauses instead of adverb clauses, usually when they follow and describe a noun. Adjective clauses can be essential (no commas) or nonessential (commas). See Punctuation: Commas: Rule 15: Essential-Nonessential Elements, page G-24.

Example: *King Arthur decided to climb to the top of the cliff, where he could drink from the pool of water collected above.* This *where* clause follows a noun that it also describes; since it is nonessential, it needs a comma.

While, although, and **whereas** sometimes need a comma before them because they present a contrast to the main clause in the sentence.

Examples: You stand there with a lethal bow to shoot at my heart, *while* I have only a plain blackthorn staff to meet you with.

Hrothgar and Robert had been trying to save his life all along, *whereas* he had been too foolish to listen to them.

www.asia.b

when
while
where
as
since
if
although
because

While and *whereas* technically function as coordinating conjunctions in this case and follow the punctuation pattern **MC, cc MC**, but it is easiest to explain this as needing a comma because of the contrast.

Sentence Openers

Sentence openers are the patterns that sentences begin with. Their obvious advantage is in encouraging more complex sentence structure and variety, which greatly improves the quality of student writing. A second advantage is that openers teach lots of grammar in a backdoor fashion. By teaching the patterns and punctuation that accompany the openers, you will help students master quite a bit of grammar in the context of writing.

#1 Subject Opener

Subject openers essentially begin with the subject of a main clause, although articles and/ or adjectives may precede it. If the sentence is shorter than six words, it can be counted as a #6 vss opener instead.

> Examples: *He became livid on the subject of modern gadgets.* The subject is *He*.

> *The convivial company congregated in the great hall.* The subject is *company*, but it is still a subject opener because *the* is an article and *convivial* an adjective.

Sometimes #1 sentences invert the usual word order, placing the verb or other word first. For this reason, it helps to explain that the #1 sentence starts with a main clause.

> Example: *There were blameless, loyal men at his side who rambled with him through the greenwood shades.* The actual subject is *men*, but the sentence begins with a main clause so is still a #1 subject opener.

#2 Prepositional Opener

Prepositions begin phrases that follow this pattern:

preposition + noun (no verb)

The phrase starts with a preposition and ends with a noun, with no verb inside. Other words may squeeze in between the preposition and noun but never a verb. See under #5 Clausal Opener, page G-42, for the trick to distinguish between #2s and #5s. See also Parts of Speech: Prepositions, page G-11.

Examples:

> *During* these reflections, King Morton shook his head in abject despair.

> *After* a pause she summed it up.

Younger students should practice finding prepositional phrases before identifying the #2 opener, showing how the phrase fits the pattern. Example: After (preposition) + a (article) + pause (noun). This phrase begins with a preposition, ends with a noun, and has no verb, which fits the pattern. Remind students that the lack of a verb means it must be a phrase and cannot be a clause.

Punctuation: Prepositional phrases of five or more words take a comma after them; with fewer than five, the comma is optional. Let the pause test be your guide for shorter prepositional phrases: use a comma if you need a pause, no comma if you do not.

When short prepositional openers work transitionally (as in *For example, In addition, On the other hand*), they will need a comma, just as any transitional opener should take a comma. Usually the pause test is sufficient to determine this.

Punctuation rule note: Grammar books express the punctuation rule more vaguely: long prepositional phrases take a comma; with short ones, the comma is optional.

For most students, a clear cutoff is more helpful than this general principle, and five or more words are usually long enough to warrant a comma.

Advanced Prepositional Phrase

Disguised #2. Sentences starting with some kind of time (*Wednesday; Two weeks ago; The evening of the ball; One night*) followed by the main clause begin with what is effectively a disguised #2, in which a preposition is implied but not stated, as in "One morning…" where "In," "On," or "During one morning" is implied. The sentence sounds better without the preposition, but the opener functions as if it were there and is punctuated the same way.

Infinitives. Although infinitives do not fit the usual pattern of prepositional phrases (**preposition + noun**), the *to* in them is still a preposition, used to mark the infinitive of a verb. Infinitives starting sentences may be counted as #2 openers. E.g., *To lend* credence to this claim, one of the most respected authors related a pertinent account.

#3 -ly Adverb Opener

The main difference between an -ly dress-up and -ly sentence opener is the flow of the sentence. Beginning the sentence with the -ly adverb gives a different kind of rhythm than placing it later in the sentence.

Advanced: -ly Adverb Punctuation. LY openers take a comma after them when they modify the sentence but do not need a comma when they modify the verb. The best way to tell what they modify is to put the sentence in two patterns that use the adjective form of the -ly adverb.

> Did the subject act in the [adjective] manner? **If so, the -ly modifies the verb: no comma.**
>
>> Example: *Resentfully the stranger answered him.* The stranger answered in a resentful manner, so this -ly modifies the verb and therefore does not take a comma.
>
> Is it [adjective] that the rest of the sentence is true? **If so, the -ly modifies the sentence: comma.**
>
>> Example: *Unfortunately, Queen Mary was traveling with him at the time.* It is unfortunate that she was traveling with him at the time, so this -ly modifies the whole sentence and needs a comma.

Sometimes, both the comma and no comma are correct but affect the meaning.

Sorrowfully Chanticleer acceded to the counsel of his wife. He acceded, but he did so sorrowfully, with regret.

Sorrowfully, Chanticleer acceded to the counsel of his wife. This opener is the narrator's warning that Chanticleer made a mistake in acceding to his wife's advice. It is sorrowful that Chanticleer acceded to his wife's counsel.

#4 -ing Participial Phrase Opener

Sentence opener #4 sounds easy but can be complicated grammatically. Teach this pattern:

-ing word/phrase + comma + subject/-inger + main verb

It begins with an -ing word (participle) or phrase, then a comma, then the subject of the main clause which is also doing the inging, then the main verb. Check that #4 openers have these four elements and teach students to ask this important question: Is the subject after the comma doing the inging?

Examples: *Gathering their three gifts, the soldiers set out on a journey to visit a neighboring king.* 1. *Gathering their three gifts* is an -ing phrase; 2. there is a comma; 3. the noun after the comma is both the subject of the main clause (*soldiers set out*) and the inger (*soldiers were gathering*); 4. *set out* is the verb. This follows the four steps and is therefore a legal, legitimate #4 opener.

Taking up his bow, Robin Hood shot with unparalleled skill. This also follows the four steps: Robin is both taking up his bow and shooting.

Advanced #4 Opener

There are two main ways students might mislabel #4s.

1. Illegal #4s look like #4s, only the person or thing after the comma is not the one doing the inging. This is known as a **dangling modifier**—an often humorous but still grammatically faulty sentence pattern.

Examples: *Hopping quickly to keep up, she let the frog traipse behind her to the resplendent dining hall.* It is not the princess but the frog that is supposed to be hopping!

Looming nearby in the harbor, she beheld a large ship. The mermaid is not looming nearby but the ship.

Scanning the noble assembly, the horse rode straight to the high dais. The horse is not the one doing the scanning but the Green Knight.

2. Imposter #4s begin with an -ing word so look like #4s but are actually #1 subject openers or #2 prepositional phrase openers. See also Parts of Speech: Verbals, page G-9.

#2s that look like #4s begin with one of these prepositions: *during, according to, regarding, concerning.* The four steps reveal that the pattern does not work.

Examples: *According to state history, the only indisputable test for real princess blood is the mattress test.* The subject after the comma is *test*, which is not doing the *according*, so this sentence does not fit the #4 pattern. It is actually a #2.

During the obligatory dance after dinner, she twirled him around. She is not doing the inging. In fact, nobody can "dure" because *during* is not a participle derived from a verb but a preposition.

#1s that look like #4s begin with an -ing word, but it functions as the subject of the sentence. (We call -ing nouns gerunds, not participles). These have no place for a comma and no person or thing mentioned doing the inging.

Examples: *Living at the splendid castle cheered the soldiers.* There is no comma or place for one, nor is there a subject that is doing the inging. The context makes it clear that the soldiers are living there, but the sentence does not use *soldiers* as the subject doing that action. The subject-verb pair is *Living cheered.*

Peering through the curtain left Gawain in wonder. Again, no comma or place for one. The subject-verb pair is *Peering left*.

Invisible #4s are sentences that follow the same pattern as regular #4s, but the -ing word is hidden. These sentences begin with an adjective or adjective phrase followed by a comma plus main clause, with the word *being, seeming,* or *appearing* implied at the beginning of the sentence. They are more elegant without the -ing participle but function and are punctuated just like a #4.

IEW instructors sometimes add a seventh opener for sentences starting with a past participle ending in -ed, but it is unnecessary to create a separate category for this since it follows the same pattern as an invisible -ing opener.

Examples: *Quick-witted and agile, Robert compensated for his limitation by an eagerness to please.* Implied: *Appearing* quick-witted and agile, Robert compensated for his limitation.

Relaxed and untroubled, the stranger genially waited for him. Implied: *Being* relaxed and untroubled, the stranger genially waited for him.

Energized by boyish blood, Arthur did not care to lounge at his ease. Implied: *Being* energized by boyish blood, Arthur did not care to lounge at his ease.

#5 Clausal Opener

This is the same as the dress-up and uses the same www words (subordinating conjunctions), except that now this dependent clause starts the sentence and needs a comma after it. Teach the simple pattern: **AC, MC**

Examples:

If possessions were plundered, the yeomen would recapture the goods and return them to the poor.

As he approached, Robin Hood noticed a tall stranger resolutely striding toward the bridge.

When he demanded it back, Dorinda mumbled something about not being able to locate it.

Advanced: #5s versus #2s. The problem with accurately identifying #5s, #2s, and www.asia.b dress-ups is that a few words might be either a preposition or a subordinating conjunction. *After, before, since, until* and *as* can function as either, and while *because* is a subordinating conjunction, *because of* is a preposition.

Two tricks help tell the difference, both bouncing off the fact that prepositional phrases never have a verb and clauses always do.

1. Drop the first word of the phrase or clause in question and look at what is left. If it is a sentence, the group of words is an adverb clause; if it is not, the words form a prepositional phrase.

2. Look for a verb: only #5s and adverb clause dress-ups can have a verb.

Example:

a. After supper, King Morton ordered Dorinda to prepare the Golden Guestroom.

b. After they finished supper, King Morton ordered Dorinda to prepare the Golden Guestroom.

Drop *After* and see what is left in the opener. Sentence *a* starts with a #2 prepositional opener because *supper* is not a complete sentence; sentence *b* starts with a #5 clausal opener because *they finished supper* is a complete sentence. Also, we know that sentence *b* starts with a #5 because the opener contains a verb (*finished*).

#6 vss, or Very Short Sentence

An occasional short sentence can pack a punch in paragraphs that otherwise have intricate and lengthy sentences.

Examples:

"Tarry for me here."

Robin Hood set off.

The blow inflamed him.

King Morton esteemed values.

The trick to #6s is that they must be short (two to five words) and they must be sentences (subject + verb and be able to stand alone).

They should also be strong: a vsss = Very Short Strong Sentence!

#T or Transitional Opener

#T works for sentences beginning with interjections, interrupters, or transitional words and expressions. Transitional openers are usually followed by a comma.

Common words and phrases in this class include the following: *however, therefore, then, thus, later, now, otherwise, indeed, first, next, also, moreover, hence, furthermore, henceforth, likewise.* Also included are interjections, such as *oh, ouch, wow, ha*, which can be followed by a comma or an exclamation mark.

Tip: When you add one of these words or phrases to a main clause, the clause remains a main clause.

#T "Moreover, the august Macrobius explained that his dreams were clear portents." (transition)

#T Oh, how gladly she would have shaken off all this pomp and laid aside the heavy wreath! (interjection)

#T "Alas! For this, you have forfeited my heart and all my love." (exclamatory interjection)

#Q or Question

#Q takes care of sentences that ask questions. This teaches students not to mark questions beginning with *who* or *which* as their *who-which* dress-up or questions beginning with words like *when* or *where* as their clausal openers.

#Q Did you ever hear the story of the three poor soldiers?

#Q "What name do you go by, good fellow?"

#Q Where is fair Pertelote?

Advanced Style

Duals and Triples

Deliberate use of dual or triple adverbs, adjectives, or verbs, especially when the words add a different nuance, enriches prose and challenges students to be precise with words chosen. Classic writers of the past like Charles Dickens and persuasive essayists like Winston Churchill have used duals and triples to convey their meaning most powerfully.

Examples:

All who beheld her wondered at her *graceful, swaying* movements.

The ship glided away *smoothly and lightly* over the tranquil sea.

Noun Clauses

A noun clause is a dependent clause used as a noun. It can function in any of the ways that nouns function: subject, direct or indirect object, or object of a preposition. See also Sentences, Clauses, and Phrases: Clauses: Dependent Clauses (Advanced): Noun Clauses, page G-18.

Although noun clauses may begin with many words, those starting with *that* are the main ones highlighted in IEW because students sometimes confuse them with essential adjective clauses.

To tell the difference: If *that* begins an adjective clause, you can substitute *which* and it will still make sense. If *that* begins a noun clause, *which* does not work in its place. Also, noun clauses follow verbs and answer the question "What?" after a verb. Adjective clauses usually follow a noun and describe the noun they come immediately after.

Example:

"I know well that I am the weakest of these illustrious knights." Can you say, "I know well which I am the weakest of knights"? No, so it is not an adjective clause but a noun clause. It follows a verb (*know*) and answers the question "What?" E.g., *I know*. What does he know? That he is the weakest of these knights.

Invisible Noun Clause: This is a noun clause with the word *that* understood, not stated directly. Example: *He could tell [that] he was going to relish his palace stay.* Sometimes it is more elegant without *that*: *He could tell he was going to relish his palace stay.*

Decorations

Used sparingly, as an artist might add a splash of bright color to a nature painting, these stylistic techniques daringly or delicately decorate one's prose. You can introduce the decorations at any time when teaching IEW writing.

The six decorations are questions, conversation/quotation, 3sss (three short staccato sentences), dramatic opening-closing, simile/metaphor, and alliteration. In *Fix It! Grammar*, you will see the last two.

Similes and Metaphors

A simile is a comparison between two unlike things using the words *like* or *as*. A metaphor, harder to create, is a similar comparison but without the *like* or *as*.

Examples:

> The ship dived like a swan between them. (simile)

> The waves rose mountains high. (metaphor)

The key to recognizing these figures of speech is that they compare unlike things. For example, to say that a cat is like a tiger is a comparison but not a simile.

Alliteration

Alliteration is the repetition of the same initial consonant sounds in two or more words in close proximity. It adds flavor to writing when used judiciously.

> Example: *Arthur was **seeking some** shady relief from the **sweltering sun**. Shady* is not part of the alliteration because it does not have the same initial sound as the other *s* words. It is not the letter that matters but the sound. Thus, *celery* and *sound* are alliterative, but *shady* and *sound* are not.

Stressed syllables in the middle of words that carry the same sound can contribute to the alliteration. Example: *I **will** a**ward** you **what** I **win** in the **woods**.*

In academic writing, alliteration usually sounds awkward unless found in a title or the first or last sentence of a paper, where it can appropriately dramatize those parts.